BASIC LAW FOR SMALL BUSINESSES

Susan S. Jarvis
University of Texas—Pan America

WEST PUBLISHING COMPANY
Minneapolis/St. Paul   New York   Los Angeles   San Francisco

WEST'S COMMITMENT TO THE ENVIRONMENT

In 1906, West Publishing Company began recycling materials left over from the production of books. This began a tradition of efficient and responsible use of resources. Today, 100% of our legal bound volumes are printed on acid-free, recycled paper consisting of 50% new fibers. West recycles nearly 27,700,000 pounds of scrap paper annually—the equivalent of 229,300 trees. Since the 1960s, West has devised ways to capture and recycle waste inks, solvents, oils, and vapors created in the printing process. We also recycle plastics of all kinds, wood, glass, corrugated cardboard, and batteries, and have eliminated the use of polystyrene book packaging. We at West are proud of the longevity and the scope of our commitment to the environment.

West pocket parts and advance sheets are printed on recyclable paper and can be collected and recycled with newspapers. Staples do not have to be removed. Bound volumes can be recycled after removing the cover.

Production, Prepress, Printing and Binding by West Publishing Company.

 TEXT IS PRINTED ON 10% POST CONSUMER RECYCLED PAPER ∞

COPYRIGHT © 1997 by   WEST PUBLISHING CO.
610 Opperman Drive
P.O. Box 64526
St. Paul, MN 55164–0526

ISBN 0–314–20139–4

Dedication

To Bruce

Whose confidence and support
made this book possible

and to Ian, Colin, and Ted

May the children of their generation
grow up in a global community
where tolerance and cooperation
replace all tensions and conflicts

TABLE OF CONTENTS

PART I. THE LEGAL ENVIRONMENT FOR TODAY'S SMALL BUSINESS 1

PART II. TYPES OF LAWSUITS FREQUENTLY BROUGHT AGAINST SMALL BUSINESSES 33

Chapter 12. Going Global 181

PART III. COMMONSENSE APPROACHES TO AVOID LAWSUITS 195

Chapter 13. Keeping Up With the Law 197

Chapter 14. The Asset of Ethics 205

PREFACE

An increasing number of individuals today are choosing to set up their own business rather than work for a large corporation. A major concern for these entrepreneurs is the risk of facing a lawsuit. This book was written to acquaint business students and those currently involved in operating small businesses with the general areas of law that frequently form the bases for these lawsuits. Each chapter highlights "red flag" situations that may arise in a small business and lead to a lawsuit. In addition, the book offers guidelines for reducing the risks of a lawsuit.

Laws are constantly changing and this book is not intended to offer legal advice for specific legal problems. The reader is advised to seek competent legal counsel when a specific legal problem arises.

The author wishes to thank the following for their invaluable support in the preparation of this book: Dr. Donald Ball; Peggy Ferrin; Mary Moore; and Danita Rincones-Alamia. Special thanks to Stephanie K. Johnson and John Szilagyi of West Educational Publishing and Rob Dewey of South Western College Publishing. Thanks also to the reviewers whose comments helped to shape this book and make it a more effective learning tool:

Susan Demers
St. Petersburg Junior College

Norman Heyboer
Southwest Florida College of Business

Jay Hollowell
Virginia Commonwealth College

Tim Krumm
Meardon, Sueppel, Downer & Hayes

Kate Oberholtzer
Kelsey-Jenny College

Roger Reinsch
Emporia State University

Anne Schacherl
Madison Area Technical College

Allan Sheets
Indiana Business College

Kim Tyler
Shasta College

INTRODUCTION

Lawsuits are a major concern for small businesses today. The plaintiffs, or parties bringing the lawsuits, come from such diverse groups as employees, dissatisfied customers and clients, suppliers, and governmental agencies. Frequently the lawsuit is based on a law that the defendant does not know about. Unfortunately, ignorance of the law is usually not a valid defense in a courtroom.

The purpose of this book is threefold: (1) to acquaint students and those involved in the operation of small businesses with certain general areas of the law that are frequently the bases of lawsuits (2) to help the reader recognize "red flag" situations that can arise in a small business and lead to lawsuits and (3) offer guidelines and suggestions for reducing the risks of these lawsuits.

Chapters include the following sections to assist the reader in reaching these goals:

1. The "Chapter Objectives" outline what the reader should learn by the end of the chapter.

2. "Red Flag Situations" describe typical situations that can arise in a small business and which have the potential to result in a lawsuit.

3. "Going Global" points out foreign laws and practices that can impact the small business that enters the international market.

4. The "Home-Based Business" section explains how the chapter's legal principles apply to the business operating out of the owner's residence.

5. "Reducing Your Risks" contains specific suggestions for reducing the risks of a lawsuit in the area of law the chapter covers.

6. "Key Words and Phrases" lists key terms the reader should learn in the chapter.

7. A "Chapter Summary" outlines the basic concepts of the chapter.

8. "Discussion Questions" include hypothetical situations requiring the reader to apply legal principles discussed in the chapter to typical problems facing small businesses today.

9. "Is It Ethical?" challenges the reader to evaluate specific actions that are considered legal but may be considered unethical.

This book does not attempt to offer legal advice for specific legal problems. Instead, it focuses on preventive law by assisting the small business owner in conducting business in a manner that will avoid costly lawsuits.

PART I

THE LEGAL ENVIRONMENT FOR TODAY'S SMALL BUSINESS

CHAPTER 1

SOURCES OF LAWS THAT AFFECT SMALL BUSINESSES: EVEN LAWS HAVE "ROOTS"

CHAPTER OBJECTIVES

In this chapter you will learn to:

1. Recognize the essential characteristics of a law and how laws are classified.

2. Identify the various sources of laws in this country and which law prevails in case two laws are in conflict.

3. Understand how the Federal Interstate Commerce Clause can impact a small business even if the business is strictly local in nature.

4. Recognize rights of the small business that are protected by the U.S. Constitution.

5. Identify sources of information that can provide information relevant to proposed and recently adopted laws to assure compliance with any changes in the law that may impact your business.

Today's news is full of stories about the **"law"** and how it affects every aspect of one's personal and business activities. A new "law" may become effective today that has immediate impact on the operation of a small business. In learning of this new restriction on operating a business, the owner may ask exactly what is the "law" and where does it come from?

Many owners of small businesses feel that they are encountering a new and unfamiliar language when they start reading about legal issues. This confusion over legal terms is understandable. By carefully analyzing certain basic legal terms and concepts, a businessperson can more easily grasp a basic understanding of the "law" and its sources.

This chapter will examine the term "law" and its essential elements. The various sources of laws will also be examined.

DEFINITIONS

If five legal scholars were asked to define the word "law" the chances are good that five different definitions would result. Despite their differences, certain basic characteristics would be found in each definition. These characteristics are essential to any definition of the term "law".

Basically, a law requires the following elements or characteristics:

(1)   a <u>rule</u> which is

(2)   <u>handed down</u> (or passed) by a person or group

(3)   <u>with authority</u> for which

(4)   <u>noncompliance</u> (breaking the rule) results in

(5)   <u>sanctions</u> (punishment)

Based on this definition, a "law" can be a court decision handed down by a judge, a statute passed by Congress or state legislature, or a regulation passed by a state administrative agency. A "law" can also be an ordinance passed by a local council. In all of these examples, a source of authority passes a rule, and failure to comply with the rule can result in certain consequences.

Laws are classified in several ways. One classification is based on the type of wrong committed. **Criminal laws** involve wrongs committed against society as a whole. For example, if Smith throws a rock and injures his employer, Jones, then Smith has violated a criminal law. Even though there is technically only one victim, all of society has been injured. Smith will be charged with violation of a state criminal law and tried in a criminal court. The state will file a case and a prosecutor or district attorney will represent society in the lawsuit.

The employer, Jones, may also sue Smith based on an area of "civil" or private law. The term "civil" or private law in this context refers to a wrong committed against a private individual or business. Jones' suit would claim Smith had committed a "civil" wrong (in this case an intentional private wrong called a "tort") against the individual Jones. The plaintiff (Jones) will hire a private attorney to file the case. The case will be heard in a civil court. The defendant (Smith) will be represented by a private attorney.

CONSTITUTIONAL LAW

The term **"constitutional law"** in the United States refers to laws based on either the federal constitution or on a state constitution. The federal constitution is considered the "supreme law of the land." Consequently, no law passed by Congress or a state legislature can conflict with this Constitution.

The federal constitution and state constitutions give Congress and state legislatures the power to pass laws regulating small businesses. Comparatively speaking, the federal constitution is much shorter in length than the Constitutions of the various states. The federal constitution was intentionally written as a short document to enable it to be a "living" constitution that can be interpreted in accordance with the current times.

Commerce Clause

The **Interstate Commerce Clause** of the federal Constitution (Article I, Section 8) has significant impact on small businesses. This clause grants Congress the power to regulate commerce "with foreign Nations, and among the several States, and with the Indian tribes." The Commerce Clause further authorizes Congress, "To make all Laws which shall be necessary and proper for carrying into Execution the foregoing Powers, and all other Powers vested in the Government of the United States, or in any Department or Office thereof."

Many small businesses have little or no direct business contacts beyond their city limits. These businesses are surprised to learn that the federal courts have determined they are nevertheless engaged in "interstate commerce" and therefore subject to federal laws.

In recent years the federal courts have greatly expanded the interpretation of the term "interstate commerce". For example, in the case *Heart of Atlanta Motel vs. United States*, the U.S. Supreme Court ruled that the federal Civil Rights Act of 1964 can apply to a small privately owned business that operates only one establishment in one state.

HEART OF ATLANTA MOTEL VS. UNITED STATES

379 U.S. 241

85 S.Ct. 348 (1964)

Facts:

The Heart of Atlanta Motel was a small local motel that denied accommodations to African Americans. The federal Civil Rights Act of 1964 prohibited racial discrimination by privately owned businesses that affected interstate commerce. The owner of the motel claimed the law was unconstitutional because Congress had exceeded its power to regulate interstate commerce by imposing the Act on privately owned local businesses.

Issue:

Does Congress's power to regulate interstate commerce extend to the regulation of small, locally operated businesses?

Decision:

The U.S. Supreme Court upheld the constitutionality of the Act and its application to plaintiff's business. The Court referred to the extensive evidence of racial discrimination practiced by hotels and motels throughout the U.S. prior to the passage of the Act and the negative impact this discrimination had on interstate commerce.

In delivering the Court's opinion, Mr. Justice Clark specifically stated:

"... It is said the operation of the motel here is of a purely local character. But, assuming this to be true, if it is interstate commerce that feels the pinch, it does not matter how local the operation that applies the squeeze... the power of Congress to promote interstate commerce also includes the power to regulate the local incidents thereof, including local activities in both the States of origin and destination, which might have a substantial and harmful effect upon the commerce."

Reason:

The Court determined that the motel's operation was not strictly local in nature. The motel advertised nationally, accommodated tourists from other states and was accessible from interstate highways. Therefore, the application of the Act to plaintiff's business was constitutional.

Discussion Questions:

 1. Do you agree with the Supreme Court's decision?

 2. Can you think of any type of small business today that is not engaged in some form of interstate commerce?

Another example of a case challenging a federal law's application to a local business activity involved a real estate board in the New Orleans area.

In 1980, the U.S. Supreme Court ruled in *McLain vs. Real Estate Board of New Orleans, Inc.* [444 U.S. 232, 100 S. Ct. 502, 62 L. Ed. 2d 441 (1980)] that the federal Sherman Antitrust Law applied to a real estate board located solely in one parish (county) in Louisiana. The board had been charged with violating the Sherman Act by setting real estate commission rates. The board argued that the Sherman Act did not apply because there was no interstate activity involved.

The Supreme Court disagreed, pointing out that buyers and sellers of the properties involved came from other states; the title policies issued came from title companies operating in other states; and the mortgage monies used for purchasing the properties came from investors and lending institutions throughout the nation. Based on this reasoning, the Supreme Court held that the federal Sherman Antitrust Act applied because Congress did in fact have authority over this case.

These two cases illustrate how the term "interstate commerce" has been expanded in the past few years, thus allowing the federal courts to apply federal laws to small, locally owned businesses.

Bill of Rights

The first ten amendments to the U.S. Constitution (the Bill of Rights) provide specific guarantees to individuals. These include freedom of speech and religion (Amendment I) and freedom from unreasonable searches and seizures (Amendment IV). The Fourteenth Amendment to the Constitution prohibits states from abridging these rights and from depriving "any person of life, liberty, or property without due process of the law." The Supreme Court has determined these rights and protections extend to businesses.

An example of the Supreme Court's application of the right of free speech to a business corporation is found in *First National Bank of Boston vs. Bellotti* [435 U.S. 765, 98 S. Ct. 1407 (1978)]. A Massachusetts law provided that corporations could not make political contributions that were permissible for individuals. The Supreme Court ruled the state law was unconstitutional because it deprived businesses of their First Amendment right to free speech.

State Constitutions are also the basis for laws affecting small businesses. For example, a State Constitution will give the state legislature the power to protect the safety, health, and general welfare of a person within the state. Assume the operator of a small business decides to buy an existing building, open a new restaurant on the first floor and convert the second floor into a rental apartment. The new building owner must comply with state laws relevant to rental property. The state laws, for example, may require smoke detectors to be placed in certain locations and specific types of locks be placed on each door of the rental unit. The state is exercising its police power to protect the safety of tenants.

Statutory Law

The term "**statutory law**" refers to a law passed by a law-making body such as a state legislature or the federal congress. These laws cannot conflict with the provisions of the federal constitution or the individual state's constitution.

An example of a federal statutory law is the Occupational Safety and Health Act of 1970. This federal law places certain requirements on businesses engaged in interstate commerce. These requirements are relevant to the health and safety of workers in the workplace. The courts have interpreted the term "interstate commerce" broadly as it pertains to this Act. As a result of this broad interpretation, small businesses that operate in only one location are covered by the requirements of this Act.

An example of a state statute would be a state law requiring each new business to register its business name with the appropriate local or county office. The various states have hundreds of statutes that affect small business operations. These include fire protection codes, state health codes, and state workers' compensation laws.

Unfortunately, ignorance of changes in the law usually provides no defense for a small business that violates a law. It is therefore important to keep abreast of any changes in the laws that will impact a business.

There are a number of ways to learn of any proposed or adopted changes in state or federal laws. Besides following media stories of statutory changes, those involved with small businesses can benefit from joining local, state-wide, and national trade groups or associations. Examples of such groups include Retail Grocers Associations and Restaurant Owners' Associations. Many of these groups closely monitor any proposed changes in state or federal laws that may impact their members. Frequently these groups will lobby their state legislatures or Congress if there are proposed laws that may negatively impact their trade group.

Relevant magazines and trade journals can be a valuable source of information relevant to state statutes also. Many city and university libraries subscribe to these publications. Examples include Arizona Business Magazines and Florida Grocer. National magazines include American Advertising; HR News; and Sign Business.

COMMON LAW

The term **"common law"** refers to laws that are based on a judge's decision. Frequently "common law" is referred to as "judge-made law." These judicial decisions are handed down when there is no statute on the books to govern a certain type of dispute. From a realistic point of view, it would be both impractical and impossible for either the Congress or a state legislature to adopt laws that address every conceivable area of conflict between individuals.

The common law system followed in the United States is based on the common law system of England. All of the states in the U.S. follow the common law system except for the state of Louisiana, which still follows what is referred to as the **civil law** system. The civil law system is based on statutes that also address conflicts between individuals. This statutory approach is frequently referred to as "codified law."

In those states which follow the common law system, the judge may have no statute to determine if a particular wrong has in fact been committed. The judge will then turn to prior court decisions in the jurisdiction. In a majority of cases, the presiding judge will follow the prior decision made in a similar dispute in that jurisdiction. This prior decision is called "precedent." Occasionally, a judge will hand down a decision that is contrary to prior decisions. This is a "precedent-setting" case.

Types of disputes which are frequently decided based on the common law include certain breach of contract disputes, defamation suits, malpractice suits, and suits involving an employer's liability for the wrongful actions of an employee.

These common law decisions frequently reflect the changes in attitudes of the public. For example, in recent years more judicial decisions have held third parties (such as social and business hosts) liable for the damages caused by the driving of a drunk guest. These decisions have reflected the public's concern over the high number of innocent victims killed or injured by drunk drivers. Frequently, the public will lobby a state legislature to pass statutes relevant to liability for a particular activity. As a result of this procedure, many state legislatures have now passed statutes regarding third party liability for drunk drivers.

Some countries that currently follow the common law system include the U.S., Great Britain, India and Nigeria. Some civil law countries include France, Germany, Mexico and a majority of other Latin American countries.

GOING GLOBAL

ADMINISTRATIVE LAW

A majority of the laws that impact small businesses are based on **administrative law**, which comes from regulations handed down by federal, state, county and even city regulatory offices. These agencies have been authorized by either Congress or a state legislature to regulate a particular aspect of a business activity. When Congress passed the Occupational Safety and Health Act in 1970, for example, it also established the Occupational Safety and Health Administration (OSHA) and authorized OSHA to write and enforce regulations necessary to carry out Congress's mandate as found in the Act.

For example, in 1991 OSHA promulgated a new rule titled, "Occupational Exposure to Bloodborne Pathogens" (29 C.F.R. 1910.1030). The agency had concluded that exposure to the Hepatitis B virus, Human Immunodeficiency Virus (HIV) and other bloodborne pathogens "can be minimized or eliminated using a combination of engineering and work practice controls, personal protective clothing and equipment, training, medical surveillance, Hepatitis B vaccination, signs and labels and other provisions." The American Dental Association (ADA) challenged the rules' application to dental workers, claiming among other points that OSHA had not proven dental workers were at high enough risk to come under the rule. A U.S. Court of Appeals upheld the application of the rule to dental workers [*American Dental Association vs. Martin*, 985 F.2d 823 (1993)].

Among the dozens of federal regulatory agencies that oversee small business operations are the Internal Revenue Service, the Department of Labor, the Federal Commerce Commission, and the Equal Employment Opportunity Commission. Each of these agencies or commissions has adopted regulations that small businesses must follow.

Many state statutes also establish state agencies to carry out the mandate of state law. For example, after a state legislature passes an environmental protection bill, the legislature will then establish an environmental protection commission or agency to carry out the state law. The commission or agency will write and enforce regulations necessary to implementing the state environmental law.

Small businesses are regulated by dozens of state agencies. Frequently both state and federal agencies have regulations relevant to the same area of business activity. For example, a business must comply with both federal and state environmental regulations. Proposed or adopted changes in administrative regulations can be monitored in the same manner as one monitors state and federal legislation: following media stories; joining trade groups or associations; and reading relevant magazines and journals.

SOURCES OF LAWS FOR THE HOME–BASED BUSINESS

The home-based business can be subject to the same laws as the small business operating in the local strip mall or the multinational company with a multimillion dollar annual income.

The owner of a home-based business may engage in interstate commerce and become subject to certain federal laws even though all of the business customers are from the local neighborhood. For example, a home-based florist may order flowers from another state or a home-based caterer may order and sell birthday candles manufactured in another state or another country.

It is important for the owner of a home-based business to monitor changes in the law that impact the business to assure compliance with the current law. Ignorance of the law is not a valid excuse for noncompliance no matter how small the business operation.

REDUCING YOUR RISKS

Applying the material in this chapter may help reduce the possibility of future legal problems for small businesses operating within the U.S. (domestic operations) and those conducting business in other countries (international operations).

Preventive measures include the following:

Domestic Operations:

(1) Know the sources of domestic law, monitor those sources on a regular basis and make sure any new business decisions will be in compliance with present or proposed laws. For example, the latest provisions in the state and local fire codes may require sprinkler systems that are not included in the specifications for the business's renovation.

(2) Review relevant proposed laws prior to their adoption, in order to have a voice in explaining their impact on your business operations. Joining trade and business associations frequently affords access to the proposals and the opportunity to learn more about them through experts retained by the organization.

(3) Understand the general rule that "Ignorance of the law is no excuse" and thereby reduce the risk of being sued by staying informed.

International Operations:

(1) Understand that laws and legal systems may be quite different in other countries. For example, the charging of any amount of interest on a credit sale may be totally illegal in a certain country; this information can have a significant impact on determining price and sales terms in that country.

(2) Seek competent legal advice prior to entering into any international agreement to assure the agreement is both legal and in the best interest of the small business.

*KEY WORDS AND PHRASES

Administrative Law	Criminal Law
Civil Law	Interstate Commerce Clause
Common Law	Law
Constitutional Law	Statutory Law

CHAPTER SUMMARY

1. Characteristics of a Law
    a. A rule which is
    b. Handed down by person or group
    c. With authority for which
    d. Noncompliance results in
    e. Sanctions

2. Classification of Law
    a. Criminal law involves a wrong against society as a whole.
    b. Civil law refers to a wrong against a private party.

3. Sources of U.S. Law
    a. Federal and state constitutions
    b. Statutes
    c. Common law decisions
    d. Administrative regulations

4. Sources of Information
    a. Trade groups and associations
    b. Trade journals and publications
    c. Consultations with a qualified attorney

DISCUSSION QUESTIONS

1. <u>Elements of a Law</u>. Rick Retailer, candidate for mayor, hands out a circular stating he has just passed a law providing that any retail business that remains open after 7 p.m. is subject to sanctions that Rick will determine after he is elected mayor. Has Rick passed a valid law? Why or why not?

2. <u>Commerce Clause</u>. Rick Retailer employees 100 employees in his store. He argues that he is not subject to the federal Age Discrimination in Employment Act because a majority of his customers are local residents. Is Rick correct? Explain.

3. <u>Freedom of Speech</u>. Rick, the newly elected mayor, again encourages the City Council to pass an ordinance that prohibits local businesses from mak-

ing any political contributions to Rick's opponent in the upcoming election. Fern, owner of Fern's Florist, brings suit against the city, claiming her business has been deprived of its constitutional right of freedom of speech. Who will win? Why?

4. <u>Common Law Disputes</u>. Sam Salesman is injured when Fern from Fern's Florist runs a stoplight and slams into Sam's car. When Sam brings a lawsuit, Fern claims there is no cause of action because the state legislature has not passed a statute relevant to careless driving. Is Fern correct? Why or why not?

5. <u>Sources of Information</u>. Enrique Entrepreneur wants to set up a new upscale retail store in town. He is not certain what state and federal laws apply to his business since he will be employing only 5 employees. How can Enrique learn more about the applicable laws?

Is It Ethical?

1. Statutory laws are passed by state legislatures and the federal congress. Frequently a business organization will lobby members of a legislature or congress to pass a law that is favorable to the interests of the organization. Is this practice ethical? Why or why not?

2. A newcomer to a community decides to open up a restaurant, unaware of the need to get a permit from the city health department. The restaurant is immediately shut down by the city because the required permit was not obtained. Is it ethical for the city to shut down the business even though the owner was unaware of the requirement? Why or why not?

3. Moe Manufacturer becomes distressed because of the increasing number of state and federal laws applicable to his small manufacturing company. Moe decides to move his company to another country to avoid the laws in this country. Is Moe's decision ethical? Are there other factors to be considered in determining your answer? Explain.

4. Many U.S. companies intentionally keep the number of employees low in order to avoid being subject to certain federal employment laws. Is this practice ethical?

5. Assume in #4 that a company would have to shut down in the near future due to the costs involved in meeting the requirements of the federal employment laws. Would this affect your answer to #4?

DISCUSSION CASE

> ## RUBIN, SECRETARY OF THE TREASURY V. COORS BREWING CO.
>
> 115 S.Ct. 1585 (1995)

Facts:

Coors Brewing Co. (plaintiff) applied to the federal Bureau of Alcohol, Tobacco and Firearms (BATF) for approval of new labels disclosing the alcohol content of the company's beers. The BATF (a part of the U.S. Treasury Department) denied the application, citing Section 205 (e) (2) of the Federal Alcohol Administration Act (the Act). The applicable section of the Act prohibited beer labels from disclosing alcohol content in order to discourage "strength wars" among the brewing companies.

The plaintiff sued, claiming that Section 205 (e) (2) violated the company's freedom of commercial speech under the First Amendment of the U.S. Constitution.

Issue:

Does Section 205 (e) (2) of the Federal Alcohol Administration Act violate the First Amendment's protection of commercial speech?

Decision:

The U.S. Supreme Court held that Section 205 (e) (2) violates the First Amendment's protection of free speech, affirming the decisions of the U.S. District Court and the U.S. Court of Appeals.

Reasons:

In reviewing a governmental regulation of commercial speech, the Court stated it must be convinced that (1) the governmental agency has a "substantial" interest in supporting the regulation and (2) the regulation directly advances that governmental interest.

In this case, the Court found a "substantial" governmental interest in discouraging strength wars between brewing companies. The Court did not find, however, that the ban on alcohol content directly advanced that interest. The Court referred to the fact that the ban applies only in those states where applicable state laws ban such advertisements. In addition, the Court pointed out that certain beers containing high alcohol content can be labeled as "malt liquor" and alcohol content is required for wine and spirit labels.

The Court ruled that Section 205 (e) (2) is overly extensive and violates the plaintiff's freedom of commercial speech.

Discussion Questions

1. Do you agree with the Supreme Court's decision? Why or why not?

2. Why did the federal law apply to plaintiff's business?

3. How was the plaintiff engaged in interstate commerce?

4. Assume the plaintiff was a small brewery with only one facility. Would it still be involved in interstate commerce? Explain.

CHAPTER 2

THE COSTS OF LAWSUITS: $'S, TIME AND STRESS

CHAPTER OBJECTIVES

In this chapter you will learn to:

1. Recognize a situation in your business that may result in a lawsuit if the situation remains uncorrected.

2. Identify the categories of damages a party may seek when bringing a lawsuit against a small business.

3. Understand the nonmonetary losses associated with defending a lawsuit.

4. Identify the steps involved in the legal process when defending a civil lawsuit.

5. Understand how state and federal courts obtain jurisdiction over the parties and subject matter in a lawsuit.

6. Recognize alternative means of dispute resolution when a lawsuit is contemplated or filed.

7. Identify certain steps that help reduce the risk of a lawsuit against your small business.

8. Understand how a home-based business may be as vulnerable to a lawsuit as a larger company.

If a small business remains in operation for an extensive length of time, the chances are extremely high the business will be sued. The plaintiff (the party bringing the suit) may be a customer who slips and falls in the store; a supplier who claims nonpayment; a competitor claiming unfair business tactics; or a governmental agency claiming noncompliance with a government regulation. The defendant retailer may even be sued for merely selling a product that was manufactured thousands of miles away because a court finds the product was unreasonably dangerous and had not been altered between the time it left the seller and reached the ultimate user. This legal theory is referred to as strict liability (Chapter 4). In every case, the small business defendant may face the same basic cost factors in defending the lawsuit, even though the business was not at fault in any way.

The first question the owner of a small business usually asks when sued is "how much will this cost?" The owner is probably referring to the monetary cost of defending the lawsuit. Unfortunately, money is only one of several costs the defendant will incur. Other costs include loss of time, physical and emotional stress, lost sales, damage to public relations and lost self-image. These latter factors may prove more detrimental than the initial court costs and attorney fees. The time factor can have a devastating effect on the defendant's business life and personal life while the stress factor can play havoc with one's physical and emotional life.

This chapter will examine several of these three cost factors individually and evaluate the potential effect on the defendant.

▶ ## "RED FLAG" SITUATIONS

Situation	Potential Problem
1. A customer loudly claims injury by a product or service provided by the business.	1. The customer may be laying the foundation for a future lawsuit.
2. An employee claims unfair treatment by a supervisor.	2. Again, a future lawsuit may result.
3. A business owner is served with a lawsuit and disgustedly throws it aside.	3. Failure to answer on time can result in a default judgment for the opposition.
4. A busy retailer does not take time to document the counseling of an incompetent salesperson.	4. Inadequate documentation can destroy any possible defense to a wrongful discharge claim.
5. The defendant to a lawsuit becomes overwhelmed by the suit and ignores customers, employees, friends and family.	5. Business and family relationships can be damaged or destroyed.
6. The defendant looks for the nearest (and cheapest) attorney to defend him.	6. Incompetent counsel can cost the defendant money, time and reputation.

THE $ FACTOR

Big Bucks to Defend

Even if the court rules for the defendant small business, the defendant may be required to pay attorney fees and court costs incurred in defending the case.

Defense attorneys usually charge their clients in one of two ways: on an hourly basis or an established fee for the entire case. If the hourly basis is used, most attorneys charge higher hourly fees for the time spent actually arguing the case in the courtroom. Hourly fees for preparing the defense may exceed $300 per hour, and courtroom fees frequently go higher. In addition, there are fees for expert witnesses, preparation of documents, transcripts, and numerous other changes. Based on these figures, it is easy to see how the monetary costs of defending a lawsuit can become so astronomical. To reduce the financial burden on the client, the defendant attorney may ask the court to order the plaintiff to pay defendant's court costs and attorney fees if the defendant prevails. There are, however, no guarantees the court will issue that order.

As mentioned earlier, the case may be brought against the small business retailer simply because the store sold an allegedly defective product that harmed the plaintiff. Potential costs from these strict liability suits (see Chapter 4 on Torts) force manufacturers and other parties in the distribution chain to buy liability insurance.

Damages Paid to Plaintiff

The monetary costs of lawsuits that grab the headlines are the dollars awarded to the plaintiff if the latter wins the suit. These awards are referred to as **damages** and fall into several categories.

Compensatory damages refer to the amount paid to the plaintiff for damages actually suffered. If the lawsuit involves a breach of contract, the compensatory damages are intended to place the plaintiff in the same position he would be in if the defendant had fully performed on the contract. For example, assume that Acme Manufacturing Co. contracts to sell 5000 toy dolls to Toddler Toys, Inc. at $5.00 per doll. Acme breaches the contract and fails to supply the dolls. Toddler has to buy the dolls elsewhere for $6.00 per doll. Toddler would be entitled to $5,000.00 in compensatory damages. This amount is based on the fact that Toddler had to pay an additional $1.00 per doll to be in the same position as if Acme had fully performed under the contract (that is, Toddler had 5000 dolls to sell in its retail stores).

Another type of damages is referred to as **consequential damages**. These damages are the losses that "flow from" or result from the defendant's failure to comply with the terms of a contract. A court may award consequential damages in breach of contract cases if the court is convinced the defendant knew or should have known that the plaintiff would suffer these consequential losses.

Assume that in the case of Toddler Toys Inc. the dolls were to be delivered on December 1, in time for Christmas sales and that Toddler was unable to find any other dolls on the open market in time for Christmas. Toddler may sue for the profits lost as a consequence of Acme's failure to deliver the dolls. If Toddler can convince a court that it would have realized a profit of $4.00 per doll, it may recover consequential damages of $20,000. The burden is on the plaintiff's attorney to convince a jury that Acme Manufacturing Company had actually known or should have known profits would be lost if the dolls were not delivered on time. This knowledge issue is a factual determination for the jury. Plaintiff attorneys frequently find consequential damages difficult to prove.

A third category of damages is referred to as **punitive damages**. These are the "big bucks" the media frequently quotes when reporting a court award against a business. Courts ordinarily award punitive damages in tort cases only when convinced the defendant's behavior was either intentional or so reckless that it was construed as intentional. Punitive damages serve a twofold purpose: they punish the defendant for what the court considered as outrageous behavior and they serve as a deterrent to potential future wrongdoers.

One of the most publicized examples of punitive awards was the case of Pennzoil Co. v. Texaco, Inc. (729 S.W.2d 768). Pennzoil had offered to buy controlling interest in Getty Oil. Following extensive **negotiations** the parties entered into an informal memorandum of agreement. The companies informed the media and attorneys for both companies began negotiating the final written document. During the interim, Texaco offered a purchase bid which Getty accepted. Pennzoil sued Texaco based on the intentional tort of wrongful interference with a contractual relationship (Chapter 4). Texaco claimed no binding agreement existed between Pennzoil and Getty. The trial court, in finding the defendant liable for wrongfully interfering with an existing agreement between Pennzoil and Getty Oil, determined the plaintiff was entitled to $7.53 billion in actual damages and $3 billion in punitive damages. The case was later settled for $3 billion. At that time the defendant emerged from twelve months in Chapter 11 bankruptcy reorganization proceedings.

Loss in Sales

In addition to the costs of legal fees and damages paid to the plaintiff, the defendant frequently suffers monetary loss in sales of goods or services. This latter loss may result even if the defendant ultimately prevails in the lawsuit. Sales losses are due to several factors: adverse publicity; loss of credit rating; and neglect of the business while defending the lawsuit.

Adverse publicity due to a lawsuit impacts both current customers and potential customers. Unfortunately the media is quick to report that a local business has been sued and reluctant to later report that the case was dismissed or the court found the defendant not liable. If the latter information is in fact reported, it is frequently found on a back page of the newspaper in contrast to the front page headlines when the suit was originally filed. The public has a long memory as to the fact that a business was sued and may never know the end results of the case.

Assume that a local restaurant is sued for allegedly serving contaminated food. Potential patrons will avoid the restaurant in droves. The court later dismisses the case after learning the plaintiff contracted the alleged illness elsewhere. Unfortunately the damage to the defendant's reputation may be permanent if the public never knows the end results of the case.

Damage to the business's credit rating is another factor that can result in lost sales. A standard question on loan applications asks if the applicant is party to a lawsuit. The defendant's affirmative **answer** may greatly decrease the chances of getting a loan to replenish inventory, make needed repairs to the store or expand current floor space. Failure to get a loan for these critical needs can drastically reduce sales and thus profits for an extended period of time.

THE TIME FACTOR

Time to Prepare the Defense

First-time defendants in a lawsuit are frequently surprised to find how much time is involved in preparing for court. Many assume they only have to call up an attorney, send the **complaint** over to the law office, and show up in court the day of the trial. Unfortunately, this assumption is quite erroneous.

As soon as the defendant receives the complaint, he should indeed notify his attorney. The complaint is the document that names the parties to the lawsuit, the basis for the court to have **jurisdiction** (power) to hear the case, the plaintiff's alleged basis for the lawsuit, and the damages the plaintiff is seeking. The complaint may be one short page in length or may be comprised of dozens of pages of allegations. In either case, the defendant has only a certain number of days which vary from state to state, in which to file an **answer** to the complaint with the court. Failure to file the answer on time can result in a **default judgment**. The result is similar to a situation where a football team fails to show up for a game and is declared the loser even if that team could in fact have defeated the opposition by several touchdowns. Due to the danger of a default judgment, business owners need to be aware of the need to notify their attorneys as soon as they receive a complaint.

The defendant's attorney immediately determines if the court in which the suit was filed has proper jurisdiction over the parties and the subject matter. Federal court jurisdiction is established by Article III of the U.S. Constitution, which provides the following cases may be heard in federal courts:

Federal Court Jurisdiction

Federal court jurisdiction is based on either:

(1)   Cases that involve a federal question. These include cases arising under the U.S. Constitution, federal laws, and treaties; cases involving

Ambassadors, public Ministers and Consuls; admiralty and maritime cases; and cases to which the federal government is a party or

(2) Cases where there is diversity of citizenship and the plaintiff is claiming at least $50,000 in damages. Diversity of citizenship exists when the parties are from different states or one party is a U.S. citizen and the opposing party is from another country.

If the plaintiff filed suit in a federal court which lacked jurisdiction, the defendant's attorney will request the case be removed to a state court. If the case was filed in a state court and there is also federal jurisdiction, the defendant's attorney may have the case removed to federal court or leave the case in state court. This dual jurisdiction is referred to as concurrent jurisdiction.

GOING GLOBAL If the owner of a small U.S. business is involved in a dispute with an individual or company from another country and the plaintiff claims at least $50,000, there is federal court jurisdiction if the case is heard in the U.S.

In Personam and In Rem Jurisdiction

Whether the case is heard in federal or state court, the court must have jurisdiction over the person involved (referred to as **in personam jurisdiction**) or over the property involved (referred to as **in rem jurisdiction**) and also have jurisdiction over the subject matter involved in the lawsuit. For example, an Oklahoma customer claims she fell and was injured while shopping in a New York department store. Claiming $250,000 damages, her attorney plans to sue in a federal court. The negligence case may be brought in a New York federal court since businesses are considered "persons" and New York courts have jurisdictions over persons located in that state and over negligence cases. This example also involves dual or concurrent jurisdiction; therefore the parties may choose to have the case heard in New York state court.

The subject matter may also determine which court within the state or federal system will hear the case. For example, the U.S. Constitution provides bankruptcy cases will be heard in federal bankruptcy courts. Cases involving distribution of property upon an individual's death are heard in state probate courts.

The defendant's attorney will need detailed information from the client in order to properly prepare the answer to the complaint. In preparing the answer the defendant's attorney may determine that the client actually has a cause of action to bring a **countersuit** against the plaintiff. For example, assume that Jones files a breach of contract suit against Salinas's Stereo Shop, alleging the latter failed to pay $5000 for work Jones did on the defendant's roof. While meeting with Salinas, her attorney discovers that Salinas did in fact pay the $5000 and furthermore that Jones did not repair the roof in a workmanlike manner.

Salinas' attorney will prepare an answer that denies Jones' claim and that also includes a counterclaim. The original plaintiff (Jones) must then answer the counterclaim with a pleading called a reply. Salinas must spend time acquainting the attorney with the facts of the case and producing the roofing contract, canceled check, and documentation as to the inadequacy of the work. All of this costs Salinas time (and money).

If the case is set for trial, Salinas must spend more time with her attorney and possibly with Jones' attorney during the discovery portion of the lawsuit. **"Discovery"** refers to the gathering of evidence to be presented at the trial. Evidence may be gathered by **depositions**. In a deposition, Jones' attorney may ask verbal questions of Salinas in the presence of a court reporter. The questions and answers are transcribed and become part of the court record. Salinas's attorney may likewise take a deposition from Jones. Expert witnesses appearing for either side may also give depositions. In complex lawsuits, depositions for each witness may last for many hours or even days.

Evidence is also gathered through written **interrogatories** served by one party to a lawsuit upon the other party. If the lawsuit is complex, a set of interrogatories may consist of hundreds of questions. Some courts limit the number of interrogatories today. The party served with the interrogatories may have to spend dozens of hours with his attorney in preparing answers to these questions. Interrogatories also become part of the court record.

Evidence is also obtained by requesting a party to produce certain documents; requesting a party to submit to physical or mental examinations; or by inspection of the site of an accident or the product that caused an injury. As indicated above, the gathering of evidence before the trial begins can cost the defendant hundreds of hours away from the business. In addition to the defendant having to devote time to preparing the defense, key employees of the business may also be subject to depositions, interrogatories and interviews with the defendant's attorney. The absence of key employees is also an expense to the business.

Time in the Courtroom

The time a business defendant will have to actually spend in the courtroom may be totally unpredictable in advance. The trial date for a case may be months after the parties have gathered evidence and may be postponed several times before the court convenes.

The actual time spent in court is frequently very short in comparison to the hundreds of hours devoted to gathering of evidence. If a jury is to hear the case, the time for jury selection usually depends on the complexity of the case. Selection of a jury to hear a complex case involving the sale of a toy that severely injured a child may take days or even weeks.

The defendant will work closely with his attorney throughout the trial and may take the stand in his own behalf.

Following the court's decision at the trial, the losing party may decide to **appeal** the case. Whether the plaintiff or defendant is appealing, the defendant will spend additional time with his attorney in preparing the appeal. An appeal is based on alleged errors of law that occurred during the trial. For example, the losing party's attorney may claim the judge issued erroneous instructions to the jury or admitted improper evidence. As a general rule, the factual determinations of the jury are not subject to appeal. Whatever the basis of the appeal, the defendant will continue to work closely with his attorney in preparing the appeal.

To avoid the expenses involved in retaining an attorney and proceeding through a formal lawsuit, a plaintiff may choose to sue in a state small claims court. The case cannot involve more than a specific amount of money, and the parties are not required to have attorneys represent them. The losing party in a small claims case can appeal the decision to a state trial court.

No Time for Family

First-time parties to a lawsuit are frequently shocked to realize the impact the suit has on the family. As discussed above, the defendant may have to spend hundreds of hours in preparing for the case, going to trial, and even during the appeals process.

Unfortunately, the legal process does not recognize family birthdays, wedding anniversaries, and graduations. Even if the defendant has spent months in preparing a surprise silver wedding anniversary party for a spouse, the "court must go on."

Lawsuits can have a particularly harsh effect on children. Explaining to a ten-year-old why a parent must miss the Little League playoffs can be very difficult for both parent and child.

Although the defendant cannot alter the fact that an extensive amount of time must be spent away from business and family, there are a few steps to take to make the situation easier:

(1)   Explain to family and friends from the beginning that a great deal of time must be spent relevant to the lawsuit. This approach is much better than running the risk that someone will feel they are being snubbed or ignored when social or family events must be postponed or cancelled.

(2)   Make sure that any free time available is spent as quality time with family and friends. It's not worth successfully defending a lawsuit at the expense of losing all personal relationships.

THE STRESS FACTOR

Numbers can be allocated to the dollars lost in defending a lawsuit and to the hours lost from business and personal activities. No quantitative value can be placed on what may turn out to be the most serious expense: the stress factor. No matter how confident a party is that he will ultimately win the suit, stress is inevitable. Stress usually results from two separate factors: excessive worry and lack of time to rest and relax.

Worry, Worry, Worry

Worrying about the ultimate outcome of a lawsuit is inevitable. No matter how much the attorney reassures a defendant, the latter will spend time fretting over the possible outcome of the lawsuit.

It is important for the defendant to recognize the need to "let go" of his worries as much as possible. For one thing, the more one dwells on a topic, the more dire the situation seems. In addition, worrying is distracting–it is a negative expenditure of time and energy. A distracted business owner may be curt to a customer or employee at the very time when support and loyalty are most important.

Although it is impossible (and impractical) to try to eliminate all worry over the lawsuit, certain positive steps may help alleviate the situation:

1.   The client can benefit from establishing a good rapport with the attorney or someone in the law office who can keep the client informed as to the progress of the case. The few dollars spent on calling the attorney's office can be cheaper in the long run than developing an ulcer.

2.   The client needs to be able to trust the attorney and "let go" of the worry. After all, if the attorney is being paid a healthy fee for defending the lawsuit, the attorney should be the one doing the worrying.

No Time for R and R

Lack of time for rest and relaxation can contribute significantly to the stress factor. A client frequently ends up devoting all the waking hours to either working on the job or working on the lawsuit. As a consequence, leisure time no longer exists. This all-work approach can actually become counterproductive. The defendant should not feel guilty about setting aside time for exercise and relaxation–both can actually be beneficial to the defense!

Costs in money, time and stress are inevitable for a lawsuit defendant. By taking a logical rather than emotional approach, regularly communicating with the attorney, and including time for rest and relaxation, these costs can be significantly reduced.

ALTERNATIVES TO THE COURTROOM

Today an increasing number of business disputes are being settled through means of **Alternative Dispute Resolution** (ADR). Many state and federal courts now require parties to consider ADR before taking the dispute to trial.

The benefits of utilizing ADR in lieu of going to trial are substantial. Besides avoiding the huge costs associated with a trial, the matter can be settled quicker and more efficiently. The parties may choose to use a third party who is an expert on the subject matter involved in the dispute. This third party expert may bring a degree of expertise and understanding to the hearing that a lay jury would lack.

Means of alternative dispute resolution include negotiation, **mediation**, and **arbitration**. Determining which means to use frequently depends on the complexity of the case and the potential damages.

Negotiation involves the two parties meeting and attempting to resolve the dispute in a one-on-one manner. This approach is feasible when both parties are amiable and each is willing to "give" to a certain degree in order to resolve the dispute. Advantages include the informality of the procedure, the avoidance of having to pay third parties, and the privacy of the process.

In the mediation process, a third party mediator listens to both parties and attempts to bring the parties to a resolution of their dispute. The mediator does not make a determination regarding the dispute himself. A major advantage of mediation is the expertise the mediator may bring to the matter. This expertise may allow the mediator to propose a solution to the matter that is satisfactory to both parties. The mediator usually charges a fee, which is paid jointly by both parties. Mediation is an informal process that does not substitute for a trial.

Arbitration involves a third party arbitrator selected by the parties hearing both sides of the dispute and making a determination on the matter. If a panel of three arbitrators is used, each party may select one arbitrator and the two agree on a mutually acceptable third arbitrator. If the parties agreed in advance the arbitrator's decision would be binding, the hearing substitutes for a trial and courts will not ordinarily overturn that decision. Most arbitrators charge a fee, which is paid by the parties. Advantages of arbitration include fast and efficient resolution of the dispute and the expertise an arbitrator may bring to the hearing.

Many business contracts today include an arbitration clause providing that if a dispute arises the parties will take the matter to binding arbitration. If a decision is made to arbitrate, expert arbitrators may be obtained from numerous associations, including the American Arbitration Association for domestic contracts and the International Chamber of Commerce for international contracts.

The costs in money, time and stress related to trying a lawsuit in a courtroom can be astronomical. For this reason, one of the means of alternative dispute resolution may be a viable and positive alternative to both parties.

GOING GLOBAL

Many contracts between a small U.S. business and a foreign party now include an arbitration clause. In case of a dispute, one or more arbitrators will hear both sides' positions and hand down a binding decision. This means of dispute resolution reduces the monetary expenses involved in trying a case in another country. It may also reduce the risk of having a case heard in a foreign court that may be biased against parties from other countries.

The Costs of Lawsuits and the Home–Based Business

The owner of a home-based business may be surprised to learn that the business operating out of a residence may be vulnerable to lawsuits by customers, suppliers, competitors and other potential plaintiffs to the same extent a store operating in the mall is subject to lawsuits. A customer patronizing a residential business may slip and fall on the front steps, claim illness from the catered birthday cake or allege a computer software program failed to meet the seller's warranty.

The same costs in money, time and stress apply to defending a lawsuit against a home-based business. The damage to the business's reputation can be particularly costly since the owner frequently relies so heavily on the recommendations of satisfied customers as the means of attracting new customers.

The owner of a home-based business can benefit from following the same recommendations for reducing the risks of a lawsuit that apply to the owners of small businesses operating in a commercial setting.

Reducing Your Risks

Preventive measures for reducing your risks of a lawsuit include the following:

(1) Maintain specific procedures for handling customer complaints and make certain all employees follow these procedures. A dissatisfied customer who is treated fairly and respectfully may be a repeat customer rather than a lawsuit plaintiff.

(2) Make certain all customer complaints and customer accidents are carefully documented. This information may prove invaluable if the customer later threatens a lawsuit.

(3) Become acquainted with a competent attorney before legal counsel is needed. Once a lawsuit is filed, the defendant may be unable to retain the best counsel before the deadline for filing an answer.

(4) Seek legal advice in developing company procedures for counselling and dismissing unsatisfactory employees. Lawsuits by former employees claiming wrongful discharge frequently result in large monetary damages against the former employer.

*KEY WORDS AND PHRASES

Alternative Dispute Resolution
Answer
Appeal
Arbitration
Compensatory Damage
Complaint
Consequential Damages
Countersuit
Damages

Deposition
Discovery
In Personam Jurisdiction
In Rem Jurisdiction
Interrogatories
Jurisdiction
Mediation
Negotiation
Punitive Damages

CHAPTER SUMMARY

The Costs of Lawsuits

1. Monetary Damages in a Civil Lawsuit
   a. Compensatory damages-based on loss plaintiff actually suffered.
   b. Consequential damages-foreseeable losses that "flow from" defendant's failure to comply with contract terms.
   c. Punitive damages-damages awarded in a tort case when defendant's behavior was intentional or exceedingly reckless.

2. Additional Losses in Defending a Lawsuit
   a. Loss in sales.
   b. Adverse publicity.
   c. Damage to credit rating.
   d. Loss in time away from business and family.

3. Steps in the Legal Process
   a. Complaint-document served upon defendant establishing basis for lawsuit.
   b. Answer-defendant's written response to the complaint.

c. Discovery-process of obtaining evidence to present to the court–includes depositions; interrogatories; requests to submit documents; requests to submit to physical and mental examinations; and examination of accident site.

4. Jurisdiction of the Court

    a. The court's power to hear a case;

    b. Includes jurisdiction over the person (in personam) and jurisdiction over the subject matter.

5. Alternative Means of Dispute Resolution

    a. Negotiation-parties attempt to resolve dispute in non-binding, one-on-one approach.

    b. Mediation-third party listens to dispute and attempts to bring involved parties to a non-binding resolution.

    c. Arbitration-objective third party hears dispute and issues a binding decision.

DISCUSSION QUESTIONS

1. Compensatory Damages. Rick Retailer orders 500 teddy bears from Toddler Toy Co. at $15 per bear. The bears are to be delivered to Rick's store by December 1. The seller never delivers the bears and Rick has to pay $20 per bear from another source. Rick sues Toddler Toy Co. for breach of contract. How much in compensatory damages can Rick recover? Explain.

2. Consequential Damages. Assume that in case #1 the bears are delivered on December 27. Rick had planned to make a profit of $3 per bear and finds he is now unable to sell the bears. Can Rick recover consequential damages even though the bears were finally delivered? Explain.

3. Jurisdiction of the Court. Enrique Entrepreneur is injured in an auto accident when Hapless Harry runs a stop sign and hits Enrique's car. Both parties are citizens of the same state. Enrique sues Hapless for $500,000 in damages in state district court. Can Hapless have the case removed to federal court? Why or why not?

4. Jurisdiction. Assume that in #4 Hapless is from France. Would your answer be the same?

5.   Discovery. Three pedestrians witnessed the accident in #3. Enrique is claiming a severe neck injury that will prevent him from working. What tools of discovery are available for Enrique's attorney to use in presenting the case?

6.   Alternative Dispute Resolution. Fern of Fern's Florist is considering a lawsuit against Green's Greenhouse for failure to deliver roses to the florists until February 15. (The contract called for delivery on February 12). Green has suggested submitting the matter to binding arbitration. What factors should Fern consider in determining whether to bring a lawsuit or submit the matter to arbitration?

IS IT ETHICAL?

1.   Frequently the plaintiff will agree to pay the plaintiffs attorney a certain percentage of the court award if the plaintiff wins. Assume the plaintiff's attorney requests 40% as a contingency fee. The plaintiff, the owner of a small business, receives a court award of $100,000 due to severe injuries sustained as a result of the defendant's negligent driving. Is it ethical for the attorney to seek $40,000 of the award? Discuss.

2.   Testimony of expert witnesses is frequently used in lawsuits. Assume Rick Retailer sues a supplier for failure to deliver toys in time for Christmas sales. Rick's attorney uses the testimony of an economist who projects Rick's lost profits at double the amount of profit Rick realized the previous year. Rick's attorney has carefully selected an expert witness known as a "plaintiff" witness. Is this practice ethical on the part of Rick's attorney? Is it ethical on the economist's part? What would happen if the economist was very conservative relevant to projected profits?

3.   Assume Carl Consumer is shopping in Rick's Retail Store and accidentally slips and falls due to his own clumsiness, slightly injuring his knee. Carl is currently short on cash and threatens to sue Rick unless Rick's insurance company will settle. Is Carl's action ethical? What if Carl needs the extra money to pay for his son's much-needed operation?

4.   Assume that in case #3 Rick's insurance company knows Carl could not win in court but decides to settle in order to avoid the time and cost of the lawsuit. Is the insurance company's action ethical?

5.   Ed Employee is seriously injured when Hapless Harry runs a stoplight and hits Ed at a pedestrian crossing. Ed cannot work and the medical bills are increasing. Ed files suit, but Hapless's attorney continuously postpones the trial date based on technicalities of the law. Finally Ed is about to lose his home and agrees to settle the case for one-third of the amount being sought in court. Is the defendant attorney's action ethical?

BMW of North America v. Gore

116 S.Ct. 1589

(Decided May 20, 1996)

Facts:

Plaintiff Gore bought a new BMW auto from a BMW dealer in Alabama. After finding the new car had been repainted prior to his purchase, the plaintiff sued, claiming fraud based on the defendant's failure to disclose the fact the car had been repainted. During the trial the defendant acknowledged a policy of not advising dealers of predelivery damage if repair costs did not exceed 3% of the new car's suggested retail value.

The case was tried before a jury, which found defendant liable. The jury awarded plaintiff $4,000 in compensatory damages and $4 million in punitive damages.

Defendant filed a post-trial motion to set aside the punitive damages, claiming the award was so excessive that it violated the Fourteenth Amendment's Due Process Clause.

The trial judge denied the motion. The Alabama Supreme Court affirmed but found the jury had erred by multiplying compensatory damages by national sales rather than Alabama sales. The Alabama Supreme Court reduced the punitive damages to $2 million.

Defendant appeals the $2 million in punitive damages.

Issue:

Was the $2 million award in punitive damages grossly excessive and in violation of the Fourteenth Amendment's Due Process Clause?

Decision:

The Supreme Court held that the $2 million in punitive damages was grossly excessive and therefore unconstitutional. The Court found that due process requires a defendant have fair notice of (1) conduct that is punishable and (2) of the potential severity of the State's penalty. The case is reversed and remanded.

Reason:

The court award of punitive damages is measured relevant to the State's interest in (1) punishing illegal conduct and (2) in deterring repetition of the conduct. The plaintiff's award in this case is to be analyzed relevant to the interests of Alabama customers and not customers throughout the nation. The Supreme Court addressed three guideposts leading to the finding that the award was grossly excessive: (1) There was no finding that BMW's performance was reprehensible nor that the defendant engaged in deliberately false statements. (2) Plaintiff's $2 million award is 500 times the actual harm and ratio exceeds an acceptable range. (3) The difference between the $2 million and other civil or criminal sanctions that could be imposed for comparable misconduct is excessive.

Discussion Questions

1.   Do you agree the punitive damages were excessive?

2.   In your opinion, why did the jury award such large damages?

3.   Was BMW's practice of repainting and repairing acceptable?

4.   Should the dealer have been informed of the practice?

PART II

TYPES OF LAWSUITS FREQUENTLY BROUGHT AGAINST SMALL BUSINESSES

CHAPTER 3

BREACH OF CONTRACT LAWSUITS

CHAPTER OBJECTIVES

In this chapter you will learn to:

1. Recognize situations that may later lead to a breach of contract lawsuit.

2. Define contracts according to their enforceability in court; according to their stage of completion and according to the number of promises exchanged.

3. Understand the basic elements of a valid contract and each element's effect on the enforceability of a contract.

4. Recognize which contracts must be in writing to be enforceable.

5. Determine when Article 2 of the Uniform Commercial Code applies to your contract and understand the special provisions of Article 2.

6. Identify the levels of performance the courts consider when determining the seriousness of a breach of contract.

7. Understand how contractual duties are discharged based on agreement of the parties; conditions precedent or conditions subsequent; and based on operation of law.

8. Carefully review all terms before entering a contract to make certain all relevant terms are included; otherwise, a court may "fill in the gaps" in a manner that is unfavorable to your business.

One of the most common legal claims against small business owners is based on breach of contract. Small businesses are entering into contracts every day with customers, suppliers, wholesalers, manufacturers and numerous other parties. A small grocer selling a pound of potatoes to a customer is contracting with the buyer just as a large auto manufacturer contracts when selling one million dollars in cars to a major retailer. In either case, the requirements for a **valid contract** are the same and the consequences for breaching the contract are the same.

This chapter lists certain "red flag" situations that may alert small business owners to potential trouble when contracting. Different types of contracts are defined. The elements of a "good" contract and what's wrong in a "broken" contract are discussed. The special rules that the Uniform Commercial Code applies to the sale of goods are explained. The chapter concludes with an explanation of defenses to breach of contract claims and penalties for the breach.

► "RED FLAG" SITUATIONS

Situation	Potential Problem
1. One party to a contract insists there's no need to put it in writing.	1. If the parties later disagree, it's one party's word against the other's, and the court must decide who's telling the truth.
2. The contract doesn't "spell out" important terms.	2. The law may "fill in the gaps" in a way the parties never intended.
3. A seller is too busy to proof a contract before sending it out and understates a price.	3. The law may have no sympathy with this type of error, and the seller may suffer a loss on the sale.
4. A party fails to verify if the other party is sane, sober, and over 18.	4. The other party may be able to avoid the contract (and even keep the benefits without paying).
5. The owner lets an inexperienced employee contract in his name.	5. The owner can still be liable on the contract, no matter how much it costs.

WAYS OF DEFINING CONTRACTS

Contracts are defined in several ways. One category of definitions is based on whether either or both parties can enforce the contract in a court of law.

A contract is defined as a valid contract if it meets all of the legal requirements for a contract (discussed below) and is enforceable by either party in a court of law. A small business owner needs to be sure the company's contracts are always valid.

A **void contract** is one that is "no good" in a court of law. This means that the court will not enforce the contract for either party. Contracts that break the law (illegal contracts) are void. For example, Pat's Pub sells $300 in alcoholic beverages to a group of minors and the latter refuse to pay. Pat's cannot force the minors to pay (even though they consumed the alcohol) because the sale violated the law prohibiting the sale of alcohol to minors.

Contracts to commit crimes are void. Assume that the owner of Carl's Cafe pays Tony Trespasser $500 in advance if Tony will break into Pat's Pub (Carl's competition) and steal Pat's famous recipe for jalapeno juleps. Tony takes the money but never performs. Carl cannot enforce the contract in a court of law because the contract is void.

Contracts entered into by persons who have been declared insane by a court of law are also void. Assume Ed's Electronics Store sells a $1000 satellite dish on credit to Cathy Customer, who has been adjudicated insane by a court of law. That contract is void, and Ed cannot force her to pay for it, but Ed may be able to get the dish back.

Some contracts are **"voidable"**, which means that one or both parties have the power to avoid performing the contract without suffering any legal consequence. The determination as to which contracts are voidable is based on public policy: the law attempts to protect certain categories of persons from being exploited in contractual relationships. The law protects minors, those under the influence of alcohol or drugs and those who are temporarily insane (but not adjudicated insane) by allowing them to avoid their contractual duties.

Assume that Wang's Electronics sells a $700 stereo system to fourteen-year-old Mary Minor. The contract is voidable on Mary's part until she turns 18 and for a reasonable time thereafter. If Mary decides to avoid her duties to pay by disaffirming the contract, she can demand her money back. If she still has the stereo, many states require her to return it to Wang's in its used condition. As a general rule, Wang cannot force her to pay for any damages to the stereo. After Mary becomes an adult (18 for contractual purposes), she has a reasonable time in which to decide whether to disaffirm (avoid) the contract or ratify it. If she keeps the stereo for six months after reaching eighteen, the court will probably determine that she has kept it beyond a reasonable time and has therefore ratified the contract. In that case, she no longer has the power to disaffirm the contract and get her money back.

Contracts may also be classified as **"unenforceable"**. In this case, a contract has all of the elements of a valid contract but for some other reason cannot be enforced. Assume that a contract meets all of the requirements for validity but does not conform to the **Statute of Frauds**, which requires that certain contracts must be in writing to be enforceable. For example, the Statute of Frauds requires that contracts that cannot possibly by performed within one year be in writing. Assume Wang's Electronics enters into a three-year verbal contract with Super Sales, the top salesman in the area. Super walks off the job after six months and

Wang claims breach of contract. The court will hold the contract unenforceable since it was not in writing.

Contracts are also defined according to their stage of completion:

An **executory contract** exists when one or both parties have yet to perform their duties. Assume Antonio orders two dozen roses from Fern's Florist. Antonio pays for the roses, which are to be delivered the following day to Antonio's mother. The contract is executory on Fern's part until she actually delivers the flowers.

The contract is **executed** once Fern delivers the flowers. At that time, both parties have performed their duties under the contract.

Another way of defining a contract is based on the number of promises exchanged.

In a **unilateral contract**, one promise is exchanged for an act. Assume that Fern tells Gabe Gardener, "I will pay you $50 if you will transplant these roses for me." Fern is promising Gabe money if he will perform an act (the transplanting of the roses). Gabe is under no duty to move the roses; if he fails to do so, he suffers no legal consequences. In another example, Fern loses an antique ring and runs an ad in the newspaper offering a $100 reward for the ring's return. Rick Reader sees the ad, finds the ring and returns it. In this unilateral contract, Fern must pay Rick when he returns the ring. Rick had no legal duty to search for the ring and return it.

In a **bilateral contract** one promise is exchanged for another promise. Assume in the above example that Fern tells Gabe "I will pay you $50 if you agree to transplant these roses by Monday morning." She is asking for Gabe's promise to perform the act. Once Gabe makes the requested promise, he is legally bound to do the work. If he fails to transplant the flowers by Monday morning, he has breached a contract with Fern.

Cathy Client tells Ace Accountant "I will pay you $500 if you promise to audit my store's books by April 10." Ace agrees to perform the audit within the required time period. A bilateral contract is formed and if Ace fails to perform he will suffer legal consequences.

WHAT "MAKES" A CONTRACT?

As mentioned above, a party wants to be certain that the contract is valid. In order to be valid, a contract must contain certain required elements and also be enforceable in a court of law. The basic elements of a valid contract are:

(1)   Agreement

(2)   Consideration (with exceptions)

(3)   Genuine Assent

(4)   Capacity

(5)   Legality

Each of these elements will be discussed separately.

(1) Agreement

The agreement is comprised of the offer and acceptance. The offeror makes an offer to the offeree.

Offer:

In order for the offer to be valid, the courts require (1) the offeror intended to make the offer (2) the offer was communicated to the offeree and (3) the offer was sufficiently clear and complete.

In determining if the offeror intended to make an offer, the courts apply an objective test. In applying an objective test, the court asks "would an objective third person reasonably determine that a serious offer was made?" The courts therefore do not look at the offeror's owns intent. For example, assume that Jack Jokester calls up his friend Ned Naive and offers to sell the latter a prize horse for $300. Jack has no intention of selling his horse and is merely playing a prank. If Ned believes the offer is serious and a court concludes a reasonable third party would believe the same thing, Jack is bound by his offer. If Ned accepts, Jack must go through with the sale.

The offer must be communicated to the offeree. If the offeree is unaware of the offer, he does not have the power to accept. For example, Ralph Rich loses his diamond watch and runs an ad offering to pay $500 to whomever finds and returns the watch. Ned Naive, unaware of the reward, finds and returns the watch to Ralph. Since Ned did not know of the reward, he cannot force Ralph to pay the reward.

The last requirement for a valid offer is that it contain sufficient information so that a court can enforce a remedy if the contract is breached. Assume Randy Retailer offers to sell Carlos Customer "one of the cars in my lot for $5000." This is not a valid offer because a court could not determine which car had in fact been offered for sale at $5000.

Special problems relevant to offers involve advertisements, auctions, and invitations to bid.

Assume Wang's Electronics runs an advertisement in the newspaper offering a certain brand of VCRs for $200.00. Cathy Customer comes into the store to buy one of the VCRs and Wang tells her they are no longer available. Cathy claims Wang made a binding offer to sell her a VCR for $200.00. As a general rule, the courts hold that advertisements are not binding offers but are considered "invitations to negotiate." In that case, Wang has invited Cathy into the store, and Cathy becomes an offeror by offering to buy the VCR for $200.00. (In some states, Wang may be liable under a consumer protection law requiring the store have an adequate number of advertised goods).

An exception to the general rule holding advertisements are mere "invitations to negotiate" involves advertisements that are very specific as to the product being offered or the action the offeree must take to buy the product.

Lefkowitz v. Great Minneapolis Surplus Store, Inc.

Supreme Court of Minnesota, 1957

86 N.W.2d 689

251 Minn. 188

Facts:

Mr. Lefkowitz saw Saturday's ads in the newspaper where defendant offered fur pieces for sale for $1 on Saturday mornings on a "first-come, first-serve" basis. The plaintiff answered the ad for two weeks, being the first in line at the counter each week. The store refused to sell to him, claiming the ad was for women only. The first Saturday's ad offered, "...3 brand New Fur Coats Worth to $100.00..." The second ad offered "...1 Black Lapin Stole. Beautiful. Worth $139.50...$1.00." The plaintiff sued claiming breach of contract.

Issue:

Did the newspaper ads create binding offers or were they merely invitations to negotiate?

Held:

The court held the store had made a binding offer in the second ad and must sell the fur to Mr. Lefkowitz. The first advertisement did not provide a basis for recovery for the plaintiff because of the indefinite value attached to the three fur coats.

Reasoning:

The court held the second advertisement was so clear and definite that it left no room for the parties to negotiate. In addition, the advertisement requested the offeree to perform, and the offeree did so.

Discussion Questions

1. Do you agree that a binding offer was made through the second advertisement?

2. Aside from the legal issue involved, was the defendant's refusal to sell to men an ethical practice?

When an auction is conducted, the courts generally hold that the auctioneer is inviting the bidder to negotiate and that no binding offer to sell the item to the highest bidder has been made. Assume Al Auctioneer places a rare book worth $5000.00 on the auction block and Bob Bidder offers the highest bid of $75.00. Bob cannot force Al to sell the book for $75.00. An exception to the rule occurs if the auction is conducted "without reserve", "with no minimum bid" or with similar language. In that instance, a binding offer has been made to sell to the highest bidder.

Invitations for bids may pose a special problem for building contractors. Assume Carl's Construction Company places an Invitation for Bids notice in the newspaper. Carl is seeking bids from subcontractors to do the plumbing work on a shopping mall Carl is building. Pat's Plumbing submits the lowest bid, which Carl refuses to accept. Pat claims Carl has made a binding offer to accept the lowest bid. As a general rule, invitations for bids are considered invitations for bidders to negotiate and not binding offers. An exception exists when certain governmental agencies solicit bids. Governmental regulations frequently require the bid of the lowest responsible bidder be accepted by the agency.

Duration of Offers:

As a general rule, the offeror can revoke (terminate) the offer any time before the offeree accepts. There are two exceptions to this rule:

If the parties have entered into an option contract, the offer cannot be revoked. In an option contract, the offeree pays the offeror in order to keep the option to buy open for a period of time. For example, Betty Buyer may deposit $500 with Larry Landowner for an option to buy Larry's land if Betty can get the necessary financing. If the contract provides the option will remain open for 90 days, Larry cannot revoke the offer during that time.

Another exception involves a firm offer made by a **merchant** of goods. If a merchant promises in a signed writing that an offer will remain open for a stated period of time, which cannot exceed 90 days, he cannot revoke the offer during that time period. The law considers a merchant someone who is in the business of selling the goods being offered or someone who claims a special expertise in that type of goods.

The offer is also terminated in certain other circumstances:

(1) The offeree rejects the offer.

(2) Either party dies or becomes incapacitated.

(3) The specific subject matter of the offer is destroyed.

(4) It is impossible for the contract to be completed.

(5) The specified time for the offer to remain open passes. If no time is specified, the offer terminates after a reasonable period of time.

Acceptance:

There are two requirements for a valid acceptance:

(1)   the offeree's acceptance must be unequivocal and (2) the acceptance is communicated to the offeror. It should be noted that the offeree has the power to accept an offer, and the acceptance must be certain. Assume Ralph Retailer offers to sell Carlos Customer a specific car for $5000 and Carlos responds "I accept providing I'm still in the mood to buy a car tomorrow." This is not a valid acceptance because Carlos is not unequivocally committing to buy the car. If Carlos writes a letter accepting the offer but never sends it to Ralph the acceptance is not valid. In that case, Ralph can sell the car to a third party and Carlos has no legal recourse.

The general rule is that an acceptance is effective when received by the offeror. An exception is the mailbox rule. The rule provides that if the offeree uses a means of acceptance that is expressly or impliedly "authorized" by the offeror, it is effective upon dispatch. A means is expressly authorized when the offeror designates the means of acceptance. A means is impliedly authorized if it is the same medium the offeror used in making the offer (by letter for example) or a faster means. Assume Rick Retailer writes a letter to Cathy Customer, offering to sell her a new television for $300. Rick does not specify means of acceptance. Cathy puts her letter of acceptance in a mailbox which is blown away by a tornado. Cathy's acceptance is still effective. An exception to the mailbox rule occurs when the offeror specifies the acceptance must actually be received.

A special problem may arise when an acceptance is communicated by fax machine. If the acceptance is either impliedly or expressly authorized and the offeror did not specify the acceptance must be received to be effective, then the mailbox rule applies. The acceptance is effective when sent by fax. The offeror therefore is bound by the agreement even if the fax sits unread in the office over the weekend or after the office has closed for the day.

(2)   Consideration

Another requirement for a valid contract is **consideration**. The general rule is that, in order for one party to sue and enforce a contract, that party must prove he gave consideration to the other party. The courts refer to consideration as "legal detriment." Basically, a party gives consideration when (1) he promises to do an act or performs an act he had no prior duty to perform or (2) he promises to refrain from an act or refrains from an act he had a legal right to do. In each of these situations, the party has experienced a "legal detriment."

Assume Ricardo Retailer calls up Fern Florist and states he will pay her $50 if she will deliver an orchid to his home by 5 p.m. Fern delivers the flower but Ricardo refuses to pay. Fern can sue for the $50 because she has experienced a "legal detriment" by delivering an orchid to Ricardo's home. This was an act she had no prior duty to do.

In another instance, Paul Policeman offers to patrol the block around Ricardo's store in exchange for Ricardo's promise to pay Paul $500 per month. (Ricardo's store was already part of Paul's assigned "beat"). At the end of the month, Paul comes to collect but Ricardo refuses to pay. Paul sues but loses because he gave no consideration to Ricardo; Paul had a preexisting duty to patrol that area.

In another instance, Ricardo promises his nineteen-year-old son $2000 if the young man will refrain from playing his video games for one year. The son complies but Ricardo refuses to pay. The son can successfully sue the father because the son gave valid consideration: he refrained from playing his video games, which he had a legal right to do.

The courts do not consider "past consideration" valid for contractual purposes. Assume Grandfather tells Grandson "I will pay you $500 because you made four A's in business school last semester." Grandson cannot enforce the promise because his consideration (making four A's) was given before Grandfather's promise.

Exceptions

The courts recognize certain exceptions to the consideration requirement. Assume a customer has had all debts discharged by a bankruptcy court. If the customer comes to a former creditor and makes a new promise to pay the discharged debt, the promise is enforceable if the bankruptcy court approves the promise despite the fact the creditor gave no new consideration for the promise.

Another exception to the consideration requirement is based on the legal theory of **promissory estoppel** or detrimental reliance. The doctrine, which is not followed in some jurisdictions, requires the following:

(1)   One party makes a promise to another, reasonably expecting the other party will rely on the promise

(2)   The second party justifiably relies on the promise and

(3)   The second party suffers consequences.

(3)   Genuine Assent

In order for a contract to be valid, the parties must voluntarily enter into it with full knowledge of the terms. These conditions are necessary in order for assent to exist.

Assent is lacking if one of the following conditions exist: **undue influence; duress; fraudulent misrepresentation; mistake;** or **unconscionability**. A victim of undue influence enters into a contract due to vulnerability to the excessive influence of the other party. For example, Lance Lawyer convinces his elderly client Wanda Widow to sell him 1000 acres of her prime ranchland for $5 per acre. Wanda has come to rely on Lance for business advice and is easily convinced this is a superb price for her land. Wanda is a victim of undue influence.

A party is the victim of duress when forced to enter into a contract under threats of harm by the other party. Assume the owner of Carl's Cafe is forced to buy meat from Blackmailing Bill's Packing Plant because Bill threatens to harm Carl's family if the meat is not ordered. Carl is the victim of duress and the contract is voidable on Carl's part. Carl has the power to either enforce the contract or disaffirm it.

If a party to a contract is the victim of fraudulent misrepresentation, the contract is avoidable and the victim can either enforce or disaffirm the contract. Sam Salesman assures Cathy Customer that the used car he is selling has never been in an accident. Cathy, who drives three children to school each day, would not buy a car that had previously been damaged. Sam is well aware the car has been in a serious wreck and suffered serious damage, although the damage is not obvious. He nonetheless lies to Cathy and makes the sale. A short time after the purchase, the car malfunctions due to its previous damage. Cathy, upon learning of the history of the car, can disaffirm the sale and get her money back. To avoid the contract based on fraudulent misrepresentation, Cathy must prove the following:

(1)   Sam misrepresented a "material fact" about the car. A "material fact" is an assertion of a factual nature that is material to Cathy's decision to buy the car.

(2)   Sam intentionally deceived Cathy.

(3)   Cathy was justified in relying on Sam's statement. If the car had an obviously bent frame and crumpled fender, Cathy probably could not be able to convince a court she was justified in relying on Sam's statement. Whether Cathy's reliance was justifiable is judged in an objective manner.

(4)   As a result of justifiable reliance, Cathy suffered damages.

She may also sue based on the tort of fraud (See Chapter 4).

A contract may be voidable based on mistake in certain situations. A unilateral mistake involves a mistake as to a material aspect of the contract on the part of one of the parties. A mistake is bilateral if both parties are mistaken.

As a general rule, a unilateral mistake does not allow the mistaken party to disaffirm the contract. There are exceptions to this rule. One exception involves an error that the other party knew or should have been aware of. Assume Smith's Satellite Manufacturers sends a letter to Ed's Electronics offering to sell an eighteen foot satellite dish for $700. Ed recognizes the mistake, realizing that Smith intended to offer the eighteen inch satellite dish for that price. Ed cannot take advantage of the mistake and force Smith to sell the larger dish for $700.

In many states if a party makes a mathematical error, the other party cannot enforce the contract. For example, Smith's Satellite sends Ed's Electronics a letter offering to sell ten of the smaller dishes for a total of $70.00 rather than $7000.00. Ed cannot take advantage of the mathematical error and force Smith to sell the ten dishes at the reduced price.

A bilateral mistake about a material fact allows either party to avoid the contract. In an early English case, a merchant bought a shipment of cotton scheduled to arrive on the ship "Peerless" from Bombay. The buyer was referring to a ship named "Peerless" that sailed from Bombay in October. The seller intended the goods to be on another ship named "Peerless" which left Bombay in December. By the time the cotton arrived on the later ship, the buyer refused to accept and the seller sued for breach of contract. The court held that as a result of a bilateral mistake of fact, no contract was formed. The defendant therefore had no legal duty to accept the cotton. (Raffles v. Wichelhaus, 159 Eng. Rep. 375).

Lack of assent to a contract may also be based on unconscionability. A contract is unconscionable if the parties are not in equal bargaining positions and the party with the most power takes unfair advantage of the other. Assume Wayne Widower is a single parent on a limited fixed income. His refrigerator breaks down and the only store that will sell him a new one on credit is Sleazy's Home Appliances. Sleazy's contract provides that if Wayne is one hour late in making a payment Sleazy can reclaim the refrigerator. After Wayne has paid $750 of the $850 due, he misses a payment deadline by two hours. Sleazy tries to reclaim the refrigerator. A court may rule that the contract was unconscionable and Sleazy cannot enforce the late payment provision.

In determining if a contract is unconscionable, courts look very closely at the bargaining power of the two parties. If the agreement was an adhesion contract, where the customer could "take it or leave it" with no right to negotiate, the court may find unconscionability exists.

(4)   Capacity

A valid contract requires that both parties have the legal **capacity** to enter into the contract. Lack of capacity may be due to minority of age, contracting while under the influence of alcohol or drugs, or temporary or permanent insanity.

As a general rule, contracts entered into by those under the age of eighteen are voidable on the minor's part. Assume Rick Retailer sells a $300 television set on credit to Marco Minor, 14 years old. Marco has the power to disaffirm the contract throughout the time he is a minor and for a reasonable time after reaching majority. If he chooses to disaffirm, he can return the set in its used condition and Rick must reimburse him the $300. In some states, if a minor has intentionally misrepresented age, the minor can no longer disaffirm the contract.

An exception to the general rule allowing minors to disaffirm their contracts applies to contracts entered into by minors for **necessaries**. Courts have held minors cannot disaffirm contracts for goods or services that are necessary for a minor to maintain one's standard of living. Absent this rule, business may refrain from selling to minors those goods or services that are actually necessary for the minor's livelihood. If a minor enters into a contract for what is considered a necessity, the minor must pay the reasonable value of the goods or service. The reasonable value test prevents businesses from charging excessive prices to minors.

In the past, necessaries usually included food, basic clothing and housing. In recent years, the courts have expanded the definition of necessaries in accordance with the individual minor's needs. A computer may be necessary for a minor who earns an income through the computer work done at the minor's apartment. A contract with an employment agency may be a necessary for a minor who must have a job in order to support the minor. The determination of what is a necessary is determined on a case-by-case basis, and usually is only effective when the minor is "emancipated."

A contract entered into by a person under the influence of alcohol or drugs is voidable in limited situations. Assume Frank Farmer contracts to sell 10 acres of valuable farmland to Bret Buyer after Frank has consumed an extensive amount of alcohol one evening. Upon gaining sobriety the next morning Frank realizes his mistake and wants to disaffirm the contract. The law may determine the contract is voidable on Frank's part and allow him to disaffirm based on his intoxication in limited instances. The court must be convinced that Frank was so inebriated that he did not understand the legal consequences of the action. Courts very rarely allow a party to avoid a contract based on intoxication.

(5) Legality

A valid contract must be for a legal purpose. A contract may be illegal because it violates a specific statute or it violates a public policy.

Statutes that may affect the legality of a contract include usury laws (that set the maximum interest rate for lending money or selling on credit); closing laws (that provide certain items cannot be sold on Sundays); gambling regulations; other laws designating certain activities as illegal; and laws requiring specific permits or licenses for the operation of a business or profession. As a general rule, contracts that violate a statute are void and the courts have a "hands off" attitude toward the agreement.

Gary Gambler and Dick Dodger enter into a $5000 wager over a boxing match. Gambling is illegal in the state in which they bet. Gary's boxer wins and Dick refuses to pay. Gary sues in state court. The court will not enforce the wager because the agreement was illegal.

There are special considerations for the laws requiring permits or licenses. If the purpose of the law is to protect the public from an unqualified person rendering services, the unlicensed individual cannot enforce her contract. Assume Dora Dropout, who never finished law school, hangs out a shingle proclaiming herself a licensed attorney. Carl Client retains her to prepare a will. Dora spends ten hours on the will, delivers it to Carl and sends him a bill for $400. He refuses to pay and she sues for breach of contract. The court will hold that Carl owes Dora nothing because the purpose of the statute which she violated was to protect the public from unqualified persons such as herself.

Assume instead that Dora completed law school and had been licensed for ten years. While in her office Carl overhears her mention that she had forgotten to send in her $200 license renewal fee for the state bar association. The law requires that all licensed attorneys send in a fee each year to maintain a current license. Carl refuses to pay and Dora sues. In this case, Dora can recover because the purpose of this statute is strictly revenue raising.

Certain contracts may be illegal because they violate public policy. Examples include certain contracts with covenants not to compete; contracts containing **exculpatory clauses** and contracts to commit torts.

At one time, courts held all **covenants (agreements) not to compete** were illegal. Today, covenants not to compete are a standard part of employment contracts. Assume Cal's Computer Company hires Super Salesman, the top computer salesperson in the city. The five-year employment contract includes a clause providing that if Super leaves Cal's the salesman will not compete with Cal's for one year within the city limits. After five years, Super leaves and immediately sets up a competing computer store directly across the street from Cal's. Cal sues for breach of the **covenant not to compete**.

Most courts will uphold the covenant if the employer gave consideration for the covenant and it meets the reasonableness test: the covenant is reasonably necessary to protect the employer's business interest and must be reasonable as to time and as to geographic area. The reasonableness factor is a fact determination made by a jury. A contract providing Super could not compete for 10 years may be held unreasonable as to time length, whereas the one-year limit would probably be reasonable. If a court determines the time or geographic area is unreasonable, the court may "reform" the contract rather than declare the entire contract void. The "reforming" would incur adjusting the time span or geographic area to what the court determined was reasonable.

Frequently a contract to sell a business will include a covenant wherein the seller agrees not to compete with the new buyer. When the buyer is paying extra money for the goodwill, or name and reputation of a business, the courts frequently expand the time span or geographic area in determining what is reasonable. The rationale is based on the fact the business's goodwill will be of little value if the previous owner can immediately set up a competing business.

Contracts with exculpatory clauses may be contrary to public policy. An **exculpatory clause** is a "hold harmless" clause where one party agrees not to hold the other party liable for anything that may happen, even if due to the second party's negligence. Assume Ace's Amusement Park sells tickets to the roller coaster. On the back of the ticket in small print is a provision that the purchaser will not hold Ace liable for any injuries or damages the purchaser may suffer, even if due to Ace's own negligence. Ralph Rider buys a ticket and is seriously injured when his seat on the roller coaster comes flying off onto the park grounds. The seat's malfunction was due to Ace's negligence. Ralph sues and Ace produces the ticket.

The court will not enforce the exculpatory or "hold harmless" clause because it is against public policy to allow a business such as Ace's to have no responsibility to the public for its own negligence. The court will allow Ralph to sue despite the exculpatory clause.

The courts will enforce exculpatory clauses in limited circumstances when both parties are in equal bargaining positions and each fully understands the contents of the clause.

HOFFMAN V. RED OWL STORES, INC.

133 N.W.2d 267 (1965)

26 Wis. 2d 683

Facts:

The plaintiffs sold their grocery store and bought a lot for the site of a new store based on defendant's representation that for $18,000 the defendant franchisor would set plaintiffs up in a store. The price was raised to $24,100 and then $26,100. Relying on defendant's assurances relative to the store, plaintiffs then sold their grocery store fixtures, inventory and bakery building. The arrangement was not finalized due to defendant's failure to fulfill its promise regarding the franchise store.

The plaintiffs claimed they were induced by the defendant to sell their assets in order to run one of defendant's franchises. The parties never signed a contract. Based on the theory of promissory estoppel or detrimental reliance on defendant's promises, plaintiffs sought damages for recovery of the losses they suffered in selling their assets.

Issue:

Can plaintiffs recover damages based on promissory reliance?

Decision:

The Court ruled in plaintiff's favor.

Reasoning:

The Court determined the defendant made promises that plaintiffs could reasonably be expected to rely on. In addition, the plaintiffs justifiably relied on the promises and suffered damages. The Court held the elements for promissory estoppel existed.

Another example of a court applying promissory estoppel involves promises to donate to a charity. Assume City Charity calls up Rick Retailer and explains the charity needs to buy a new van to transport elderly citizens to a medical clinic. Rick promises to donate the $20,000 needed for the van, knowing the charity will immediately purchase the van relying on his assurance. The charity buys the van on credit, but Rick never pays. The charity sues Rick for breach of his promise. As a general rule, the charity would not win because it had given Rick no consideration in return for his promise.

Under promissory estoppel, however, the charity could win the lawsuit. Rick had promised the charity $20,000, knowing the charity would rely on his promise. The charity had in fact justifiably relied on his promise and had suffered legal consequences as a result. In this case, the court will force Rick to fulfill his promise.

PROPER FORM

In addition to having the required elements discussed above, a valid contract must be in the proper form to be enforceable. The Statute of Frauds requires that certain contracts be in writing to be enforceable. Among those contracts that must be written are contracts to convey interests in real estate, contracts to be secondarily liable for another party's debts, marital contracts, and contracts that cannot possibly be performed within one year.

Assume that Larry Loser is having difficulty obtaining a loan to buy inventory for his new business. The lending institution may ask Larry to bring in a guarantor, a party who guarantees to pay the loan if Larry defaults. Mike Millionaire agrees to guarantee the loan. The lending institution must have Mike's promise in writing to enforce it against Mike.

Rick Retailer hires Elaine Employee to work for him for eighteen months. The contract must be in writing for either party to enforce it. Assume instead that Rick orally promises Elaine a job "for all her life" and then wrongfully fires her six months later. Elaine sues and Rick pleads the Statute of Frauds, claiming the contract should have been written. Elaine will prevail because it was possible for the contract to have been performed in less time than one year: had Elaine died before the year was up, the lifetime commitment would have been fulfilled.

Some contracts between a small U.S. company and a foreign conmpany may contain a "choice of law" clause which designates what country's law will apply in case of a contractual dispute. Otherwise, the court hearing the case must decide whether to apply domestic contract law or the law of another country.

GOING GLOBAL

What "Breaks" a Contract?

As mentioned earlier, a "good" contract is one that has all of the elements required for a valid contract and is in the proper form. Lack of one of the elements or improper form can "break" a contract and render it unenforceable.

When the owner of a small business is contemplating entering into a contract, the time and money spent in having at attorney review the contract prior to signing may save extensive losses in the future.

Assume Fern's Florist contracts to buy $5000 in imported orchids from Overseas Orchids Company. Fern pays in advance and then learns that the importation of the flowers from the seller's company violates a U.S. import regulation. Fern sues to recover her money. The court will hold that the contract was illegal and she will have no recourse.

In another situation Larry Landowner agrees verbally to sell ten acres to Rick Retailer for the latter's new store. A better offer comes along and Larry sells to another party. Rick sues to enforce the oral contract. The court will apply the Statute of Frauds and hold the verbal contract unenforceable.

These situations illustrate how a business owner operating in good faith may find himself party to a "bad" contract and thus suffer extensive losses.

The Sale of Goods: Special Rules of the Uniform Commercial Code

Special rules apply to contracts for the sale of goods. The Uniform Commercial Code (U.C.C.), which contains these rules, has been adopted by all of the states except Louisiana, which has adopted part of the Code. "Goods" are items of personal property (in contrast to real estate) that are tangible. This basically means that goods are movable items that have a physical existence (they can be seen and touched). The U.C.C. includes growing crops and unborn animals in its definition of goods. Therefore a contract to sell ten tons of oranges still on the trees is covered by the U.C.C.

A **merchant** seller under the U.C.C. has special responsibilities. According to the Code, a merchant is one who is in the business of selling the type of goods being offered or one who holds himself out as an expert in dealing in that particular type of goods.

The U.C.C.'s special rules include provisions for the "firm offer"; Statute of Frauds; and modification of the contract without new consideration.

According to common law, the offeror can revoke his offer any time until the offeree accepts the offer unless the agreement is an option contract. Under the U.C.C., if the seller is a merchant and has promised in a signed writing to keep an offer open for a certain length of time, he cannot revoke it during that time up to 90 days. Assume Dan Dealer writes Cathy Consumer, offering her a specific new car for $12,000 and providing the offer will remain open for 60 days. Since Dan is a merchant of cars, he cannot revoke the offer during those 60 days.

The Statute of Frauds under the U.C.C. provides that as a general rule, contracts for the sale of goods priced at $500 or more must be in writing to be enforceable. There are several exceptions to the U.C.C.'s Statute of Frauds. A verbal contract for the sale of goods priced at $500 or more is enforced in the following situations:

(1) The buyer has ordered specially manufactured goods that are not suitable for resale and the seller has substantially begun to manufacture the goods or made commitments for the manufacture.

Assume Betty Q. Bride verbally orders a set of specially monogrammed silk bedspreads at a cost of $1000 from Sol's Silk Shoppe. Sol specially monograms the letters "BQB" in each corner of the bedspreads. Betsy refuses to accept the goods, claiming the Statute of Frauds. Sol can enforce the contract based on the specially manufactured goods exception.

(2) The party against whom the enforcement is sought admits to the contract under oath.

(3) Verbal contracts covered by the Statute of Frauds are enforceable up to the amount paid for or extent of goods delivered.

The U.C.C. also provides that modification of a contract does not require new consideration. Assume Dan had contracted with Cathy to sell the car for $12,000 and then Cathy requests that a stereo priced at $300 be added to the car. Dan agrees to add the stereo then refuses to do so. At common law, Cathy could not enforce the new promise to add the stereo unless she had given new consideration in exchange for Dan's new promise. According to the U.C.C., however, Dan's new promise is enforceable without Cathy giving new consideration.

The purpose of the U.C.C. is twofold: to provide a basically uniform set of rules for sellers of goods throughout the states and to enforce a contract whenever possible to enhance commerce. Due to this latter purpose, contracts covered by the U.C.C. are frequently enforceable when they would not be enforceable under the common law.

The U.S. has ratified the Convention on Contracts for the International Sale of Goods (CISG). The CISG applies to the international commercial sale of goods between parties whose places of businesses are in countries that have signed the Convention. A small U.S. business that may be subject to CISG may "opt out" of its provisions if the other party agrees.

GOING GLOBAL

BEST DEFENSES AND PENALTIES FOR BREACH

When a small business is sued for breach of contract, defenses include performance of duties and discharge from duties.

If the defendant party has fully performed his duties under the contract, the plaintiff has no viable cause of action. There are several levels of performance the courts consider.

Full performance means the defendant completely performed all of his contractual duties. Assume Clyde's Construction Company agreed to build a new store for Rick Retailer as per specification. Rick is to pay Clyde $300,000. Completion date was to be May 1. Clyde completed the job on April 29 as per specification. Clyde has fully performed and Rick is entitled to no damages if he sues. Clyde in turn is entitled to the full $300,000.

Substantial performance occurs when the defendant has substantially complied with the contract and the plaintiff receives substantial benefit from the defendant's performance. Assume that Clyde completes the job discussed above but leaves one door handle off one of the 30 doors in the store. Clyde has substantially performed and Clyde will receive the $300,000 minus the cost of the one door handle.

A **material breach** occurs when the defendant's performance has been so inferior that the plaintiff receives little or no benefit. Assume Rick Retailer contracts with Ace Accountant for the latter to prepare a comprehensive financial statement on Rick's store for Rick to present to the bank. The contract provides the work will be done by April 1, so Rick can take advantage of the low interest rates on the bank loan he seeks. Ace does a terrific job but does not complete the work until June 1 and the interest rates have soared. Ace has materially breached the contract. If he sues Rick, Rick will owe the plaintiff nothing (and will probably countersue for malpractice).

Even if the defendant did not completely or substantially perform a contract, he may have been discharged of his duties. Discharge may occur due to agreement of the parties; occurrence or nonoccurrence of a condition or due to operation of law.

In some circumstance, the parties may agree "to call the agreement off." For example, Rick may decide he does not want a new store at the same time Clyde's Construction decides it only wants to build residential structures. Each party is discharged from performance due to the agreement of the other party.

Many contracts have conditions. A **condition precedent** provides a specific condition must be met before a party is obligated on a contract. For example Fern decides she wants to buy a racehorse from Harry's Horse Farms. The contract provides she will pay Harry $100,000 for Dapple Gray if the horse wins the Fourth of July race. The horse comes in last, and Harry sues for breach of contract. Fern has a valid defense because the condition precedent (that the horse win the race) did not occur.

A contract may have a **condition subsequent**. Assume Sam Salesman promises to work for Dan Dealer unless or until Sam passes the bar exam. On his sixth attempt, Sam passes the bar exam and quits his job. Dan sues for breach of contract. Sam has a valid defense because the condition subsequent occurred.

A party may also be discharged from contractual duties by operation of law. In this instance, the law has provided that certain events or situations will automatically relieve a party of his contractual duties. Discharge based on operation of law may occur due to the statute of limitations (the time limit to bring a breach of contract case); the defendant had obtained a discharge from the bankruptcy court of the debt owed; the other party materially altered the contract without the innocent party's permission; or performance is impossible or commercially impracticable.

Assume Farmer Fred has contracted to sell ten tons of oranges from his Northridge Grove and the grove is leveled by an unprecedented earthquake. Since the specific subject of the contract was destroyed, it is impossible for Fred to perform. In certain cases, the courts will excuse performance due to commercial impracticability.

Courts are frequently hesitant to excuse performance based on commercial impracticability. The following case is such an example.

SYROVY V. ALPINE RESOURCES, INC.

841 P. 2d 1279

68 Wash. App. 35 (1992)

Facts:

The plaintiff, the George Syrovy Trust, agreed to sell to Alpine Resources, Inc. all timber Alpine produced on Syrovy property over two years for $140,000. Due to bad weather and the fact it couldn't cut timber during hunting season, defendant harvested less timber than anticipated and paid plaintiff only $50,000. Plaintiff sued for the remainder and defendant claimed commercial impracticability.

Issue:

Should defendant be excused from paying the remaining $90,000 based on commercial impracticability?

Held:

The Court ruled in plaintiff's behalf.

Reasoning:

The bad weather was a risk factor that was part of the bargain and defendant should have considered it when agreeing to the price. The Court explained, a defendant can successfully claim commercial impracticability if the contingency was unforeseen and its nonoccurrence was assumed by both parties. In this case, the defendant's negotiator was "a logger with considerable experience in purchasing timber. It would be unreasonable to suggest that weather conditions were an unforeseeable event."

As mentioned earlier, many factors can determine the validity of a contract and the consequences for breach. Small businesses can often prevent later losses by having a contract reviewed by competent counsel before entering into the agreement.

BREACH OF CONTRACT LAWSUITS AND THE HOME–BASED BUSINESS

The home-based business regularly enters into contracts with customers, suppliers, employees, lessors, and other third parties. These contracts must meet the same requirements for enforceability as contracts entered into by larger businesses located in a commercial setting.

Frequently the home-based business enters into contracts for the buying and selling of goods, including foods and beverages. These contracts are covered by Article 2 of the Uniform Commercial Code. If the contract does not contain certain relevant terms, the Code may fill in the gaps in a manner unfavorable to the home-based business. It is therefore important for the owner of the home-based business to carefully review and include all relevant terms in these contracts.

It is important for certain contracts to be in writing even if the contracts are not covered by the Statute of Frauds. Assume Fern of Fern's Florist agrees to deliver a floral arrangement to Cathy Consumer's home. Fern remembers the agreed upon price as $75 while Cathy thought the price was $25. Written evidence of the agreement could have prevented the inevitable dispute that arises.

Owners of home-based businesses can benefit from a consultation with a competent attorney prior to entering into large contracts. In addition, a legal review of the contracts the business proposes to use prior to their use may avoid legal problems at a later date.

REDUCING YOUR RISKS

Preventive steps the small business owner may take to reduce the risk of breach of contract lawsuits include:

(1)   Always take time to fully understand all the terms of a contract. Don't let the other party rush you into any contract before you are completely satisfied you understand the entire agreement.

(2)   The best approach is "put it in writing." Even if the verbal contract can be enforceable, committing the agreement to writing can avoid later disputes.

(3)   If the contract comes under the U.C.C., make certain all important terms are agreed to in the contract. Otherwise, the U.C.C. may "fill in the gaps" in an unsatisfactory manner. For example, if the parties fail to specify place of delivery, the U.C.C. provides delivery shall occur at seller's place of business.

(4)   Make certain the other party has legal capacity to contract; otherwise the other party may avoid the contract.

(5)   Have a competent attorney review any important contract before you sign. Also, have counsel review any form contracts you plan to use before your company enters into such a contract.

* KEY WORDS AND PHRASES

Bilateral Contract

Capacity

Condition Precedent

Condition Subsequent

Consideration

Covenant Not to
  Compete

Duress

Executed Contract

Executory Contract

Exculpatory Clause

Fraudulent
  Misrepresentation

Impracticability

Material Breach

Mistake

Merchant

Necessaries

Promissory Estoppel

Revocation

Statue of Frauds

Undue Influence

Unenforceable
  Contract

Unconscionable
  Contract

Unilateral Contract

Valid Contract

Void Contract

Voidable Contract

CHAPTER SUMMARY

Breach of Contract Lawsuits

1. Types of Contracts
    Based on Enforceability

    a. Valid—enforceable in a court of law
    b. Void—lacks one of the essential elements and is never enforceable
    c. Voidable—one or both parties have the power to avoid performance
    d. Unenforceable—includes the essential elements but court will not enforce it for some other reason; frequently applied to verbal contracts that should be in writing

2. Types of Contracts
    Based on Stage of Completion

    a. Executory—one or both parties have yet to perform
    b. Executed—both parties have fully performed

3. Types of Contracts
    Based on Number of Promises

    a. Unilateral—a promise is exchanged for an act
    b. Bilateral—a promise is exchanged for another promise

4. Elements of a Contract

    a. Agreement—comprised of offer and acceptance
    b. Supported by consideration (with exceptions)
    c. Genuine assent
    d. Capacity
    e. Legality

5. Contracts Covered by Statute of Frauds

    a. Contracts to convey interest in real estate
    b. Contracts to be secondarily liable for another's debts
    c. Marital contracts
    d. Contracts that cannot possibly be performed within one-year
    e. Contracts for goods priced at $500 or more

6. Article 2 of the U.C.C. and Its
    Special Provisions

    a. Covers the sale of "goods"
    b. Special rules for the "merchant" seller
    c. Irrevocability of the "firm offer"
    d. Statute of Frauds under the U.C.C.
    e. No new consideration required for modification of terms
    f. U.C.C. will "fill in gaps" if certain terms are left blank

7. Degrees of Performance

    a. Full performance-party has met all contractual requirements
    b. Substantial performance-party has complied to extent other party receives substantial benefit
    c. Material breach-defendant's performance is so inferior plaintiff received no benefit

8. Discharge of Duties

    a. Based on agreement of parties
    b. Based on a condition precedent or condition subsequent
    c. Based on operation of law—includes statute of limitations; bankruptcy discharge; material alteration of contract by other party; impossibility or commercial impracticability of performance.

DISCUSSION QUESTIONS

1. <u>Categories of Contracts</u>. Rick Retailer offers Fern's Florist $300 if the florist will deliver ten dozen roses to the retail store for its Valentine's Day promotion sale. Fern delivers the roses on time. Was the contract unilateral or bilateral? If the florist had failed to deliver the roses, could Rick sue for breach of contract? Explain.

2. <u>Consideration</u>. Rick Retailer tells Ed Employee "Because of the terrific work you've done for the store the past year, I will pay you a bonus next week." Rick never pays the bonus and Ed wants to sue for breach of contract. Has Ed given valid consideration? Why or why not?

3. <u>Acceptance</u>. George's Greenhouse faxes an offer to Fern's Florist, offering to sell tulips at $15 per dozen. Fern immediately faxes an acceptance. George is too busy to check his fax machine until the following day. In the meantime, he has sold all of his tulips to another buyer. Has George's Greenhouse breached a contract with Fern's Florist? Explain.

4.   <u>Covenants Not to Compete</u>. Rick Retailer hires Dynamic Dan to sell electronics in the store. The contract provides that if Dan leaves the store, he will not compete with Rick for ten years in the entire county. Is this covenant enforceable? Why or why not?

5.   <u>Article 2 of the Uniform Commercial Code</u>. Denise Designer is well-known for the formal gowns she personally designs and makes for her client. Suzanne Star hired Denise to design and make a gown for the actress to wear to an awards ceremony. Does Article 2 cover the contract? Explain.

6.   <u>Article 2 and the Statute of Frauds</u>. Assume that in case #5 Suzanne Star verbally agreed to pay Denise Designer $1500 for designing and making the gown. Denise makes the gown but Suzanne refuses to pay, claiming that the verbal agreement is unenforceable. Does the Statute of Frauds apply? Is the contract still enforceable? Explain.

7.   <u>Condition Precedent</u>. Ace Accountant agrees to audit Rick Retailer's books provided Ace's new super computer comes in by March 15. The computer is never delivered. Rick sues for breach of contract. Does Ace have a valid excuse for nonperformance? Explain.

IS IT ETHICAL?

1.   Terry Teen, age 15, buys $300 in computer games from Rick's Retail Store. Terry tires of the games within a few months and returns them to the store, asking for his money back. Based on the fact that Terry is a minor and the contract is voidable on Terry's part, Rick returns the money. Was Terry's action ethical? Assume Terry's father, Mike Millionaire, encourages his son's action. Is Mike's performance ethical?

2.   Mike Millionaire verbally agrees to buy $2500 worth of office equipment from Naive Ned, who has just opened his first store and is naive about business practices. Mike knows about the Statute of Frauds and is also aware of Ned's inexperience. In the meantime, Mike has learned he can buy the same type of equipment from another retailer for a cheaper price. When Ned is ready to deliver the equipment, Mike refuses to accept delivery, laughingly informing Ned the contract is unenforceable. Is Mike's performance ethical?

3.   Mike Millionaire loses his expensive all-leather briefcase in the airport. He runs an ad in the newspaper, offering a $100 reward for the return of the case. Ned Naive, unaware of the reward, finds the case and returns it. Mike refuses to pay because Ned was unaware of the offer. Is Mike's refusal ethical?

4.   Edwina Employer tells Eduardo Employee, "You were such a valuable employee last year that I will pay you a bonus next week." Edwina, knowing her promise is unenforceable because Eduardo has not given valid consideration, has no intention of paying the bonus. Is her action ethical?

5.   Ed Entrepreneur decides to sell his gift shop to Sonia Speculator for $100,000. The sales price includes the goodwill of the business. The covenant not to

compete in the sales contract provides that Ed will not set up a competing gift shop in the large city for the next ten years. Ed suddenly incurs extensive medical bills due to his wife's unexpected illness. Ed approaches Sonia about his opening a small gift shop on the other side of the city. Sonia emphatically says she will enforce the covenant if Ed attempts to open the new shop. Is Sonia's action ethical? If Sonia's gift shop were in a very small town would your answer be different? Explain.

DISCUSSION CASE

PARK 100 INVESTORS, INC. V. JAMES T. KARTES AND NANCY KARTES

650 N.E. 2d 347 (Ind. App. 5 Dist. 1995)

Facts:

Nancy and James Kartes were part owners of a rapidly growing Indianapolis business, Kartes Video Communications, Inc. (KVC). They were contacted by an agent of the Park 100 industrial complex relevant to leasing at Park 100. Lease negotiations were delegated to a senior vice-president at KVC. No mention of personal guaranty was made during negotiations nor included in the lease agreement approved by the KVC attorney and signed by the KVC agent on or before July 27. On the evening of July 27, the Park 100 agent went to KVC offices as James and Nancy Kartes were entering their car. They explained they were late for their daughter's wedding rehearsal. The agent told the couple they must sign "lease papers" before they could move into Park 100. James Kartes went into the lobby of KVC's current locations, called the KVC agent, asked if the lease had been approved by KVC counsel. The Park 100 agent said nothing. Both Karteses then signed the signature page of a paper entitled "Lease Agreement," never being informed they were signing a personal guaranty to pay the lease.

Several years later they learned of the personal guaranty and disavowed it. The Karteses subsequently sold their KVC interest and the new buyers failed to pay the rent. Park 100 sued the Karteses based on their personal guaranty.

Issue:

Were the signatures of the Karteses on the guaranty of lease obtained by fraud?

Finding:

The Indiana Court of Appeals affirmed the trial court's finding that the personal guaranty of lease was obtained by fraudulent means. The appellate court found that the trial court's findings supported the judgment and that judgment was not erroneous based on the findings of fact by the trial court.

Reason:

According to Indiana law, the elements of fraud are the following:

(1) material misrepresentation of fact

(2) falsity of the material misrepresentation

(3) the material misrepresentation was made with knowledge of the falsity or with reckless ignorance.

(4) complainant relied on the misrepresentation and

(5) the misrepresentation was the proximate cause of plaintiffs injury.

The appellate court affirmed the trial court's finding that all elements of fraud were present. In addition, the appellate court confirmed the finding that the plaintiffs used ordinary care and diligence in believing they were signing a lease and their reliance on the Park 100 agent's statements was reasonable. The appellate court pointed out that a guarantee cannot enforce a guaranty contract when the guarantor is induced into the contract by fraudulent misrepresentation.

Discussion Questions

1. Do you agree that the plaintiffs were reasonable in relying on the assertion that the contract was a "Lease Agreement"?

2. What evidence was relevant to the trial court's decision?

3. The trial court found the Park 100 agent had a duty to inform plaintiffs the document was not a lease but a guaranty. Do you agree?

CHAPTER 4

TORTS

CHAPTER OBJECTIVES

In this chapter you will learn to:

1. Recognize situations in your business that may lead to a tort claim.

2. Understand the elements of the different intentional torts and the defenses available when a small business is sued for an intentional tort.

3. Identify the elements required for liability based on negligence and the defenses to negligence claims.

4. Recognize ultrahazardous activities and potentially dangerous products that may lead to claims against the small business based on strict liability.

5. Understand the potential liability for the unauthorized use of the intellectual property belonging to another party.

The lawsuits against small businesses that result in the largest monetary awards to the plaintiff occur when the defendant commits a tort. This chapter will define a "tort," explain the three major categories of torts, and identify specific torts in each of those categories which frequently involve small business.

▶ # "RED FLAG" SITUATIONS

Situation	Potential Problem
1. An employee has a "short fuse" and frequently loses his/her temper.	1. That employee may commit assault/battery against a customer/client/other third party.*
2. An employee frequently "tells others off" or criticizes others.	2. That employee may defame the reputation of a competitor/customer/other third party.*
3. An overly aggressive marketing employee will "do anything" to increase sales.	3. The employee's marketing tactics may include invasion of privacy by misappropriating a public figure's name or picture in an advertisement.*
4. An extremely zealous security guard will "stop at nothing" to catch shoplifters.	4. Unreasonable detention of a suspected shoplifter can result in liability for false imprisonment.*
5. A Human Resource director's goal is to have the best sales team possible and will therefore "stop at nothing" to reach that goal.	5. Wrongful interference with an existing employment contract can result.*
6. Any of the conditions exist as shown in right column.	6. Any of these situations may result in liability for **negligence***.
	(a) store is unsafe for customers (slippery floors, inadequate lights, unmarked glass doors)
	(b) surrounding premises are unsafe (inadequate lights in parking lot, failure to provide needed security)
	(c) food or beverages served are unwholesome
	(d) delivery employees drive in an unsafe manner

*The employer faces potential liability even if the act is committed by the employee.

7. An employee is driving while conducting business on a cellular phone and negligently hits a pedestrian.

7. The telephone call may bring the accident within "the scope of employment" and the employer becomes liable.

8. Goods sold in a retail store are defective or dangerous (a doll with buttons that can be pulled off and swallowed).

8. The seller may be strictly liable for injuries

DEFINITIONS

Today's legal definition of a "tort" is based on the French term meaning "twisted" or "to twist". Today, a "tort" refers to a civil (private) wrong committed against the plaintiff's personal or property rights. Tort actions are separate from breach of contract actions. As mentioned in an earlier chapter, a civil case is brought in a civil court (rather than a criminal court), and the plaintiff is represented by a private attorney.

Torts are divided into three categories: (1) **intentional torts** (2) torts based on the legal theory referred to as negligence and (3) torts based on the legal theory referred to as **strict liability**.

Decisions in tort cases are usually based on prior common law decisions rather than on statutory laws.

INTENTIONAL TORTS AND THEIR DEFENSES

A tort is classified as "intentional" when the defendant actually intended the action which resulted in harm to the plaintiff's personal rights or property rights. The defendant may have intended no actual harm to the plaintiff, but if the intended action results in harm, the defendant is liable. For example, Allen may intentionally pull a chair out from under Baker as the latter is sitting down. Allen was only playing a joke on Baker and intended no actual harm. If, however, Baker is injured by the prank, Allen is liable for his tort.

Small businesses are especially vulnerable to lawsuits based on certain intentional torts. These specific torts include **assault** and **battery**, **defamation**, **false imprisonment**, **invasion of privacy**, **trespass** and wrongfully interfering with a contractual relationship or an economic expectation.

Assault and Battery: The Fear and the Fist

The intentional tort categorized as an "assault" is different from the criminal activity also labeled as an "assault". The definition of a criminal assault is found in state or federal statutory criminal laws, and the case is brought by a state or federal prosecutor in the name of society as a whole. Conviction for a crime requires proof the defendant had some intent to cause the injury that harmed the victim. Liability for an intentional tort requires proof the defendant intended the act that caused the injury. The defendant may not have intended the harm that resulted from the act. In the case of an assault based on tort law, the plaintiff sues in a private capacity and is represented by a private attorney. Further discussions in this chapter relate to assault as an intentional tort.

An assault requires four elements:

(1)   the defendant intentionally does the act which threatens or places the plaintiff in fear,

(2)   the harm perceived or feared is imminent,

(3)   the plaintiff experiences apprehension and,

(4)   the apprehension is reasonable.

For example, if an employee comes at an employer waving a baseball bat and the employer is genuinely fearful for her personal safety, an assault occurs. The assault occurs even if the employee never hits the employer. It is also irrelevant whether the defendant employee could have actually injured the plaintiff employer. Assume the bat was actually made of papier-mâché and was incapable of hurting anyone. If the plaintiff was unaware of this fact and was actually fearful for her safety, an assault has occurred.

Another example of an assault is a situation where a clerk becomes angry with a customer and approaches the customer with her hand raised in a threatening manner. If the customer is actually fearful for her safety, an assault occurs.

The intentional tort of battery requires the following:

(1)   the defendant or an extension of the defendant intentionally touches the plaintiff,

(2)   the touching is without plaintiff's consent,

(3)   the touching is offensive to plaintiff and,

(4)   the touching would be offensive to a person of normal sensibilities.

This definition is different from the criminal term "battery" and the following material refers only to the tort of battery.

As mentioned earlier, an intentional tort occurs if the defendant intended the action which caused the injury, even though the defendant did not intend actual harm to the plaintiff. For a battery to occur, the defendant does not have to personally touch the plaintiff; for example, the defendant may throw an inanimate object which hits and injures the plaintiff. Even though the defendant did not physically touch the plaintiff, an "extension" of the defendant has caused the injury. Placing a harmful substance in plaintiff's food or beverage constitutes a battery.

In certain situations, owners of businesses are held liable for the intentional torts of their employees, including the tort of battery. This occurs when the tort occurred while the employee was "within the scope of his employment." (See Chapter 5 on

Agency Law). In a recent case, the employer company was held liable for battery when one of its route salesmen became angry and struck a store manager.

There are several defenses which the defendant may raise in assault and battery cases. Consent is the first defense. If the plaintiff actually consented to the action taken by the defendant, there is no tort. A second defense is defense of oneself or of others in the presence of real and apparent danger. The defendant may also claim defense of property in certain circumstances provided the force will not cause serious bodily harm or death.

Defamation: Lies that Harm

A tort based on defamation involves harm to the plaintiff's personal or business reputation. Defamation occurs when the defendant intentionally makes a false statement that holds plaintiff up to public contempt, ridicule or hatred.

Defamatory statements can be written (**libel**) or spoken (**slander**). For a plaintiff to succeed in a libel suit, she must prove three elements regarding the statement made by the defendant: (a) the statement was false, (b) the statement harmed plaintiff's reputation and (c) the statement was "published" to at least one other person. Courts have held that by dictating a letter to one's secretary, the publication requirement has been met. For example, Amy dictates a letter to her secretary that contains false and harmful statements about her competitor Baker (the addressee of the letter). Baker may win a libel suit if he can convince a court that the statement was false and was injurious to his reputation. The mere dictation of the letter to her secretary met the requirement that Amy must "publish" the statement to a third party.

Slander involves a verbal or spoken statement that is defamatory. The "publication" of a slanderous statement can occur by the defendant making the defamatory statement directly to a third party or by a third party overhearing the defendant make the statement to the plaintiff.

An example of a slanderous statement would be Amy, owner of a small restaurant, telling all of her customers that Baker, owner of a competitive restaurant, uses horsemeat in his hamburgers. If Baker can prove the statement (a) is false; (b) is injurious to his business reputation and (c) was heard by others, Baker may win in a slander suit.

Certain statements are considered so harmful they are referred to as defamatory *per se*. If a statement is defamatory *per se*, the plaintiff does not have to show actual damages were suffered. Both of the examples above are considered defamatory *per se* because they allege the plaintiff engaged in wrongful business practices.

The ultimate defense available to a defendant in a defamation suit is truth. In other words, for a statement to be defamatory, the plaintiff must show it is a false statement. For example, if Amy tells Joe that Baker sells horsemeat in his restaurant, Amy is not liable for slander if the statement is true. Other defenses include privilege and absence of **malice**. Certain statements, although defamatory, are privileged (or protected). Statements that are privileged include statements made by attorneys in courtroom procedures and statements by members of Congress during a debate on the floor of Congress.

Absence of malice is a defense available when the plaintiff is a public figure. A public figure, such as a politician or movie star, must prove not only that the statement was false but also that there was malice on the defendant's part. Malice has been interpreted to mean that the defendant either (1) knowingly made a false statement or (2) made a false statement "with reckless disregard for the truth" (not properly verifying the facts).

Invasion of Privacy: The Truth is No Defense

Business operators should be aware of another tort that can occur even if the statement is true. This intentional tort is called invasion of privacy and occurs in several different situations. There is invasion of privacy if information, although truthful, is of a private nature and is disseminated to other parties. An example would be a newspaper running a story about Smith, a local businessman, which states that Smith had been treated for a mental disorder when he was in college. The story is true, but unless the newspaper can prove a compelling reason for the public to know this fact, it is an invasion of Smith's privacy.

Invasion of privacy suits also involve "placing a person in a false light." An example is a local store running an advertisement in a newspaper showing a national sports celebrity standing in front of the store. The ad suggests that the sports figure is endorsing the store. If the celebrity had not agreed to his picture being used to endorse or advertise the store, he had a cause of action based on a category of invasion of privacy referred to as appropriation. Courts have also held that "sound alikes" in ads may result in appropriation. A plaintiff may win an appropriation suit even if his full name or picture was never used by the defendant.

> # CARSON V. HERE'S JOHNNY PORTABLE TOILETS, INC.
>
> 698 F.2d 831 (1983)

Facts:

A company referred to the portable toilets it rented and sold as "Here's Johnny" toilets in its advertisements. Television host Johnny Carson sued, claiming appropriation of his identity. The plaintiff's nightly television show was opened with the phrase "Here's Johnny" and Carson claimed the public associated the phrase with him and would assume he was connected with the business offering the goods.

Issue:

Had the defendant violated plaintiff's right to privacy through appropriation by using a phrase so closely associated with plaintiff even though neither the plaintiff's name nor picture was used in the advertisements? Lower court dismissed the case.

Decision:

The appellate court found for the plaintiff, holding appropriation had occurred.

Reasoning:

The term "Here's Johnny" was so closely connected to the plaintiff that the public could erroneously assume he was in fact endorsing the defendant's product.

Discussion Questions:

1. Should a celebrity be allowed to sue for appropriation even though the celebrity suffered no financial loss?

2. Do small businesses sometimes engage in the tort of appropriation in their advertisements?

3. Should small businesses also be liable for the tort of appropriation?

False Imprisonment: When the Suspected Shoplifter Can Sue (and Win)

The tort of false imprisonment involves the defendant depriving the plaintiff of his right of freedom of movement. The plaintiff must be detained by the defendant without a reasonable way of escape for an unreasonable period of time. This tort frequently occurs when a store owner or employee detains a suspected shoplifter. Even though the suspect is not literally tied up and prevented from leaving, the courts have held that the detention required for a false imprisonment case has occurred because the plaintiff cannot leave without facing possible legal consequences (for example, the store owner may call the police).

A problem arises when it turns out that the suspect had not in fact shoplifted anything from the store. Before states passed special laws protecting store operators, the suspect could successfully sue for false imprisonment. Today, however, there are state laws that protect the business operator from liability for false imprisonment. These statutes provide a limited privilege (or protection) for the detention of a suspected shoplifter who did not in fact shoplift. The statutes are very specific as to when this protection is available. The business operator must have had reasonable grounds to suspect shoplifting, detained the suspect in a reasonable manner and for a reasonable period of time. For example, the reasonable manner test prohibits the person who detains the suspect from using physical force, or from yelling "Stop thief!" across the store. (The latter action can result in an action for slander against the business).

The state laws also require that the suspect not be detained for an unreasonable period of time. What is an unreasonable time depends on what the courts in that particular jurisdiction have determined to be unreasonable. Detention for only a few minutes has been held to be unreasonable in some cases.

The monetary damages awarded in false imprisonment cases are frequently large. Punitive damages, where the court is attempting to punish the defendant and deter similar action in the future, are frequently awarded in false imprisonment cases when malice on the defendant's part is proven.

Small businesses are well advised to carefully train employees who are responsible for detaining suspected shoplifters. If a court later finds the suspect has not shoplifted and the detention was conducted in an unreasonable manner or for an unreasonable period of time, the business could face large monetary damages.

Interfering With a Competitor's Contract or Prospective Customer: or "Hands Off" the Competition's Employee and Customer!

Intentional torts based on wrongfully interfering with an existing contractual relationship or an economic expectation are relatively new torts. They are based on damage to the plaintiff's rights under an existing contract or interfering with plaintiff's expectation of an economic benefit yet to come.

Liability for wrongfully interfering with a contractual relationship requires that the plaintiff prove three elements: (1) That the plaintiff had an existing contractual relationship with a third party (2) That the defendant knew of this relationship and (3) That the defendant knowingly interfered with the relationship for the defendant's own monetary gain.

An example of this tort may involve a local computer salesman. Assume that Sam, the best computer salesman in the city, is midway through his five-year contract with The Komputer Store, a small local store. A competitor, Hardware House, is losing money and needs a dynamic salesperson like Sam. The Hardware House, aware of Sam's current contract, approaches him and persuades him to leave The Komputer Store and come to work for the floundering store. As a result, The Komputer Store can sue Hardware House for wrongfully interfering with the contractual relationship with Sam. (Sam also faces possible liability for breach of contract with The Komputer Store).

Interference with an economic expectation arises when the plaintiff has a relationship with a potential customer or client that may result in economic benefit to the plaintiff. For example, assume that Sally is looking at computer hardware in The Komputer Store. Mable, owner of the Hardware House, enters The

Komputer Store, approaches Sally and persuades her to leave The Komputer Store and shop at Mable's store. Even though Sally had not yet entered into a contract with The Komputer Store, a court may find that The Komputer Store had an expectation of economic benefit from Sally and that the Hardware House had wrongfully interfered with that expectation.

In this last tort, the courts will frequently determine if the defendant's behavior was predatory in nature. If so, the plaintiff may recover for this tort.

Small businesses are well advised to refrain from interfering in any way with a competitor's existing contractual relationships and to also refrain from interfering with a competitor's prospective relationship with a potential customer or client. These actions go beyond normal competition. For example, if Sally quits shopping at The Komputer Store and buys at Hardware House solely because of the latter's convincing television ads, The Komputer Store has no legal remedy.

Trespass and Fraud: Places and Actions That Are "Off Limits"

Other intentional torts include trespass and **fraud**. Trespass involves the intentional interference with a person's right to enjoy his property. For example Bill's Bar-B-Que regularly cooks beef on an open pit next to Mary's Boutique Shop. The smoke from the pit enters Mary's air conditioning system and permeates the clothes in her inventory. A trespass has occurred because Bill intentionally performed an act (cooking) which interfered with Mary's use of her store. It is immaterial under tort law that Bill did not intend to harm Mary's inventory.

In order for a plaintiff to prevail in a case involving fraud, certain specific elements must be proven:

(1)   The defendant made a false or misleading statement of fact.

(2)   The statement was made intentionally or with reckless disregard for the truth.

(3)   The statement was material to the plaintiff entering into the contract or taking other action.

(4)   The plaintiff relied on the statement and the reliance was justified.

(5)   The reliance caused the damages the plaintiff suffered.

Misrepresentation involves all of the above elements except intent or recklessness on the defendant's part. If a salesperson innocently makes a false statement, misrepresentation has occurred.

An example of fraud occurs when Ace, a used car dealer, tells Connie, a customer, that a car will get 30 miles per gallon of gasoline. Mary, wanting an economic car, reasonably relies on the statement and buys the car. Ace knew the car gets 15 miles per gallon and intentionally made the false statement. Fraud has occurred.

Assume Ace shows Connie a used car with numerous rust holes, several large dents, and a twisted frame. Ace tells Connie the car has never been in an accident and has never sat out in bad weather. Connie buys the car and then finds it has been in several accidents and sat out in the weather for extended time periods. Connie cannot succeed in a suit based on fraud because her reliance on Ace's statements was not justified.

Entering Business for the Wrong Reasons May Not Be "Right"

A relatively unknown intentional tort involves setting up of a business strictly to drive another party out of business. For example, Zelda inherits a large sum of money and decides to fulfill a longtime dream: ruin the boutique business of her old high school rival Clara. Zelda opens up a competing business right next door to Clara's Shoppe and sells clothing at a deep discount. Clara, unable to match the low price, is forced to close her business. Having accomplished her mission, Zelda immediately closes her own boutique. Clara can sue Zelda for setting up a business strictly to have Clara close her own shop. Clara must prove Zelda's motive was predatory in nature.

It is often difficult for the plaintiff to prove a predatory motive when the defendant is claiming she was only engaged in normal business competition. When a court is convinced the defendant had no legitimate business reason to open the new business, the plaintiff will win.

TUTTLE V. BUCK

Supreme Court of Minnesota, 1909

119 N.W. 946

107 Minn. 145

Facts:

The plaintiff had operated a barbershop in a small town for ten years. He claimed the defendant, a local banker, opened a competing barbershop solely to drive the plaintiff out of business. Plaintiff alleged defendant used his influence as a banker and other tactics to deter customers from going to plaintiff's barbershop and that defendant had no legitimate business purpose in opening a barbershop.

Issue:

Did defendant open the barbershop without any legitimate business purpose and therefore commit a tort?

Decision:

The court ruled for the plaintiff, holding that the defendant had committed an actionable tort.

Reason:

The court held that the defendant opened his business solely to destroy the plaintiff's barbershop business and the action has materially injured and threatens to destroy plaintiff's businesses. The court reasoned that this simulated competition had no legitimate business purpose and was an actionable tort.

Discussion Questions:

1. Do you agree that wrongfully entering into a business should be an actionable tort?

2. Would this tort be hard to prove?

3. What type of evidence would plaintiff seek to use to win the case?

UNINTENTIONAL TORTS AND THEIR DEFENSES: "I DIDN'T MEAN TO DO IT" DOESN'T MATTER TO THE COURT

Negligence Suits: It Doesn't Pay Not to Pay Attention

Unintentional torts can also result in liability. These torts are based on negligence and strict liability; neither requires intentional behavior on defendant's part. For example, Sibyl is daydreaming while driving down the street. She absentmindedly runs a stop sign and hits Pam, a pedestrian. Sibyl in no way intended to hit or harm Pam. She can still be liable for the tort of negligence if the plaintiff can prove certain elements.

The elements required for a plaintiff to win in negligence include the following:

(1) Proof that the defendant owed a duty to the plaintiff... (In the above example, Sibyl had a duty to all pedestrians to drive carefully).

(2) Proof that the defendant breached (broke) that duty. (Sibyl breached her duty to Pam by running a stop sign).

(3) Proof that the defendant's breach of duty was the proximate (foreseeable) cause of plaintiff's injury. (It was foreseeable that if Sibyl ran a stop sign, she may hit and injure a pedestrian such as Pam).

In determining defendant's liability for negligence, the courts apply a "reasonable person" standard. This standard is based on the assumption that an objective "reasonable person" is always careful and never breaches a duty owed to another. For example, in applying the "reasonable person" standard, a court would conclude that the hypothetical "reasonable person" would never run a stop sign and hit a pedestrian.

Frequently negligence cases involve customers slipping and falling in stores. Assume that Carol is shopping in Hometown Grocery Store. She slips and falls on a banana peel that has been on the floor for several hours. Carol suffers severe injuries and sues Hometown Grocery for negligence. Carol must prove the following:

(1) that Hometown owed a duty to its customers. (In this case, the duty to keep its floors clean and safe).

(2) that Hometown breached its duty to Carol. (The breach was in allowing the peel to remain on the floor for several hours), and

(3) that the breach was the proximate (foreseeable) cause of Carol's injuries. (It is foreseeable that a banana peel allowed to remain on the floor will cause a customer to fall and injure herself).

If Hometown Grocer could prove that the peel had just fallen on the floor, it is possible that the plaintiff would lose her case. The fact that the peel had remained on the floor for several hours indicates that Hometown had breached its duty to inspect and clean the floors regularly.

Customers and prospective customers who visit businesses open to the public are referred to as **business invitees**. The courts have found these businesses have a duty to business invitees to maintain the property in a reasonable manner. If a business invitee is injured on the business premises, the courts will determine if reasonable care was exercised in maintaining the property.

BRAY V. KATE

Supreme Court of Nebraska, 1990

454 N.W. 2d 698

235 Neb. 315

Facts:

The plaintiff slipped and fell on ice as he was about to enter defendant's restaurant. He claimed the restaurant was negligent in failing to remove the ice at the entrance to the restaurant. Plaintiff was a business invitee, entering a business that was open to the public.

Issue:

Did the defendant restaurant breach its duty to the plaintiff by failing to remove the ice?

Decision:

The court ruled for the plaintiff, holding that the defendant had breached its duty by not clearing the ice.

Reason:

The court held that it was foreseeable that a customer such as plaintiff would either fail to see the ice, or fail to protect himself, slip and suffer injuries. The defendant was therefore negligent.

Discussion Questions:

1. Should the defendant be liable even though the plaintiff should have been aware of the ice?

2. Can you think of a situation where a customer may slip and fall and yet the court would not hold the business liable?

Another example of negligence may involve a 24-hour fast-food restaurant. Cathy Customer drives into the restaurant's parking lot at midnight planning to go in and order a hamburger. The parking lot is poorly lit, and a robber approaches Cathy's car, robs and shoots her. She may successfully sue Happy Hamburger for negligence if certain facts are proven. The requirements for a negligence suit will require the customer prove that (1) Happy Hamburger had a duty to provide a safe parking lot for its customers, (2) that duty was breached and (3) that the breach was the foreseeable cause of the customer's injury. In this case, Cathy will try to prove that other robberies had occurred in the area at night and that it was therefore foreseeable that Happy Hamburger may be robbed.

Another negligence case may involve the owner of an apartment building. Pat's Properties owns and manages a ten unit apartment building. Timmy Tenant, who lives in one of the apartments, is attacked and injured by a third party stranger in the unlit hallway of the building. Timmy may successfully win a negligence case against Pat's Properties if Timmy can prove (1) Pat's Properties had a duty to provide a safe building for its tenants (2) Pat's Properties breached that duty (by not having adequate lightning and other security measures) and (3) it was foreseeable that an injury such as Timmy's would occur. Timmy would attempt to show that other robberies had occurred in the neighborhood recently.

Frequently a plaintiff has difficulty in proving that it was foreseeable that the defendant's breach of duty would result in an injury such as the one the plaintiff suffers. Two legal theories are sometimes applied in such a situation. These theories are *res ipsa loquitur* and *negligence per se*.

The term *res ipsa loquitur* comes from the Latin phrase, meaning "the thing speaks for itself." This theory is applied under the following circumstances: (1) The "thing" that caused the injury was in the exclusive control of the defendant, (2) The "thing" does not ordinarily cause injury unless there was negligence on the defendant's part and (3) The "thing" did in fact cause plaintiff's injury.

Assume that Careful Construction Company is building a house for Harry Homeowner. While Harry is standing on the ground inspecting the construction work, a bag of nails falls from the second floor window and injures Harry. There are no witnesses to the accident. Harry may successfully use the theory of *res ipsa loquitur* because (1) The "thing" that caused the injury (the bag of nails) was in the defendant's control, (2) The "thing" does not ordinarily cause injury absent negligence (bags of nails do not ordinarily fall out of windows absent negligence) and (3) The "thing" caused the plaintiff's injuries. *Res ipsa loquitur* creates a rebuttable presumption that the defendant was negligent.

The legal theory *negligence per se* is used when the plaintiff may have difficulty in proving proximate causation. This theory requires that the plaintiff prove that (1) there was a statute already in effect that prohibited defendant's action (2) the defendant violated that statute and (3) the statute was passed to protect persons such as plaintiff from the type of injury that the plaintiff suffered.

A negligence *per se* suit may be brought against a small business by a third party stranger. For example, assume that a clerk at Gus's Gun Shop sells a firearm to a customer without obtaining the identification required by law. The customer proves to be a convicted felon who could not legally buy the gun. The customer takes the gun and shoots Betty Bystander in a robbery across town. Betty can sue Gus's based on negligence *per se*. She would claim (1) there was a law on the books requiring proper identification before selling a gun (2) Gus's Gun Shop violated that statute and (3) the statute was intended to protect innocent victims such as Betty from being shot by persons such as the customer.

Two defenses available in negligence suits are (1) assumption of risk and (2) **contributory** and **comparative negligence**. To successfully defend a case based on assumption of risk, the defendant must prove the plaintiff knowingly and willingly assumed the risks. Harold, knowing his business partner Jacob is intoxicated, willingly gets into the car Jacob is driving. Harold, injured in a wreck caused by Jacob's drunk driving, sues Jacob for negligence. Jacob can claim the defense of assumption on risk because Harold knowingly and willingly assumed the risk of riding with a drunk driver.

Contributory and comparative negligence apply when the plaintiff's own negligence contributed to plaintiff's injury. In jurisdictions that follow the defense of contributory negligence, a plaintiff cannot recover any damages if plaintiff's negligence contributed in any degree to the injury.

Most jurisdictions have adopted the comparative negligence defense. Assume Sibyl runs a stoplight and collides with Carl's car in an intersection. Carl was driving 35 miles per hour in a 30 mile per hour zone. A jury may determine Carl's speeding contributed 20% in causing the accident. Rather than recovering the full $100,000 the jury awarded, Carl would receive $80,000; his award is reduced by 20% based on his own degree of negligence.

Strict Liability: Courts Are Tough on Dangerous Products and Activities

The third category of torts is based on strict liability. The term "strict liability" means that the defendant will be held strictly liable under certain circumstances even though the defendant did not intend the action (intentional torts) and the defendant was not negligent. Strict liability applies to activities that are unusually dangerous. The theory is based on public policy: if a person or business chooses to undertake these unusually dangerous or "ultrahazardous" activities, then they will be liable for any injuries to third persons as a result of the activity.

Activities that are ultrahazardous include blasting activities, fumigation, crop dusting, and hauling dangerous cargo on the public roads.

Assume that Dan's Demolition company is hired to demolish an old downtown building. Dan's follows all the applicable ordinances and guidelines for demolishing a building. Nevertheless, the blasting blows out all of the windows of Randy's retail store across the street. Although Dan's Demolition Company did not intend to blow out the windows and the company was not negligent in any way, the court will still hold Dan's liable based on strict liability. The theory is applied because Dan's undertook an activity that is considered ultrahazardous.

Assumption of risk is a defense to strict liability cases. For example, Dan's Demolition Company has posted signs around a building warning the public of the blasting activities and to stay away from the site. Sidney is curious about how the demolition works, sees the signs and decides to risk injury anyway. If Sidney is injured from the blasting activity, Dan's has a defense.

Strict liability may also be applied to the sale of certain defective goods. The product liability theory applies if (1) the goods were defective when the defendant sold them, (2) they were not substantially altered in any way before they reached the plaintiff, (3) the plaintiff was injured by the goods, (4) defendant is normally a merchant seller of the goods, (5) product is unreasonably dangerous (most states) and (6) the defect was the proximate cause of injury. For example, a manufacturer designs a new baby doll that has buttons that can be easily removed and swallowed. The doll is not altered from between the time it leaves the manufacturer and the time it reaches the user. If a child is in fact injured by swallowing the button, a court may apply strict liability holding that the doll was an usually dangerous item. A plaintiff claiming strict product liability may sue the manufacturer, the wholesaler, the retailer, and any other seller of the product. The retailer who sold the doll with the easily removable buttons can therefore be liable even though the retailer was in no way involved in the manufacture of the doll.

Strict product liability may be imposed based on improper labeling; improper warning and instructions; design defects; and improper packaging. Failure to include warnings/instructions written in the language of the target market may also result in strict product liability. Defenses include (1) misuse of the product in an unforeseeable manner (2) assumption of risk and (3) contributory and comparative negligence. (Strict product liability is also discussed in Chapter 9: Consumer Law).

Small businesses are constantly vulnerable to the threat of lawsuits based on tort claims. These businesses can reduce the risk of those suits by recognizing situations and conditions that may result in a tort claim and eliminating or correcting the problem before a claim arises.

HOW TORT LAW IMPACTS MICKEY MOUSE: PROTECTION OF INTELLECTUAL PROPERTY

A special area of tort law involves infringement of an individual's or business's rights in **intellectual property**. Examples of intellectual property include a new invention, a painting, a computer software program and a fanciful name for a new product. In each case, the creator has property rights that can be protected by law. Anyone who infringes on these rights can be liable for infringement. Intellectual property can be protected by **patents, trademarks,** and **copyrights**.

Patents

Patents are granted to inventors of new products, designs or processes. Product patents are valid for seventeen years. A patent holder can bring an infringement suit against anyone who duplicates, uses or sells the subject matter of the patent without his permission. The federal laws relevant to obtaining patents are quite specific. Inventors can benefit from working with qualified attorneys who understand the intricacies of patent law. Often applications for patents are denied by the U.S. Patent Office due to improper wording in the patent application.

Trademarks

Trademark protection is available for trademarks used by a specific product; trade names used by a specific business; and certification, collective and service marks.

Consumers frequently identify a particular trademark with a favorite product. The trademark may be in the form of a word or group of words; a picture or mark; an implement attached to the product; or even a logo. "7-up" is an example of a trademark identifying a specific product. If a new soft drink company used the same name for its product, it could be sued for trademark infringement. "Rice Krispies" is another example of a trademark identifying a particular product.

The public also identifies providers of goods and services by their trade names. For example, "Kellogg's" is the registered trade name of the company that produces the product "Rice Krispies".

Certification, collective and service marks may also be the subject of trademark protection. For example, a product cannot claim it holds the "Good Housekeeping Seal of Approval" without having actually been awarded the seal.

Small businesses can benefit from seeking advice before adopting a name, logo or mark for a new store or product. A consultation fee can be much cheaper than the costs involved in defending an infringement case later. In addition, the business can benefit from advice as to how to properly register its own trademark before its store or product becomes famous.

Copyrights

Copyrights are available to creators of literature; dramas; music; pictures; graphics and sculptures; audiovisual works; sound recordings; pantomimes and dance choreographies and computer software. Examples of copyrightable material include menus, architectural plans and product packaging. A copyright is valid for the life of the creator plus 50 years.

One area of special concern for small businesses today involves the showing of videos or the playing of music in their establishments. Assume a small commercial campground has a recreation room and shows exercise videos for its customers. If the campground has not paid a copyright fee, it can be held liable for copyright infringement. A small grocery store that shows a commercial video in the "kids' corner" while the parents are shopping can also be liable for infringement. It is possible for businesses to pay an "umbrella fee" to associations that represent artists and thereby have the right to show videos or play music without being liable for infringement.

Trade Secrets

Trade secrets are comprised of any information or process that gives a business an advantage over the competition. Subject matter for trade secret protection includes recipes, customer lists, and formulas. A plaintiff can sue for misappropriation of a trade secret even though the information was not protected by a patent, trademark or copyright. Assume the owner of Rick's Restaurant breaks into the computer system of George's Gourmet Shoppe and copies one of George's famous recipes from the files. Rick can be liable for misappropriation of a trade secret.

As technology evolves and competition increases, small businesses may become more and more vulnerable to lawsuits involving intellectual property. Consulting with an attorney before naming a business, a product or engaging in any activity that may involve another's intellectual property can save much time and money in the future.

International piracy of intellectual property rights is of increasing concern to businesses of all sizes. Before introducing goods or services into a foreign market, the small business owner should seek competent legal advice on ways to protect the owner's rights in the host country.

GOING GLOBAL

TORTS AND THE HOME–BASED BUSINESS

The home-based business faces potential tort liability from the same potential claimants as the retail business operating in a downtown store. For example, the owner of a home-based business may be sued for the intentional tort of defamation by making allegedly untrue and harmful statements about a competing business.

A negligence suit may be brought by a customer or delivery person who slips and falls on the icy sidewalk leading up to the home/business. Selling a customized computer software program that has not been properly debugged may lead to a negligence suit by the dissatisfied customer. Strict liability may be imposed on the owner of a home-based business who sells a product that proves to be unreasonably harmful.

Owners of a home-based business can also be sued for violating the intellectual property rights of others. For example, naming the business after a famous cartoon character may result in a copyright infringement lawsuit. Prior to opening a home-based business, the entrepreneur can benefit from a legal consultation to make certain the name and logo of the business do not infringe on another's rights.

REDUCING YOUR RISKS

The following steps may reduce the risk of a tort action against a small business:

(1)   Acquaint employees with potential tort liability that may result from threatening (assault) or touching (battery) a customer or co-worker.

(2)   Make certain employees understand that false and injurious statements about customers or competitors may result in a defamation suit.

(3)   Review all prospective ads to make sure they don't lead the public to believe a celebrity has endorsed the goods or services unless you have the celebrity's endorsement (misappropriation).

(4)   Have your store procedure for handling suspected shoplifters reviewed by an attorney to help avoid a false imprisonment claim.

(5)   Don't interfere with an existing contract between a competitor and a customer or employee (**wrongful interference with contractual relationship**) or with a competitor's negotiations with a third party (wrongful interference with a prospective relationship).

(6)   Make certain that statements made by salespeople are true so a customer can't later claim fraud.

(7)   Check the business premises regularly and immediately correct safety and health hazards before a customer brings a negligence suit.

(8)   Obtain the proper license before showing videos or playing music in your business to avoid a copyright infringement claim.

(9)   Make certain the name or architectural design of your business does not infringe on another business's copyright or trademark.

(10) Carefully select your employees since the employer can be liable for an employee's business torts.

* KEY WORDS AND PHRASES

Assault	Intellectual Property	Strict Liability
Battery	Intentional Torts	Tort
Business Invitees	Invasion of Privacy	Trademark
Contributory and Comparative Negligence	Libel	Trade Secret
	Malice	Trespass
Copyright	Negligence	Wrongful Interference With Contractual Relationship
Defamation	Negligence Per Se	
False Imprisonment	Patent	Wrongful Interference With Economic Expectations
Fraud	Res Ipsa Loquitur	
	Slander	

CHAPTER SUMMARY

Torts

1.   Categories of Torts

    a.   Intentional torts-the defendant intended the action that resulted in the harm

    b.   Negligence-based on breach of duty

    c.   Strict liability-liability without fault

2.   Intentional Torts

    a.   Assault and battery; defenses-consent and defense of oneself
or
others

    b.   Defamation; defense-truth

c. Invasion of privacy; defense-public right to know

d. False imprisonment; defense-compliance with state's protection statute

e. Wrongful interference with a contractual relationship or economic expectation

f. Trespass

g. Fraud

h. Wrongfully setting up a business

3. Negligence

a. Elements:
    Defendant owed a duty to plaintiff
    Breach of that duty (was the)
    Proximate causation of plaintiff's injuries

b. Defenses:
    Assumption of risk
    Contributory and comparative negligence

c. Special doctrines:
    Negligence per se
    Res ipsa loquitur

4. Strict Liability

a. Applies to ultrahazardous activities such as blasting and fumigation

b. Applies to sale of certain defective goods; retailer may be liable as well as manufacturer

c. Defenses:
    Misuse of product in unforeseeable way
    Contributory and comparative negligence

5. Infringement of Intellectual Property Rights

a. Patent infringement

b. Trademark infringement

c. Copyright infringement

d. Misappropriation of trade secrets

DISCUSSION QUESTIONS

1.   Battery. Ed Employee notices Sly Sam slinking around the jewelry department in Rick's Retail Store. Sly reaches out to pick up a chain necklace on the counter. Ed, assuming Sly is about to steal the necklace, rushes up and slaps Sly's hand. Sly, claiming great pain, immediately calls up Ace Attorney regarding a possible lawsuit. Has a tort been committed? Explain.

2.   False Imprisonment. Assume that in #1 Ed does not touch Sly but instead forces Sly into a small office, locks the door and leaves the accused there for three hours to "think things over." During that time Ed learns that Sly won the state lottery yesterday and is now a millionaire. Ed decides to release Sly and actually try to sell him the necklace. Does Sly have grounds for a lawsuit? Explain your answer.

3.   Negligence. Fern's Florist receives an order for two dozen fresh roses to be delivered to Sly's newly purchased mansion. Sly's wife Sylvia will arrange the roses herself. When Sylvia pulls the first flower out of the wrapping paper, she severely cuts her finger on a large thistle on the flower stem. Claiming the florist had a duty to remove the thistles, Sylvia retains Ace Attorney and sues for negligence. Will the plaintiff prevail? Why or why not?

4.   Strict Liability. Sly purchases an expensive electric train for his son Sylvestor at Tomas' Toy Store. The train was manufactured in a foreign country. Due to a design defect, little Sylvestor receives an electrical shock while playing with the train and is seriously injured. Does Tomas face potential liability even though the train was in no way altered between the time it left the manufacturer and the time it reached little Sylvestor? Explain.

5.   Copyright and Trademark Infringements. Ed Entrepreneur has a terrific idea for a new video store. He names it Micki and Minnie Mouse's Video Store and has pictures of the famous couple on the front door. Can Ed be sued for the store name and the pictures? Explain.

6.   Copyright Infringement. Rick Retailer decides to video tape a number of children's programs off his home television set and take them to the store. He runs the tapes to entertain the customer's children to allow the parents more time to shop. Has Rick violated the law? Explain.

IS IT ETHICAL?

1.   Cathy Consumer orders a bowl of hot chili at Charley's Chili Corner. Fearing she will be late for a formal tea, Cathy places a cover on the styrofoam bowl of chili. She places it in her lap and drives off, planning to eat the delicious food en route. (She does not care for the finger foods she will be offered at the tea). Due to Careless Cal's careless driving in front of her, Cathy is forced to slam on her brakes. The hot chili spills in her lap, ruining her expensive new designer dress. Cathy sues Charley's for failure to put the bowl of chili in a spill-proof box. Is Cathy's action ethical? Discuss. Should Charley's be legally liable? Why or why not?

2. Charley, the owner of Charley's Chili Corner, has been known for years for the high quality meat used in his chili. Unfortunately, Charley's meat supplier recently made a mistake and sent Charley an order of the poorest grade meat available. Charley made up one large batch of chili before learning of the problem and correcting it. Cathy Consumer ate a bowl of the lower quality chili and told the owner of Dan's Deli about the meat. Dan, seeing a way to hurt his main competitor' business, immediately spread the word about the meat. Even if the statement was true, was it ethical for Dan to tell others? If Charley regularly used poor quality meat would your answer be different?

3. Melanie Mogul owns the copyright to the latest box office hit for children. While driving her Rolls Royce through town she notices that Ed Entrepreneur is showing her movie in his store for the children of his customers. Melanie immediately files a multimillion dollar lawsuit against Ed. Is her action ethical?

4. Assume that in #3 Ed owns a chain of retail stores throughout the country and is showing Melanie's movie in all his stores. Would your answer be any different?

5. Simon Shopper goes into the local cafeteria and orders a chef's salad. Halfway into the salad, Simon spots an ant on the lettuce. Simon claims extreme mental distress and sues the cafeteria for negligence. Is Simon's action ethical?

Discussion Case

Qualitex Co. v. Jacobson Products Co., Inc.

115 S.Ct. 1300 (1995)

Facts:

For years, plaintiff Qualitex Co. had used a certain shade of green-gold color for its dry cleaning press pads. Defendant, one of plaintiff's rivals, started using a similar shade for its press pads. Plaintiff then obtained trademark registration for its color and claimed trademark infringement in its challenge to defendant's use of the color. The U.S. District Court ruled for plaintiff but the Ninth Circuit Court of Appeals ruled the federal Lanham Trademark Act does not allow trademark protection for color alone.

Issue:

Does the Lanham Trademark Act permit registration of a trademark consisting only of a color?

Decision:

The U.S. Supreme Court ruled that color alone can be registered for trademark protection.

Reason:

The Supreme Court pointed out that the Lanham Trademark Act (the Act) requires a mark identify seller's goods from the competition and the mark not be "functional". Both lower courts held that plaintiff's use of the green-gold color identified its product to the point the color had acquired a secondary meeting and also that the color has no other function.

Defendant's arguments included assertions that (1) trademark protection for a color will lead to unresolvable disputes over shades of color protected and (2) the limited supply of colors will be depleted. In a unanimous decision, the Supreme Court did not agree.

Discussion Questions

1. Do you agree that a color alone should receive trademark protection?

2. Can you think of certain businesses where the use of a color is an important factor of the "total dress" of the company?

3. In your opinion, will all colors receive trademark protection in the future?

4. Can you think of any goods where a particular color is functional?

CHAPTER 5

AGENCY LAW

CHAPTER OBJECTIVES

In this chapter you will learn to:

1. Understand how an agency relationship can be created through the express or implied action of the parties.

2. Recognize the duties owed by the principal and the agent to each other in an agency relationship.

3. Recognize the rights of the principal and the agent in an agency relationship.

4. Identify the factors a court will consider in determining if an independent contractor has become an employee of the principal and thereby subjected the principal to tort liability for any torts committed within the scope of employment.

5. Understand how the agent obtains express and implied authority to enter into contracts on the principal's behalf.

6. Recognize how a principal can ratify a previously unauthorized contract.

7. Understand how a court will determine if apparent authority existed when the agent acted on the principal's behalf.

8. Identify situations when the principal must notify third parties of the termination of the agency relationship.

9. Recognize situations where a court may hold the employee's actions were "within the scope of employment."

As a small business grows, it becomes impossible for the owner to conduct every business transaction individually. Assume Frank's Furniture Store expands and opens a second store in the suburbs. Frank must hire a salesperson to handle sales in the new store. That person, who represents Frank in dealing with third party customers, is referred to as an **agent**, while Frank is referred to as the **principal**. Contracts entered into by the agent can bind Frank to the same extent as if Frank had entered into the contract himself. In addition, if Frank has the right of control over the salesman, Frank can be liable for torts committed by the salesman in certain situations. It is therefore important for Frank to select his agents carefully.

This chapter will examine "red flag" situations that can alert Frank to potential problems in agency relationships. The chapter also examines the parties to an agency, the definition of an **employee**, and when the principal becomes liable for the actions of the agent and employee.

▶ "RED FLAG" SITUATIONS

Situation	Potential Problem
1. An employee with a "short fuse" intentionally hits a customer	1. The employer can be liable for the tort of battery if it was committed "within the **scope of employment**"
2. An agent places a large order for merchandise without the principal's authorization	2. The principal may still be liable on the contract if the agent had **apparent authority**
3. An agent takes a customer's order, pockets the cash and skips town	3. The principal can still be liable to deliver the merchandise if the agent had apparent authority
4. An employee drinks too much at an office party and negligently hits a pedestrian on the way home	4. The employer may be liable for the tort of negligence if the court finds the accident occurred "within the scope of employment"

AGENCY RELATIONSHIPS: THE PARTIES AND THE RULES

An agency relationship exists when one party (the agent) is authorized to act on behalf of another party (the principal) in dealing with third parties. Assume Carl, the owner of Carl's Computers, hires Sam Salesman to sell computers at the store. Carl is the principal and Sam is the agent.

In an agent relationship, the principal may agree to pay the agent, or the relationship may be gratuitous. In either case, the agent has the power to bind the principal in certain contracts. Each party owes certain duties to the other, whether the agency is gratuitous or for compensation. The principal's duties include payment of compensation (if agreed upon); reimbursement for the agent's expenses incurred in the course of the agency; cooperation in all aspects of the agency business and providing a safe work environment for the agent.

The agent's duties to the principal include performing the job in a reasonable manner; following the principal's reasonable instructions; loyalty; disclosure to the principal of all information relevant to the agency; and accounting for all monies received on behalf of the agency. The agent cannot make any secret profits or divulge private information about the agency without violating the duty of loyalty. The agent must keep agency funds in a separate account to assure a proper accounting of agency funds.

If an agent violates one of these duties, the principal can sue. For example, assume Lawrence Landlord hires Alice Agent to visit his rental properties and collect the rents. While visiting Lawrence's Garden Grove apartment complex, Terri Tenant points out a missing board in the stairway. As soon as Alice learns of this problem, the knowledge is imputed to Lawrence. This means that when the agent acquires knowledge about the business, it is the same as if the principal had the knowledge. Alice forgets to tell Lawrence about the missing board and a tenant falls on the stairway. The tenant can successfully argue that Lawrence was negligent due to his failure to repair a broken stairway he knew about. In other words, the court will hold Alice's knowledge about the missing board was imputed to Lawrence. Lawrence can in turn sue Alice for violation of her duty to inform him of information relevant to the rental business.

Assume that Lawrence retains Alice Agent to sell an apartment complex for him. The property is listed at $500,000 but Lawrence tells Alice in confidence he will take $400,000. Alice's listing contract with Lawrence is coming to an end and Alice does not want to lose her sales commission. She divulges this confidential information to Bette Buyer, who offers the $400,000 and gets the property. Alice has violated a duty to her principal and Lawrence has a cause of action against his real estate agent.

WHEN AN AGENT IS AN INDEPENDENT CONTRACTOR

An employee is basically someone who works for and under the close supervision of another (the employer). An agent may be the principal's employee or may be referred to as an **independent contractor**. For example, Sam Salesman works in Carl's Computers eight hours daily, five days a week. Carl assigns Sam his duties and pays him a salary plus commission. Sam is considered Carl's agent and also Carl's employee. Carl is liable for torts of his agent/employees in certain situations discussed later.

Carl also retains Raylene Realtor as his agent to sell the current store so the business can move to a larger site. Carl does not supervise Raylene's work schedule, does not provide her a place to work, and will pay her a commission only upon the sale of the property. Raylene is an independent contractor and not Carl's employee. Assume Raylene is driving a prospective buyer to Carl's warehouse and negligently hits a pedestrian. In this case, Carl is not liable for the pedestrian's injuries. As a general rule, principals are not liable for an independent contractor's torts. An exception exists when the independent contractor is engaged in an ultra-hazardous activity for the principal.

It is possible for an employer-employee relationship to develop even though a contract states the other party is an independent contractor. Assume Carl hires Roy's Roofing to put a new roof on the store. At the beginning of the relationship, Roy is an independent contractor. If, however, Carl starts supplying Roy with supplies and tools to use, employs him full-time and closely supervises Roy's work, a court may conclude that Roy has become an employee. If a customer is injured by shingles Roy negligently drops, Carl may be liable as the employer. Courts examine a long "laundry list" of factors in determining on a case-by-case basis if an employer-employee relationship exists. The factors include degree of supervision; provision of work tools and supplies; method of payment; degree of special skills required; and whether the worker is also employed by other parties. A plaintiff attorney looking for a "deeper pocket" may try to prove that Roy has in fact become Carl's employee and recover damages from Carl.

WHEN THE BOSS IS LIABLE

Contractual Liability

The law provides that the principal is liable for a contract entered into by an agent if the agent had authority to contract. The courts categorize this authority as actual or apparent.

Actual authority may be either express or implied. **Express authority** is based on what the principal expressly authorizes the agent to do. For example, Carl promotes Sam Salesman to the position of store manager of Carl's Computers in the suburbs and specifically authorizes Sam to order inventory for the store. This is referred to as express authority. In addition, Sam's **implied authority** is based on whatever actions Sam reasonably believes are necessary to carry out his duties as store manager. Sam may therefore have implied authority to hire employees to work in the store. Carl's Computers is liable on any contracts Sam enters into based on Sam's express or implied authority. If Sam orders $5000 worth of computer hardware from Metro Manufacturing as inventory, Carl's is responsible for paying as per the contract. If Sam agrees to pay Cathy Clerk $200 per week to work in the store, Carl's is liable for paying Cathy.

In determining whether or not the agent had implied authority to enter into a contract in the principal's behalf, the court inquires as to whether it was reasonable for the agent to believe she had such authority. Assume that Charlotte's Clothes Closet sends Betty Buyer to Paris to purchase dresses for the spring season. While in France Betty attends an antiques auction and buys a rare vase in

Charlotte's name. Betty lacked implied authority to buy the vase because it was not reasonable for a clothes buyer to assume her authority extended to purchasing antique vases. Betty is therefore personally liable to the seller of the vase. Charlotte is liable only if the seller convinces a court that Betty had "apparent authority" to buy the vase. (Apparent authority is discussed below).

If, however, Charlotte is pleased with the successful bid, she may be able to **ratify** the contract and keep the vase. When an agent enters into a contract in the principal's name without authority, the principal may ratify the contract if certain requirements are met:

(1) The principal had the legal capacity to enter into the contract when the agent contracted

(2) The other party has not withdrawn the offer

(3) The principal knows all of the facts of the contract and

(4) The principal ratifies the entire contract.

If all of the requirements are met, Charlotte can pay for the vase and retain it.

Apparent Authority

Apparent authority is based on what a third party reasonably believes an agent is authorized to do, despite the fact that the agent lacked both express and implied authority. It is based on what the principal has impliedly "communicated" to the third party by words or actions.

Assume that Carl fires Cathy Clerk but allows her to "hang around" inside the store. Brenda Buyer comes in, approaches Cathy, with whom she has dealt in the past, and orders a new computer. Brenda pays Cathy $500 based on Cathy's assurance the store will deliver the computer to Brenda's home the following day. Cathy takes the cash and skips town. Carl's Computer is still liable on the contract based on apparent authority. A court would conclude that it was reasonable for Brenda to believe that Cathy had authority to accept money and promise delivery of the computer on behalf of the store.

Whether or not it was reasonable to believe apparent authority existed is a fact determination for a jury. Assume Bob Borrower owes a monthly payment of $500 to the bank on a note he took out to expand his business. He drives up to the bank, cannot find a parking place, and hands $500 cash to the bank's grounds keeper. The bank employee takes the cash and leaves town. Bob claims the bank must credit his account for $500 because the grounds keeper had apparent authority to take the money. A jury will probably rule that it was not reasonable for Bob to believe a grounds keeper had the authority to accept payments and credit customer's accounts.

When a principal terminates an agent's authority to contract, the principal should give notification of the termination to third parties. Notice to the general public is called constructive notice and is usually made through local newspapers.

Actual written notice must be provided to third parties the agent has previously contracted with.

Failure to provide notice to third parties may result in a court finding apparent authority still existed in the former agent. Assume Cal Carpenter has worked for Bob's Builders for years. Cal would regularly go to Lum's Lumber Yard and buy supplies on credit in Bob's name. Bob's company would pay Lum's each month for Cal's purchases. Bob fires Cal but fails to notify Lum's that Cal is no longer authorized to purchase in Bob's name. Cal goes to Lum's and purchases $3000 in supplies on credit and charges the purchase to Bob's account. Cal takes the supplies and leaves town. Lum refuses to pay, arguing that Cal no longer had authority to make the purchase. A court would find that apparent authority existed because Lum's had not been actually notified that Cal's authority had been terminated. In that case, Bob would have to pay the $3000 and then try to find Cal and recover the money. A principal has the duty to provide actual notification of termination of the agency to all third parties with whom the agent has dealt; constructive notice is required for all other third parties.

Notice to third parties is not required when the agency is terminated by operation of law. This refers to special situations that automatically terminate the agency. These situations include death or insanity of either party, impossibility of performance, bankruptcy and war between the two parties' countries.

A principal may be classified as a **disclosed principal**, **partially disclosed principal**, or **undisclosed principal**. A principal is disclosed when the third party understands there is an agency and knows the principal's identity. In this situation, the agent is ordinarily not liable on contracts entered on the principal's behalf.

If there is a partially disclosed principal, the third party knows an agency exists but does not know the principal's identity. Both the agent and principal can be liable on the contract.

In the case of an undisclosed principal, the third party is unaware of the agency and therefore unaware of the principal's identity. Both the agent and the principal face liability on the contract.

GOING GLOBAL

Some small U.S. businesses may decide to enter a foreign market and employ an agent in the host country to represent the business. If the agent is considered a "dependent agent" or employee of the U.S. principal, agency law regarding contract liability may apply, if the case is heard in a U.S. court. If the case is heard in another country, the foreign country's agency laws may be quite different. The U.S. business owner can benefit from legal counsel before engaging an agent abroad.

Tort Liability

The employer is liable for torts committed by an employee if the tort was committed "during the scope of employment." The principal is also liable for an agent's torts if the principal had the right of control and the tort was "during the scope of employment." This liability is based on the legal theory *"respondeat superior"*, a Latin term for "let the master respond." The courts have expanded the definition of "scope of employment" in recent years to hold the employer increasingly liable.

In one case, the court held the employer liable for a fire allegedly caused by an employee's negligence even though the incident occurred in the employee's motel room after midnight.

EDGEWATER MOTELS, INC. V. GATZKE AND WALGREEN CO.

277 N.W. 2d 11 (1979)

Supreme Court of Minnesota

Facts:

Defendant was an executive for the Walgreen Company who was supervising the opening of a new facility in Duluth, Minnesota. While staying at plaintiff's motel, he filled out an expense report around 1:30 a.m. He had allegedly been consuming alcohol earlier and was smoking at the time he was working on the expense report. Plaintiff claimed defendant's burning cigarette or match near or in a wastebasket started a fire that caused over $300,000 in damages. Plaintiff claimed the smoking was "within the scope of employment" and the employer was therefore liable for the employee's action.

Issue:

Was defendant's smoking "within the scope of employment?"

Decision:

The appellate court ruled for plaintiff, holding that smoking was "within the scope of employment."

Reasoning:

The court held that defendant was "a 24-hour executive" and was "within the scope of employment" when smoking and filling out the report. The court held that the employee did not abandon the job while smoking his cigarette and therefore the employer was liable.

Discussion Questions:

1.   Do you agree with the court's ruling?

2.   Do you think the ruling would have been different if the employee had been watching television rather than filling out an expense report?

Courts are finding the employer liable when an employee leaves a job-related social gathering after consuming alcohol and injures someone while driving home. It is for this reason that many businesses avoid involvement in any social functions where alcohol is served.

In addition to holding the employer liable for the employee's negligence, courts may find the employer liable for the employee's intentional torts. For example, if a salesclerk becomes angry at a customer and commits a battery, the employer may be liable if the tort was "within the scope of employment."

Due to the expanding liability of employers for torts committed by employees in the scope of employment, employers are becoming increasingly careful in their selection of employees. In addition, more employers are purchasing "all-risk" insurance coverage or similar coverage that covers losses due to liability for actions of the employee and agent under the control of the principal.

GOING GLOBAL  A U.S. company conducting business in a foreign country through a dependent agent (employee), faces potential liability for torts committed by the employee within the scope of employment in the host country.

AGENCY LAW AND THE HOME–BASED BUSINESS

Agency law can impact the owner of the home-based business just as it impacts a business operating in a commercial setting. Frequently the home-based business will employ an agent to sell goods or services in the name of the business. The owner is liable on these contracts if the agent had express or implied authority to enter into the contract. It is therefore important for the owner to properly notify third parties if an agent no longer has contractural authority.

The owner of a home-based business can also be liable for torts committed by an employee when the employee is within the scope of employment. For example, a home-based catering service may hire an employee to deliver prepared foods to residences throughout the area. If the driver negligently runs a red light and injures a pedestrian, the business owner can be liable for the tort. Courts are now holding the employer liable for intentional torts committed by an employee within the scope of employment. Assume that an employee of the home-based business becomes angry with a customer and slaps the customer. The business owner can be liable for the battery committed by the employee.

Due to the potential contractual and tort liability, the owner of a home-based business can benefit from carefully selecting agents and employees who will work for the business.

REDUCING YOUR RISKS

The following steps may reduce the potential for the business's liability due to the actions of agents and employees.

1. Carefully select agents who will be representing the business in transaction with third parties. The business may be liable on a contract even if the agent's action was unauthorized.

2. If you hire an independent contractor, do not become involved in close supervision of the assigned work. A court may later find that an employer-employee relationship exists and the employer is liable for the torts of the former independent contractor.

3. Make certain that proper notification is given to third parties when you terminate a former employee's authority to contract in your name; otherwise you can be liable on a contract entered into by an employee you just dismissed.

4. When hiring employees keep in mind the employer's potential liability if the employee commits a tort "within the scope of employment." For example, don't hire a reckless driver to deliver your restaurant's food.

* KEY WORDS AND PHRASES

Actual Authority

Agent

Apparent Authority

Disclosed Principal

Employee

Express Authority

Implied Authority

Independent Contractor

Partially Disclosed Principal

Principal

Ratify

Respondeat Superior

Scope of Employment

Undisclosed Principal

CHAPTER SUMMARY

Agency Law

1.	Parties to an Agency	a.	Principal
		b.	Agent-authorized to act on principal's behalf in dealing with third parties

2.	Creation of Agency	a.	By express agreement of parties
		b.	Implied by law based on actions of parties

3.	Principal's Duties to Agent	a.	Pay compensation (if agreed to)
		b.	Reimbursement for agency expenses incurred by agent
		c.	Cooperation
		d.	Provision of safe workplace

4.	Agent's Duties to Principal	a.	Perform job in reasonable manner
		b.	Follow principal's reasonable instructions
		c.	Disclose relevant information
		d.	Account for monies received
		e.	Loyalty to principal
		f.	Maintain agency funds in separate account

5.	Factors in Determining if Independent Contractor Has Become an Employee	a.	Degree of supervision
		b.	Who provides tools and supplies
		c.	Method of payment
		d.	Degree of skill required for job
		e.	Whether worker is employed by others

6.	Types of Authority	a.	Express-based on what principal expressly authorizes agent to do
		b.	Implied-based on what agent reasonably believes agent is authorized to do in order to carry out express authority
		c.	Apparent-based on what a third person reasonably believes the agent is authorized to do.

7. Ratification of a Contract

   a. When principal agrees to terms of previously unauthorized contract

   b. Requirements for ratification:
Principal had legal authority when contract was made
Other party has not withdrawn
Principal is aware of all contract terms
Principal ratifies entire contract

8. Principal's Duty to Notify Third Parties When Principal Terminates Agency

   a. Actual notice required for third parties who dealt with agent

   b. Constructive notice required for other third parties

9. Employer's Liability for Employee's Torts

   a. Liable if tort committed "within scope of employment"

   b. May be liable for intentional torts as well as for negligence.

DISCUSSION QUESTIONS

1. <u>Agency Relationship</u>. Rick Retailer hires Tina Teen to work in the bookkeeping department of the store. Tina's duties include running a computer software program to verify certain accounts and stamping and mailing out bills to customers. Is Tina an agent of Rick's Retail Store? Explain why or why not.

2. <u>Agent's Duties</u>. Enrique Entrepreneur decides to sell the building he is currently using for his business. He contracts with Alice Agent to represent him in selling the building. The site is listed at $150,000 but Enrique tells Alice confidentially he will take $125,000. Bob Buyer, once interested in purchasing the property, seems to be losing interest. Concerned about losing her sales commission, Alice tells Bob she can get the building for him for $125,000 provided Bob will pay her a $500 "tip". Has Alice violated her duty to Enrique? Explain.

3. <u>Torts Committed by Independent Contractors</u>. Assume that Enrique's listing contract with Alice expires and he has a new contract with Sally Salesperson, another real estate broker in the area. While on her way to show Enrique's building to a prospective customer, Ruth runs a red light and injures Paul Pedestrian. Paul sues Ruth and Enrique. Is Enrique liable? Explain your answer.

4. <u>Torts Committed by Employees</u>. Fern of Fern's Florist hires Tina Teen to make deliveries on Saturdays. While driving the florist van on a delivery, Tina is also talking on her mobile phone. Becoming more engrossed in her telephone conversation, Tina ignores a stop sign and crashes the van into the

glass front of Rick's Retail Store. Rick sues Fern's Florist. Is the shop liable for Tina's negligence? Explain.

5. <u>Undisclosed Principal</u>. Larry Landman, agent for Prize Petroleum Company, enters into a contract with Naive Ned to buy 50 acres of Ned's land. Ned thinks Larry is buying the land for his own use when in fact the land is to be owned by the oil company. Prize Petroleum fails to honor the contract. Is Larry personally liable? Explain your answer.

IS IT ETHICAL?

1. Agency law requires that the principal have legal capacity to enter into a contract; a minor with authority can therefore enter into a binding contract on the principal's behalf. Assume that Rick Retailer hires Tina Teen as a buyer and sends her to New York to the annual spring fashion shows to purchase spring dresses for the store. Denise Designer, knowing that Rick has purchased modestly priced dresses in the past, shows Tina only the most expensive dresses in the collection. Excited over her first trip to New York, Tina buys 50 dresses priced at $1000 each. Assuming that Tina was in fact authorized to buy 50 dresses (no price specified by Rick), was Denise's action ethical? Explain.

2. Assume that in case #1 Denise has just been informed by her accountant that her business must close unless she sells $50,000 worth of dresses immediately. Closing the business would result in 75 employees losing their jobs. Does this information affect your answer to #1? Why or why not?

3. Rick Retailer hires Bob Belligerent to run the men's clothing department. Sylvester Sly, millionaire, comes into the store to buy a designer tie. Bob spends thirty minutes showing ties before Sylvester decides he prefers his own bow tie and turns around to leave. Bob becomes belligerent, grabs Sylvester and breaks Sly's finger. Sylvester sues Rick's Retail Store for $10 million, knowing the lawsuit may well force Rick to close his business. Is Sylvester's action ethical? Explain. If Sylvester were disabled and on a fixed income, would your answer be different?

4. Carl's Construction Company sends notices to local supply companies that Paul Plumber is no longer working for the company and has no authority to charge to the company's account. A notice is sent to Stu's Supply House, where Paul frequently purchased items in the name of Carl's Construction Company. Stu informs all of his salesclerks about the notice. Unfortunately, Sally Salesclerk, one of Stu's employees, forgets about the notice and sells $1000 in plumbing supplies to Paul, charging the amount to the construction company's account. When the bill is sent, Carl refuses to pay. Is Carl's refusal ethical? Explain your answer.

5. Rick Retailer specifically instructs his employee Clara Careless that she is never to use any of the company vehicles. Ignoring Rick's instructions, Clara uses one of the company vans to deliver a piece of jewelry ordered by Sylvester Sly. Returning to the store, Clara fails to yield the right-of-way and crashes into Melba Motorist's new car. Melba suffers serious injuries and

sues Clara's employer. Rick argues that Clara was driving the van without his permission. Is it ethical for Melba to sue Rick? Will the court hold Rick liable? Explain your answers.

DISCUSSION CASE

> ### GLORIA BLINZLER V. MARRIOTT, INTERNATIONAL, INC.
>
> 81 F.3d 1148 (1st Cir. 1996)

Facts:

Plaintiff and her deceased husband were staying in a New Jersey hotel operated by defendant Marriott International, Inc. (Marriott). Around 8:30 p.m. the deceased had difficulty breathing. Having suffered previous heart attacks, he took nitroglycerin and his wife called the hotel operator asking for an ambulance. The request was received by 8:35 p.m. The operator told the plaintiff she would call an ambulance and the operator promptly informed the manager and hotel security officer. The court record indicated the ambulance was not called until fourteen minutes after the wife's first request. The ambulance arrived at 9:02 p.m. but the husband had collapsed and apparently stopped breathing. The plaintiff had inquired twice if the ambulance had been called and was told it had been summoned. Plaintiff's husband died three days later due to brain damage resulting from prolonged period of asystole without cardiopulmonary resuscitation.

The plaintiff sued the defendant for wrongful death, loss of consortium, and negligent infliction of emotional damages due to the delay by the hotel employee in calling the ambulance. Plaintiff sought $200,000 damages for the wrongful death, $200,000 for emotional distress and $50,000 for loss of consortium. The district judge upheld the verdicts for wrongful death and loss of consortium but granted a judgment notwithstanding the verdict (jnov) on the damages for emotional distress. Both sides appealed.

Issues:

The main issues raised in the appeals were the following:

(1)   Was there a causal link between defendant's failure to promptly call an ambulance and the death of plaintiff's husband?

(2)   Is plaintiff entitled to recover damages for emotional distress?

Decision:

The U.S. Court of Appeals held (1) there was sufficient evidence to support the finding that the hotel's failure to promptly call an ambulance resulted in death of plaintiff's husband and (2) evidence supported finding that the hotel was liable for negligent infliction of emotional distress and plaintiff was entitled to $200,000 damages. The damages for loss of consortium were also upheld.

Reason:

Relevant to the causation issue, the Court of Appeals ruled that the court record supported the jury's conclusion that the defendant's delay was the proximate cause of James Blinzler's death. The Court also found the defendant's delay in calling an ambulance negligently inflicted both loss of consortium and emotion distress on the plaintiff.

Discussion Questions

1.   Do you agree with the decision of the Court of Appeals relevant to the issue of proximate causation?

2.   Should the plaintiff recover for emotional distress? What type of evidence could be introduced by plaintiff's attorney relevant to this issue?

3.   How is this case relevant to owners and employees of small businesses?

4.   Assume a customer suffers a heart attack in a small restaurant. Does the restaurant owner have a duty to summon an ambulance immediately?

5.   What steps can the owner of a small business take to reduce the risks of this type of lawsuit?

CHAPTER 6

PROPERTY LAW

CHAPTER OBJECTIVES

In this chapter you will learn to:

1. Distinguish between real property and personal property and understand how personal property can be classified as a fixture and be included in the sale of real property.

2. Recognize the different ways of acquiring ownership of real property, including the manner in which another party can acquire title to the property through adverse possession.

3. Understand the elements of a valid gift and the different categories of gifts.

4. Recognize the need to consult competent counsel before retaining a tenant's security deposit or evicting a tenant.

5. Identify potential environmental problems relevant to property you may purchase and to condition the purchase on an environmental assessment of the property.

Owners of small businesses are frequently surprised to learn the magnitude of property rights they possess. Even if the business is situated in a small area of leased space in a shopping mall, the business owner may still possess extensive property rights. These rights relate to property holdings ranging from tangible items such as inventory and office supplies to intangible property including accounts receivables and the goodwill of the business. As lessee of the mall space, the businessperson also has specific rights relevant to the space rented. These property rights are accompanied by duties to other parties and to society as a whole.

This chapter identifies certain "red flag" situations applicable to small businesses that own or rent **real property**. Types of property are identified and the ways of acquiring property are discussed. The rights and duties of landlords and tenants are explained. The chapter concludes with an overview of environmental laws and policies that impact small businesses.

▶ **"RED FLAG" SITUATIONS**

Situation	**Potential Problem**
1. In selling a building, the seller fails to identify what items do not "go with the sale"	1. The buyer may become the new owner of items the seller never intended to sell.
2. The buyer signs an Earnest Money Contract without including a condition that he must sell his first building before he can afford the new site.	2. The court doesn't accept "I forgot" as a viable defense in a breach of contract lawsuit.
3. A property owner fails to realize that the neighboring store's new driveway encroaches on his land by three feet.	3. After the legally required period of time expires, the neighbor now owns the entire driveway, including the three feet.
4. A business tenant fails to note damage to the leased property when moving in.	4. The landlord may successfully convince a court that the renter caused the damage and thus force the innocent party to pay for repairs.
5. The purchaser of an existing commercial property does not require an environmental assessment before agreeing to buy the property.	5. The new owner may have to pay for all or part of cleanup of the environmental hazards even though he was in no way responsible for the hazards.

TYPES OF PROPERTY: WHAT IS REAL AND WHAT IS PERSONAL

The two basic categories of property are real property and **personal property**, and ownership of each category carries with it specific rights and duties.

Real Property

Real property is basically the surface of the land, crops and plants growing on the land, its subsurface, a certain amount of airspace above it and certain items that are permanently attached to it. In addition, certain items originally categorized as personal (movable) property, may be reclassified as **fixtures** by the law and be included in the definition of real property. As real property, the items are included in the purchase of the real property unless the seller specifically provides they are not included in the sale. Small business owners are frequently surprised to learn that after the sale of their building they may have also sold fixtures which they intended to take with them to their new site.

As mentioned above, the law (usually the courts) determines what items are considered fixtures. Assume that sales at Fern's Florist have been blossoming and Fern decides to sell her current store site and buy a larger store. She contacts Ronald Realtor and enters into a contract with Ronald designating him as her agent to sell the store for $350,000. Fern feels that this is a bargain price for any buyer and therefore she will naturally take certain items in the store with her. She plans to take the five ceiling fans, the tulip-shaped chandeliers, the mahogany built-in shelves where she displays vases and the beautiful mauve carpet that will look divine in her own living room. Fern knows these items must be worth at least $30,000 and no buyer is entitled to them since she's selling the store at such a bargain price. Unfortunately, Fern never mentions her plans to Ronald or to Betty Buyer, who decides to purchase the store for her new venture, Betty's Beauty Barn.

Fern and Betty enter into a written contract (usually called the Earnest Money Contract) which provides that the seller will convey the land, building and "all other property attached thereto" to the buyer for $350,000. As Fern is about to sign the **deed** at the closing of the sale, she casually mentions that she will be by the store later that day to pick up the fans, chandeliers, shelves and carpet. Immediately Betty protests, saying she would never have agreed to pay such an exorbitant price if she had thought these items were not included.

At that point, Fern stalks out of the closing, deed unsigned, and Betty rushes over to Ace Attorney's office. Ace immediately files a breach of contract lawsuit against Fern, alleging she had agreed to convey the "property" upon the buyer's offer of payment of $350,000. Ace seeks the remedy of **specific performance**, where the court will order the defendant to specifically perform the action required in the contract.

The court looks at the "laundry list" of factors it considers in determining if an item has become a fixture. The factors considered usually include:

(1)   If the item is permanently attached to the building. A small rug thrown on the floor, for example, is not permanently attached to the building, whereas a nailed-down carpet is considered permanently attached.

(2)   The uniqueness of the item relative to the building. The keys to all doors in a building and garage door opener are items that fall into this category.

(3)   The intention of the owner when the owner attached the item to the building. The chandeliers, for example, were intended to become a part of the building.

In addition to these basic factors, courts in different states frequently consider additional factors. Many of these factors frequently overlap. For example, the mahogany shelves were permanently attached to the building and also were intended to become a part of the structure.

Ace Attorney convinces the court that the items Fern intends to take are indeed fixtures and Betty Buyer is entitled to them as part of the property she is purchasing. The judge orders specific performance on Fern's part and she is forced to sign the deed conveying the store along with the ceiling fans, chandeliers, shelves and carpet for the original price of $350,000.

Many states have expanded the list of fixtures to include such items as curtains, curtain rods, drapes, valances, mailboxes, satellite dishes, jacuzzis and hot tubs. Small business owners can benefit from seeking professional advice before entering into any Earnest Money Contract relevant to what is considered a fixture in the owner's state. If the seller intends to take certain fixtures, those items need to be listed in agreements with both the realtor and the prospective buyer and excluded from the "property" being sold. Failure to specify that certain items are not to be included in the property being sold may result in the seller having to convey those items based on a court ordering specific performance.

Personal Property

Personal property is basically all property that is not classified as real property. Tangible personal property has a physical existence of its own, meaning it can be seen, touched and felt. Examples of personal property include cars, animals, VCRs, books, and pizzas. As mentioned above, items of tangible personal property may sometimes become fixtures and therefore become a part of real estate. For example, assume that Rick Retailer goes to Italy and buys a slab of superior Italian marble. Rick immediately buys another first-class seat on the return flight for his purchase to assure the marble is not scratched. At that time, the item is considered personal property. Upon his return, Rick has the marble installed as a mantel in the new fireplace in his main salesroom. Upon installation, the marble is no longer personal property but is a fixture. If Rick sells the store, the marble will be considered a part of the real estate that is included in the sale.

Intangible personal property has no physical existence of its own. Examples of intangible personal property include accounts receivable, stocks and bonds, and rights in intellectual property as evidenced by patents, copyrights and trademarks. The goodwill of a business, which includes its name recognition and reputation, is another example of intangible personal property.

PROPERTY RIGHTS: EVEN "SQUATTERS" CAN BECOME LEGAL LANDOWNERS

Once an individual or business acquires real or personal property, the new owner acquires certain rights and duties relevant to that property.

Acquiring Ownership Rights in Real Property

A small business may become the owner of real property in several ways. Acquisition may occur through purchase; inheritance (if a relative dies without a will); by being named in a will; by gift; and by **adverse possession** (using someone else's property without his permission for a specified period of time). Governmental entities also acquire rights in real property through the right of **eminent domain**, where the entity condemns the property, pays the owner the fair market value, and converts the use of the property to a public purpose.

Ownership Through Purchase

The seller of real property may or may not use a real estate broker. An advantage of using a broker is the increased exposure of the property to prospective buyers. Frequently brokers will assist prospective buyers, especially newcomers to an area, in finding a lending institution to make the necessary loan.

When the seller uses a real estate broker, the seller and broker will ordinarily enter into a Listing Agreement, which explains the rights and duties of each party. The Agreement includes the provision for the realtor's sales commission, which is usually a percentage of the Gross Sales Price. This commission is negotiable, and usually is higher when commercial property (rather than residential property) is being listed.

If the business owner is not familiar with Listing Agreements or does not understand certain provisions, the business owner may benefit from a legal consultation prior to signing the Agreement. For example, the Listing Agreement may provide that the broker has the exclusive right to sell the property and any prospective buyers that approach the seller must be referred to the realtor.

Many Listing Agreements advise the seller to inform the seller's insurance carrier if the seller plans to vacate the premises before the sale and to request a rider to the policy to cover the vacant building. The existing insurance policy may cover only damage to an inhabited building. If a vacant store is vandalized, the policy may not be applicable and the seller may incur thousands of dollars in uncompensated damages.

The buyer of business property can also benefit from a legal consultation prior to signing the Earnest Money Contract with the seller to assure that the contract includes all necessary conditions to be met before the buyer is obligated to purchase the property. For example, the buyer may qualify his purchase on the commercial building passing an inspection by a professional licensed building inspector. The buyer can specify to the inspector what areas are to be inspected, such as wiring, plumbing, load bearing walls and roof. Many buyers (and lending institutions) today require that real property also pass an environmental assessment by a professional environmental inspector.

Earnest Money Contracts also provide what closing costs each party must pay. Since the responsibility for payment of these costs may be negotiable, both buyer and seller need to be familiar with the contract before signing.

Assume Rick Retailer sells his existing building and decides to buy a fine, fifty-year-old three-story structure for his new site. He plans to use the first floor for his own business and rent out the upper floors for small shops. Unknown to Rick, the building has lead pipes, asbestos in the insulation, and a high level of radon gas. In addition, the backyard has an underground leaking gasoline tank that stored petrol for a service station that once sat next door. Unfortunately, Rick does not condition his purchase of the property on an environmental assessment. After paying $400,000 for the property, he is informed by various local and state agencies he must remove the lead pipes, the asbestos, the radon gas and either remove or reseal the leaking gasoline tank. Total costs of these removals will exceed the original purchase price of the building. Before purchasing real property for commercial purposes, the buyer must also be certain the zoning laws will allow the proposed commercial venture. This provision can also be a condition in the Earnest Money Contract.

Transfer of real property through a sale is evidenced by a deed. To be valid, the deed must contain the names of both parties; words of conveyance; legal description of the property and the signature of the seller. The deed must also be delivered to the buyer and recorded.

Ownership Through Inheritance and Wills

Ownership of real property may be acquired through inheritance from a relative. When an individual dies **intestate** (without a valid will), each state has special laws designating who will inherit the property. Owners of small businesses may be surprised to learn that a surviving spouse does not automatically inherit all the deceased's property, and the deceased's children, parents, or even siblings may be entitled to an interest in the property.

The owner of real property may designate in the will who is to become the owner of the property upon the current owner's death. For example, Fern may designate in her will that upon her death her niece Nellie will become the owner of the florist in **fee simple absolute**. This means that, as owner in fee simple absolute, Nellie can keep or dispose of the property as she chooses. If, instead, Fern leaves the property to Nellie "provided the property only be used as a florist." Nellie's interest is referred to as **fee simple defeasible**, which means that if Nellie changes the use of the property from a florist, her interest is defeated and the property will go to someone else.

A will may designate two or more persons as co-owners of the real property. Assume niece Nellie and nephew Ned are named in Fern's will as **tenants in common** of the florist. As tenants in common, each owns an individual fractional interest. If either Nellie or Ned dies, that owner's interest passes to his or her heirs. Another form of concurrent ownership is **joint tenancy**; upon the death of one joint tenant, the deceased's property goes to the remaining joint tenant(s).

Ownership by Gift

Sometimes the owner of a small business is fortunate enough to acquire real property as a gift. A valid gift requires three elements:

(1)   The **donor** (original owner) intends to convey the property as a gift to the **donee** (recipient). This element is referred to as **donative intent**.

(2)   The property is delivered to the donee. The delivery may be actual, (for example, when a donor physically hands a diamond ring over to the donee) or constructive or symbolic (when the donor hands the keys to a car to the donee).

(3)   The gift is accepted by the donee.

In order for the donee to acquire ownership of real property, all three elements must be present. The conveyance of real property by gift must also be evidenced by a deed.

Ownership Through Adverse Possession

A small business may lose its ownership of real property to a third party even though the latter's only expense is usually the property tax. Every state allows a third party to acquire real property based on adverse possession. Assume Fern's Florist continues to blossom in sales at its new site and Fern decides to add a patio on the side of the building. Fern's contractor pours the concrete not only on Fern's property but on four feet of Rick Retailer's commercial property next door. Fern regularly uses the patio without Rick's permission. Years later, Rick decides to have his property surveyed and discovers the encroachment.

Rick decides to sue Fern and contacts Ace Attorney. Ace sadly informs Rick that Fern is now the legal owner of the property based on adverse possession. Ownership through adverse possession requires the following:

(1)   The possessor's use of the property was hostile (without the owner's permission).

(2)   The possession was open for everyone to see and was solely by the party claiming adverse possession.

(3)   The use was continuous for the time required by state law. In many states, if the possessor has been paying taxes on the property, the statutorily required time is shorter.

Fern has met all of these requirements and Rick has therefore lost four feet of valuable commercial property to his neighbor.

Following his sad experience with Fern's Florist, Rick Retailer starts camping out in a national park, determined to acquire ownership of his favorite campsite by adverse possession. Unfortunately for Rick, there is an exception to the right of adverse possession: governmental property cannot be acquired by third parties in this manner.

Ownership Through Eminent Domain

Governmental entities frequently acquire ownership of real property based on the legal doctrine of eminent domain. Assume that the county decides to widen the road in front of Fern's Florist and Rick Retailer's store. The county can exercise its right of eminent domain and become owner of the property if certain conditions are met.

Property can be acquired through eminent domain provided:

(1)   The "taking" of the property is for a public purpose. For example, the county can take Fern's and Rick's frontage property for a public road. However, an individual county commissioner cannot take the property as a private road to his personal home. The private property owners have the right to challenge the taking if they feel it is for an improper purpose.

(2)   The property owners are paid a fair price for the land. If Fern and Rick are offered $5 per square foot of land when the current market price is $15 per square foot, they have the right to appeal the amount absent any special circumstances.

GOING GLOBAL   A major concern for a small business purchasing real property in a foreign country is the risk of the property being taken by the government of the host country. In some instances, the host country may pay a fair price for the property. If the property is confiscated, the owner recieves no compensation. This risk should be carefully assessed befor establishing a business abroad.

Losing Property Through Foreclosure

Once a small business owner has acquired real property, the owner must be careful to avoid losing the property through foreclosure.

The owner of a small business may lose real property through foreclosure brought by the party which loaned him the money to purchase or improve the property. Upon receiving the funds to purchase or improve the property, the borrower usually executes a promissory note and a deed of trust. A promissory note contains the maker's promise to pay the payee (the lender) a sum of money at a specific time or on demand. In addition to the promissory note, the borrower (also referred to as the **mortgagor**) executes a deed of trust which provides the **mortgagee** (lender) can foreclose on the **collateral** (the property that secures the loan) if the mortgagor fails to meet the terms of the **mortgage**. In addition to making payments on time, the mortgage may provide that the mortgagor must maintain the property in a reasonable manner and have adequate insurance coverage on the property.

Failure to meet the terms of the mortgage may result in the lender foreclosing on the property and having the property sold at public auction.

A special problem may arise when the owner sells his property and the new owner assumes an existing mortgage. In this case, the first owner may still be liable on the original debt if the second owner fails to meet the terms of the mortgage. For example, Rick Retailer sells his store to Cal's Carpenter Corner and Cal assumes the mortgage Rick executed to Friendly Finance Company. Cal's business is a calamity and he skips the country with three months back payments due on the mortgage. The total amount still due on the existing mortgage is $350,000. Rick cannot come up with the back payments so the finance company forecloses and the property is sold. Due to a depressed market, the property sells for only $275,000. Rick is distressed to learn that he is legally liable to the mortgage company for the $75,000 still due on the mortgage. In this unfortunate situation, Rick must pay the $75,000 on property that is now in the hands of a new buyer.

Owners of small business can benefit from a legal consultation prior to buying or selling real property in order to avoid surprises such as Rick encountered.

Contractors who provide goods or services to build or improve real property can also foreclose on the property. Assume Sam's Swimming Pool Company installs a pool at Rita Realtor's home. Rita agrees to pay Sam $15,000 in ninety days. Sam can obtain a **mechanic's lien** on the property. A mechanic's lien provides that if the property owner fails to pay, the lien holder can foreclose on the property. In the above example, if Rita fails to pay for the pool, Sam will be paid his $15,000 from the proceeds of the sale of Rita's home.

Small business owners who provide goods or services for real property can benefit from an understanding of the requirements of a valid mechanic's lien and where the lien must be filed in their city or county.

Failure to pay property taxes can also result in foreclosure. The taxing agency, after statutorily required notice to the owner, will foreclose and the property will be sold at public auction.

Acquiring Ownership Rights in Personal Property

Ownership in personal property may be acquired through possession; purchase, **confusion**; inheritance; by being named a beneficiary in a will; and by gift.

Ownership Through Purchase

The most common method of acquiring personal property is by purchase. A small business owner regularly purchases supplies and inventory for operation of the business. The owner may routinely go to the shopping mall to buy clothing, household items and greeting cards. In each of these transactions, the owner is contracting with the seller to purchase items of personal property.

Ownership Through Possession

In certain instances, a person can acquire ownership of personal property by attaining possession of the property. This method of acquiring ownership was especially important when fishing and hunting were the main means of providing food for a household. According to the law of possession, the hunter who mortally wounded a wild animal or the fisherman who caught a prize fish became the owner of the animal or fish through possession.

If personal property is lost, the finder (and new possessor) may become the legal owner if certain statutory requirements are met. Assume Fern loses her diamond watch while jogging one day, William Winner finds the watch and contacts Ace Attorney. Ace explains that William must comply with state law, which requires William to place notices of the finding in a certain manner. If Fern does not claim the watch in a specified period of time, William may become the owner. (William was considered a bailee until he became the legal owner).

Finders of **lost property** must comply with all the relevant statutes in order to become the legal owner. According to the law, if the original owner mislays personal property, an involuntary bailment occurs (Chapter 6). The owner of the premises where the property is mislaid is deemed to be the bailee and may become the owner after the statutory requirements regarding notice and time are met. Assume Fern takes off her watch at Ann's Aerobics Club, carefully lays it on a table, and forgets to retrieve it before leaving. An involuntary bailment results and Ann may eventually become the owner of the watch provided Fern does not reclaim it and Ann complies with relevant state law.

Ownership Through Confusion

Ownership of personal property through confusion applies when one owner's fungible goods are mixed with the fungible goods of others. Assume George Grower takes his rice to the local grain gin. George's rice is mixed or commingled with the rice of other local rice growers and it becomes impossible to determine which grains of rice originally came from George's crop. After processing all of the rice, George may become the owner of a portion of rice from a neighbor's crop because the rice was commingled. George's amount of the "commingled" rice will be equivalent to the amount of his own rice he took to the gin.

Ownership Through Inheritance

An individual can acquire ownership of personal property if a relative or spouse dies without a will or intestate. State law provides who will inherit the property and in what proportion.

Ownership Through Designation in a Will

The **testator** or one who is bequeathing the property, may designate in the will who is to become the owner of specific items of personal property just as the testator may designate who will take real property. The testator must comply with state statutory requirements regarding the making of the will to assure its validity.

Ownership Through Gift

A valid gift of personal property requires the same elements as a gift of real property; donative intent; actual or constructive delivery of the gift; and acceptance by the donee.

Gifts of personal property are categorized as either inter vivos or causa mortis. A **gift inter vivos** is basically an unconditional gift made during the life of the donor or gift giver. A gift causa mortis is made when the donor believes that, due to an illness or accident, he is in imminent danger of death. The gift is conditional upon the donor actually dying from the disease or event that motivated him to make the gift. A **gift causa mortis** is terminated if one of the following occur: the donor revokes the gift before the donee accepts; the donee predeceases the donor; or the donor survives the event or illness that motivated the gift.

LANDLORD AND TENANT: BOTH HAVE RIGHTS AND DUTIES

Owners of small businesses frequently start out as tenants and later become landlords during the course of their business careers. Certain rights and duties accompany the role of both landlord and tenant.

As the owner of property leased to a tenant, a landlord has the right to enforce the provisions of the lease. The lease usually provides the duration of tenant's habitation, the amount of rent and when it is due, and any special rules the landlord chooses to impose, so long as the rules do not violate the tenant's civil rights. These rules may prohibit keeping a pet on the premises or subleasing the property to another party. The lease may require a security deposit at the beginning of the lease period to cover any damage the tenant may cause to the property.

Many states have statutes defining the situations when the landlord is entitled to keep the security deposit and the requirements for notifying the renter of the retention of the deposit. Failure to comply with these statutes may result in liability for the landlord despite the tenant having actually damaged the rental property.

State statutes also specify the procedure for evicting a tenant who has violated the terms of the lease. Failure to comply with the eviction statute can also result in landlord liability.

The landlord has the duty to comply with his obligations under the lease. In addition, the landlord has the duty to comply with all relevant laws and to provide the tenant with safe rental property. Local and state laws today are specific as to certain duties of landlords regarding such matters as types of locks for doors, smoke detectors, fire extinguishers, and lead based paint. A small business owner will usually benefit from procuring legal consultation to help assure the owner is in compliance with existing laws in his area prior to renting property to a tenant.

The tenant also has numerous rights and duties. The right to peaceable possession of the rented property is inherent in the rental agreement. This refers to the tenant's right to use and enjoy the property without interference from the landlord or third parties.

Duties of the tenant include adhering to the terms of the lease and returning the property in the same condition as when it was rented, except for normal wear and tear. Assume Timmy Tenant has rented commercial space for a tie shop. At the expiration of the lease, the drapes have faded from the sun and the nap of the carpet is worn from customers walking on it. These are examples of normal wear and tear. A recent ink stain on the carpet, however, is not normal, and Timmy may be liable for the damage.

If the property is commercial and the tenant has installed certain items such as counters and bar stools, he must remove them in a manner that does not permanently harm the property itself.

ENVIRONMENTAL CONCERNS

Small businesses today are subject to numerous local, state and federal environmental laws that regulate activities that may harm the environment. Today's environmental laws primarily focus on air, water and ground pollution and the handling and disposal of toxic chemicals and radioactive substances.

In addition to potential liability for violation of these environmental laws, small businesses that harm the environment may be liable under tort law (Chapter 3) based on negligence and strict liability. Assume Rick Retailer owns a commercial building and decides to rent office space to Bob's Bookkeeping Service. Rick fails to adequately inspect the building for radon gas leaks and Bob develops a chronic respiratory ailment from exposure to radon gas. Bob may sue Rick claiming negligence (see Chapter 4) based on Rick's breach of a duty to provide an environmentally safe office.

Strict liability may result when the small business is handling ultrahazardous items. For example, a trucking company that transports toxic pesticides may be strictly liable or liable without fault, in the event its truck is involved in a wreck and toxic fumes are released into the air.

The National Environmental Policy Act (NEPA) (42 U.S.C. Sections 4321-4370d) established the Environmental Protection Agency (EPA), the federal agency primarily responsible for enforcing federal environmental laws. Among the federal environmental laws that may impact small businesses are the following:

(1)   Clean Air Act (42 U.S.C. Sections 7401-7671q)

(2)   Noise Control Act (42 U.S.C. Sections 4901-4918)

(3)   Toxic Substances Control Act (15 U.S.C. Sections 2601-2692).

(4)   Comprehensive Environmental Response, Compensation, and Liability Act (also establishes the Superfund for payment for cleanups of hazardous waste sites) (42 U.S.C. Sections 9601-9675)

(5)   Federal Insecticide, Fungicide, and Rodenticide Act (7 U.S.C. Sections 134-136y)

A small business may be required by the National Environmental Protection Act to prepare an Environmental Impact Statement (EIS) if the business proposes an activity that involves a federal action and may have a significant impact on the environment. Assume a construction company plans to fill an area of wetlands and build new homes on the site. The Clean Water Act requires the company obtain a permit from the Corps of Engineers before dredging or filling in wetlands. Obtaining this permit from a federal agency is a federal action and the company may be required to prepare an EIS. State environmental agencies may require a similar environmental impact statement.

The Endangered Species Act (16 U.S.C. Sections 1531-1544) may also impact the construction company. The Act protects species of birds and animals that are on the endangered list.

Each state has adopted environmental laws that complement the federal laws. Laws at both the federal and state levels are constantly being changed and new laws adopted. Due to the constant changes in such laws, small business owners can benefit from consulting with an attorney familiar with environmental law prior to undertaking any activity that may impact the environment.

As mentioned earlier in this chapter, the current owner may be responsible for environmental cleanups even though the problem was caused by a previous owner.

GOING GLOBAL

Some countries have few or no environmental regulations. Before purchasing real property abroad the business owner should make certain the property will provide a safe working site. The businessperson should also check the host country's regulations on generating and disposing of hazardous wastes; some countries require any harmful wastes generated must be removed from the host country.

PROPERTY LAW AND THE HOME–BASED BUSINESS

The owner of a home-based business acquires real property and personal property in the same manner as the owner of a retail store operating in a downtown building. The home-based business is equally vulnerable to losing its property by adverse possession. This type of loss frequently occurs when a neighbor's new driveway or building expansion encroaches on the property of the home-based business. Prior to purchasing a new site for the home-based business, the prospective owner should make certain the property is zoned for commercial use. In addition, the purchase should be conditioned on the property passing an environmental assessment.

REDUCING YOUR RISKS

Steps you can take to reduce the risk of legal liability when engaged in activities relevant to property include the following:

1. Make certain you understand what items of personal property may be considered fixtures and thereby become part of the real property you are buying or selling. If the seller fails to exclude the fixtures from the sales contract, the buyer can become legal owner of these items.

2. Know the legal boundaries of your real property and regularly check the property to make certain another party is not encroaching. After a specified period of time, the encroacher may become the legal owner by adverse possession.

3. When you are a donor or donee of property, make certain all the legal requirements for a valid gift were met. Otherwise, a third party may later attack the gift and reclaim the property.

4. Always seek legal counsel before entering into any real estate contract if you do not fully understand all the terms.

5. Do not retain a tenant's security deposit or evict a tenant until you have complied with all relevant laws.

6. Require an environmental assessment before purchasing real property that may have present or future environmental problems.

*KEY WORDS AND PHRASES

Adverse Possession

Collateral

Confusion

Deed

Donative Intent

Donee

Donor

Eminent Domain

Fee Simple Absolute

Fee Simple Defeasible

Fixtures

Gift Causa Mortis

Gift Inter Vivos

Intestate

Joint Tenancy

Mechanic's Lien

Mislaid Property

Mortgage

Mortgagee

Mortgagor

Personal Property

Real Property

Specific Performance

Tenants in Common

Testate

Testator

CHAPTER SUMMARY

Property Law

1. Categories of Property

   a. Real Property—basically the surface and subsurface of the land, a certain amount of space above the land and fixtures.

   b. Personal Property—all property other than real property; personal property may be tangible or intangible.

   c. Fixture—-formerly items of personal property that are now considered part of the real property.

2. Ways of Acquiring Real Property

   a. Purchase
   b. Possession
   c. Confusion
   d. Inheritance
   e. Will
   f. Gift
   g. Adverse possession
   h. Eminent domain

3. Elements of a Gift

   a. Donative intent
   b. Delivery (actual or constructive)
   c. Acceptance by donee

4. Types of Gifts
   a. Gift inter vivos
   b. Gift causa mortis

5. Potential Liability for Environmental Hazards
   a. Liability based on environmental statutes
   b. Tort liability to buyers, renters and employees
   c. Cleanup costs

DISCUSSION QUESTIONS

1. Rick Retailer decides to sell his current store location and move to a larger site. On top of the store is a large satellite dish Rick installed. The store has wall to wall carpeting and a handsome mahogany door. Rick assumes all of these items are his personal property and he can take them to the new site. Is Rick correct? What will be the consequences if Rick makes no reference to these items in the Earnest Money Contract?

2. The site of Rick's old store was never surveyed until Rick was ready to sell to Fern's Florist. The survey shows that the neighbor's driveway has encroached on Rick's property for the past thirty years. Rick tells the neighbor there is no way the neighbor can legally claim the property. Is Rick correct? Why or why not?

3. Soon after Rick moves into his new site he is informed by the City that the City plans to expand the street in front of the site and must take a two foot strip of Rick's property. The City offers Rick $100; the market value of the strip of land is $500. Does Rick have any recourse?

4. Fern's Florist buys Rick's store, with the buyer assuming Rick's mortgage with the bank. The florist business declines, Fern misses her mortgage payment and the bank forecloses. The property sells at foreclosure for $50,000. The outstanding balance on the mortgage is $70,000. The bank informs Rick he is liable for the deficit of $20,000. Is Rick liable?

5. Rick enters into an Earnest Money Contract for the new site. The purchase price is $150,000. Rick assumes the seller knows Rick cannot buy the new property until he sells his current place of business but this condition is not included in the Earnest Money Contract. Rick has not sold his old business when it is time for him to purchase the new site. Rick refuses to go through with the purchase and the seller sues. Is Rick liable? If so, how could he have avoided liability?

IS IT ETHICAL?

1. Wayne Widower is selling the family home. He and his late wife lived in it for fifty years. The buyer, Bob Brash, intends to convert the handsome old

home into a pizza parlor. Not realizing the antique mailbox on the front porch is a fixture, Wayne does not exclude it from the property listed in the Earnest Money Contract. At the sales closing, Wayne mentions he has removed the mailbox since it was a wedding gift to him and his wife fifty years ago. Bob demands the mailbox be returned to the property. Is Bob's demand supported by the law? Is Bob's action ethical?

2. Bob Brash decides to add a patio to the side of his pizza parlor. The patio will be adjacent to property owned by an immigrant family unfamiliar with U.S. laws. Bob intentionally builds his patio four feet onto the adjacent property. After the time required by state law for adverse possession, he declares he is the legal owner of the property. Assuming Bob has met the legal requirements for adverse possession, is his action ethical?

3. Bob Brash strongly suspects that a piece of rural land one of his companies owns was once the dump site for hazardous waste. To avoid the possible cleanup costs, he donates the land to a local charitable organization. Bob denies any knowledge of the waste. Is his action ethical?

4. Learning that the property owners adjacent to his pizza parlor are facing a serious family illness, Bob offers to buy their house for $50,000 and allow them to rent from him at $500 per month. Market value of the property is $80,000 and market rent is $300. Has Bob acted in an ethical manner? Assuming that the family will lose their home by foreclosure if they do not sell immediately, is your answer different?

5. Ruth Retailer is the only real estate broker in the area. In other communities, brokers' fees are from 5% to 8% of the sales price for residential properties. Ruth demands a 20% fee. Is this practice ethical?

DISCUSSION CASE

KLOS V. MOLENDA

513 A.2d 490 (1986)

Superior Court of Pennsylvania

Facts:

Mr. and Mrs. Klos (plaintiffs) bought a lot 50 feet by 135 feet from Mr. and Mrs. Molenda in 1950. There was no survey of the property and the parties paced off the lot and put in stakes to mark the boundaries. The plaintiffs built a house, put a sidewalk in all the way across the front and a driveway 30 inches from the property line indicated by the stake. Plaintiffs planted grass in the 30 inch area and maintained the area. Mr. Molenda died in 1983 and Mrs. Molenda had the land surveyed. The survey showed the land belonging to plaintiffs was 30 inches closer to their home than the stakes indicated. Defendant then built a fence along the new property line, with the fence being immediately adjacent to plaintiff's driveway.

Plaintiffs claimed they owned the 30 inches based on adverse possession and sued to establish their ownership.

The lower court held plaintiffs were the rightful owners of the 30 inches.

Issue:

Had plaintiffs become the rightful owners of the 30 inches of land adjacent to their driveway based on adverse possession? In order for one to become the owner of real property, Pennsylvania law required the claimant show actual, visible, continuous and hostile possession for 21 years. One of the main issues in this case was whether the possession of the 30 inches by plaintiffs was hostile since the stake line may have been the result of a mistake in location on the part of the seller/defendant.

Decision:

The appellate court ruled plaintiffs were the owners of the 30 inches, affirming the lower court's decision.

Reason:

The appellate court affirmed the lower court's decision that all of the requirements for ownership by adverse possession had been met by the plaintiffs. The court affirmed the lower court's finding that the possession of the 30 inches was hostile, open, notorious and exclusive for more than 21 years.

Discussion Question

1. Do you agree with the court's finding that the Kloses are the legal owners of the 30 inches?

2. What is the philosophy behind the concept of adverse possession?

3. How is this case relevant to the operations of a small business?

4. How can the buyer of real property reduce the risk of the problem the defendant faced in this case?

CHAPTER 7

BAILMENTS

CHAPTER OBJECTIVES

In this chapter you will learn to:

1. Recognize the types of bailments that may arise in the operation of a business.

2. Understand the duty the bailee owes toward the bailment property in each type of bailment.

3. Identify bailments that may arise involuntarily but which may still impose a duty of care on the bailee's part.

4. Understand the special liability for common carriers and innkeepers regarding bailment property in their possession.

5. Identify areas of potential liability for businesses that take possession of bailment property.

The owners of small businesses are frequently unaware of an area of law that may impact any type of business at any time: **bailment** law. Potential liability under bailment law may arise any time an individual or business takes temporary possession of an item of **personal property** belonging to another party with the understanding the property is to be returned to the owner or to a third party. Personal property refers to items that are movable in contrast to real property, which consists of items of real estate (Chapter 6). Tangible personal property can be touched and felt, such as clothing, animals and VCR tapes. In contrast, intangible personal property has no physical existence of its own and includes stocks, bonds and promissory notes. Liability may arise even though the business received no compensation for agreeing to care for the property.

Bailment situations may arise from an action as simple as taking a customer's coat while the customer dines in a small restaurant. Bailment liability may also arise when the business is compensated for processing or repairing the customer's personal property. For example, a furniture upholstery shop has a duty under bailment law to care for the furniture in its possession in a reasonable manner. The question of reasonableness is a fact determination for a jury.

This chapter will examine "red flag" situations that may arise when businesses enter into bailment relationships. Types of bailments will be identified and a bailee's duties to the bailment property will be explained. Potential damages the business owner faces for loss or damage to the bailment property are also discussed.

▶ "RED FLAG" SITUATIONS

Situation	Potential Problem
1. An employee agrees to care for a customer's pet cat while the customer shops in a health food store.	1. A bailment is created and the business may be liable if the cat is hurt or lost.
2. A restaurant has a coat check area where diners check their coats.	2. The restaurant may be liable if a diner's coat is stolen.
3. A video store rents a video tape to a customer.	3. The store may be liable if the tape is defective, damages the customer's VCR, and the customer used reasonable care.
4. A grocery store rents out carpet shampooers.	4. The store may be liable if the shampooer malfunctions, and floods the customer's carpet provided the customer used reasonable care.
5. A customer takes out a wallet, forgets and leaves it on the clothing store counter, and a third party steals it.	5. An "involuntary bailment" arises and the store may be liable for the thief's action.

TYPES OF BAILMENTS

A bailment relationship arises when the **bailor** (the owner of personal property) transfers temporary possession of the property to the bailee (the party taking possession) with the understanding that the bailee will return the property to the owner or to a third party in substantially the same condition absent instructions to change the condition. As a general rule, the bailee must knowingly and willingly take possession of the property. ("**Involuntary bailments**" are discussed later). Bailments may involve compensation paid to the bailee or may be gratuitous, where the bailee agrees to care for the property as a favor to the bailor. In either case, each party has certain duties and rights. These duties and rights are determined by the type of bailment.

The type of bailment is determined by which party benefits from the relationship. Bailments may be (1) for the benefit of the bailor (2) for the benefit of the bailee or (3) for the mutual benefit of both parties.

Bailments for the Sole Benefit of Bailor

Assume that Rick Retailer decides to take a long-anticipated trip to Europe during the summer. Rick (the bailor) asks his friend Ed Entrepreneur if Rick may park his new Rolls Royce in the driveway of Ed's home. Rick hands the key over to Ed (the bailee) with the understanding that Ed is not to drive the car for his own benefit. This arrangement is for the benefit of the bailor.

Even though Ed is taking care of the car solely for the owner's benefit and is receiving no compensation, Ed still has a duty to care for the car. The degree of care is discussed later in this chapter. Rick also has the duty to reimburse Ed for any out-of-pocket expenses the bailee reasonably incurred in caring for the car.

Bailment for the Sole Benefit of Bailee

A bailment for the benefit of the bailee occurs when the bailee borrows the property to use in the bailee's own behalf and without compensating the owner of the property in any way. Assume that Grace's Gourmet Restaurant suddenly loses its electrical power during the busy dinner hour. Grace rushes over to Al's Antique Shoppe across the street and borrows two dozen rare antique kerosene lanterns to use in the restaurant. This is a bailment strictly for the benefit of Grace, the bailee.

In another situation, assume Harry Homeowner decides his yard needs extensive work. He borrows the new powerful mower/mulcher Neighbor Ned just bought for $500. Harry's purpose is to improve the appearance of his own yard; he has no intention of doing any work on Ned's yard. This is a bailment for the benefit of the bailee. The bailor has the duty to inform the bailee of known defects. For example, if Ned knows the brakes on his new mower/mulcher are defective, he has the duty to warn Harry. If Ned fails to warn of a known defect and Harry is injured, Ned is liable (even though this was a gratuitous bailment).

Mutual Benefit Bailment

In this type of bailment, both parties receive some type of benefit. Assume Cathy Customer takes a set of drapes into Calvin's Cleaners to have the silk drapes dry cleaned and pressed. Cathy, as the bailor, will receive the benefit of having her drapes cleaned and pressed. The cleaners will receive the benefit of payment for doing the job.

The benefit to the bailee may not always be in the form of monetary pay. Assume that Rick Retailer leaves his Rolls Royce with Ed Entrepreneur with the understanding that Ed will use the vintage car as part of an ad campaign for the store. Ed will actually drive the car to pick up customers and take them to his place of business. This is an example of a **mutual benefit bailment**. Ed will be looking after Rick's car while the latter is in Europe, and Ed will also have the benefit of using the car in his marketing campaign.

Mutual benefit bailments frequently involve the rental of personal property from a business establishment. For example, Ruth Realtor decides to move to a larger city where there are more opportunities in the real estate profession. She goes to the local Moving Magic business which rents trucks for moving household furnishings. Ruth leases one of the trucks and pays the business $400 for the use of the vehicle. In this case, Ruth, the bailee, benefits from the use of the rental truck. Moving Magic benefits from the fee Mary pays to rent the truck. The bailor in a **mutual benefit bailment** must warn the bailee of any defects in the property the bailor knew or should have known about. For example, Moving Magic has the duty to carefully inspect the truck before renting it to Ruth and warn her of any defects discovered in the inspection.

In each type of bailment, the law defines certain duties each party owes to the other party.

BAILEE'S DUTIES TO CARE FOR THE PROPERTY

As discussed above, the type of bailment is determined by which party benefits from the relationship. Until recently, the degree of care owed to the bailment property was particularly dependent on the type of bailment.

Duty of Care in Bailment for Benefit of Bailor

In a bailment for the benefit of the bailor, the courts previously held that the bailee's duty was to take minimal care of the property. Today most courts require the bailee take reasonable care of the property.

In the earlier example of a bailment for the benefit of the bailor, Rick Retailer parked his car in Ed Entrepreneur's driveway with the understanding that Ed was not to drive the car. In the past, the law held that Ed had a duty to take a minimal care of the car. Today, reasonable care is required. Assume that Ed instructs Rick to park the Rolls in the driveway near a 30 foot tall dead oak tree.

During Rick's trip, Ed learns that a hurricane with 100 mile per hour winds is headed toward the area. Despite ample warning time, Ed does not move the car from its proximity to the dead tree. The storm comes through, and Rick's car is leveled. Upon his return, Rick find a car that resembles a flattened pancake and threatens to sue Ed. Ed responds that he is not liable since Rick did not compensate him in any way for taking care of the car. In this case, Ed will probably be liable for the damages to the car. A jury will make the factual determination as to whether Ed had exercised a reasonable degree of care regarding the car. The fact that Ed had ample warning regarding the approaching hurricane will probably lead the jury to determine that Ed was negligent and therefore failed to exercise reasonable care over the car.

Assume instead the car had been leveled by a tornado that unexpectedly uprooted the tree. Since Ed had no advance warning of the need to move the car, he would not be liable for failure to take reasonable care of the car.

In another situation, assume that Rick had such a delightful time in Europe that he is heading off again. This time he wants to make sure his prize goldfish, Goldilocks, is properly cared for. Rick decides to call his friend Ruth Realtor to care for the fish. Ruth agrees to take care of the pet and Ed takes the aquarium over to Ruth's home. Suddenly the real estate business starts to boom and Ruth is seldom home. Somehow she forgets to feed Goldilocks for several days and the poor fish starves. This time Rick comes back from Europe to find his pet no longer swimming. Ricks calls up Ace Attorney, who did so well in the suit against Ed, and Ace advises a lawsuit against Ruth. Once again Ed wins his suit and is compensated for the loss of Goldilocks. The jury determined that reasonable care owed in a bailment for the benefit of the bailor required that the bailee at least feed the fish to prevent it from starving.

In two of the above examples, the bailee was legally liable for damage to the bailment property even though the bailee was caring for the property strictly as a favor for the bailor. Frequently owners of small businesses will volunteer to care for the personal property of a friend, neighbor, relative or customer as a gratuitous act. Even this type of friendly gesture can lead to legal consequences in the event the bailee fails to take what a jury today considers to be reasonable care of the property.

Duty of Care in Bailment for Benefit of Bailee

Courts previously held the duty of care owed to the property in a bailment for the benefit of the bailee was extraordinary care. This extremely high degree of care was required because the bailee was using the property strictly for the bailee's own benefit. Today, reasonable care is required by the bailee by most courts.

In the earlier example, Grace's Gourmet Restaurant borrowed two dozen rare antique kerosene lanterns from Al's Antique Shoppe to use during a power failure. One of Grace's employees decides to polish a lamp and the harsh polish harms the patina. Al sues for failure to take reasonable care of the valuable lamps and will recover for the loss in value of the antique.

In another situation, Rick Retailer, still without his Rolls, borrows a sports car from Ned Neighbor. Rick is using the car solely for his own benefit. Rick parks the sports car on a city street that is being tarred with a new surface. Signs warn of the roadwork under way. The road equipment throws tar on the sports model, damaging the paint job. This time, it is Rick being sued for failure to take proper care of bailment property. Ace Attorney, arguing on Rick's behalf, claims that reasonable care of the property does not require Rick move the car off the street. The jury may disagree with Rick and Ace this time and hold Rick liable. The jury may hold that reasonable care required Rick park the car on another street to avoid damage to the paint surface in view of the fact Rick was warned of the roadwork.

As mentioned earlier, a bailment generally requires that the bailee knowingly and voluntarily accept delivery of the property. An exception to this rule exists when personal property is mislaid. Assume that Cathy Customer comes into Rick Retailer's store, selects a dress and pulls out her wallet at the check-out counter. Cathy inadvertently leaves her wallet on the counter, forgetting to replace it in her purse. The store has neither knowingly nor willingly assumed possession of the wallet. The law categorizes the wallet as **mislaid property** and holds that an "involuntary bailment" has been created. As bailee of the wallet, Rick's now has the duty to take reasonable care of the wallet. This requires Rick place the wallet in a safe place until Cathy returns for it.

Two special categories of bailment law involve **common carriers** and **innkeepers**. In the case of a common carrier, the duty of care is higher than reasonable care. The law holds the common carrier is strictly liable (the plaintiff does not have to prove intent or negligence) for loss or damage to the goods with several narrow exceptions. The common carrier is exonerated from liability if the damage or loss was due to an act of a public enemy; an act of God; order of public authority; inherent nature of the goods, or act of the shipper.

Assume that Icky's Ice Cream Company decides to ship 1000 cartons of vanilla ice cream to Alaska from Florida. Thinking of the sub-zero temperatures at the destination point for the goods, Icky decides to ship by unrefrigerated air freight, thereby saving a substantial amount of money. When the goods arrive at their destination, the buyer opens the first quart and finds sour milk rather than frozen vanilla ice cream. Icky, on the advice of Ace Attorney, sues the carrier because common carriers may be strictly liable for loss or damage to goods in most situations. Unfortunately for Icky and Ace, the carrier has a viable defense: the damage to the ice cream was due to the inherent nature of the goods. Any ice cream will melt on a long trip in an unrefrigerated container.

In another instance, Fred's Fine China Shop of New York City receives an order for eight place settings of fine French china from a new lottery winner in Montana. Fred decides to increase his profits by wrapping the $8,000 purchase himself. A little short on wrapping supplies, Fred places the 164 pieces of fine china in one large wooden box without any wrapping materials to protect the items. Unfortunately the fine china arrives in Montana as fine china slivers. Once again Ace advises his latest client Fred to sue the common carrier. Again, the carrier has a valid defense: the damage to the fine china was due to an act by the shipper. In this case, Fred's less than fine packing of the fine china was the cause of the damage to the goods and the carrier was not liable.

Innkeepers, such as hotels and motels, are also bailees of personal property. When a guest checks into a hotel, the guest will leave possession of the guest's luggage and clothing in the hotel. Based on the common law, innkeepers faced strict liability for damage or loss of the guest's possessions. States now have statutes that limit the innkeeper's liability. The statutes usually require the innkeeper to provide a safe for the guest's valuables and the innkeeper must inform the guest of the availability and location of the safe. Many statutes also limit the innkeeper's liability for goods not placed in the safe. The statutes require strict compliance on the innkeeper's part in order to benefit from this limit on liability.

DAMAGES: LOSING THE CUSTOMER'S DEAR WEDDING FILMS CAN COST DEARLY

The type of bailment that involves most small businesses is a **mutual benefit bailment**. In this situation, the customer or client compensates the business in some manner. In certain instances, the business is the bailor, as when a video store rents the newest video game to a customer. In other instances, the customer is the bailor, as in the situation where a customer takes photo films into a film processing business to be developed. In each of these examples, both parties benefit from the bailment.

As a general rule, contract law applies to **mutual benefit bailments** and damages applicable to breach of contract cases may be imposed by the court. Assume that Phil Photographer takes a roll of film of a recent tornado to Fiona's Fast Film Shop. The shop promises Phil the film will be developed within 24 hours. Phil, planning to use the film in the free-lance story he is submitting to the newspaper, must have the film within that time period in order to meet the newspaper's deadline and receive his $500 commission for the story. Fiona's does a fine job but is 24 hours late in processing the film. Phil sues for breach of contract and may recover the $500 in consequential damages for the lost commission. As discussed in Chapter 3 (Contracts), consequential damages may be recovered if they were contemplated by the parties at the time of contracting.

Frequently the plaintiff in a lawsuit involving a **mutual benefit bailment** brings a tort suit in negligence rather than suing for breach of contract. The reason for alleging negligence is due to the fact that larger damages are frequently available in tort cases.

Assume that Bridget Bride takes her bridal gown to Claude's Cleaners for cleaning and preserving after the wedding.

Unfortunately, Claude has just hired Careless Cal to clean wedding gowns. Cal carelessly puts the dress in the "Dye" stack rather than the "Clean" stack. The priceless gown emerges from the dye vat a brilliant blue. Bridget sues for negligence. A jury determines Claude's had a duty to follow Bridget's instructions. Claude's employee breached that duty and Bridget suffered foreseeable damage.

Other examples of bailments include a customer taking family films into a shop for developing and a customer taking heirloom jewelry in for cleaning and repairs. Businesses sometimes attempt to avoid liability by posting "Not Responsible for Damages" signs. The court may consider the sign as an exculpatory clause (Chapter 4) and refuse to enforce it.

BAILMENTS AND THE HOME–BASED BUSINESS

The home-based business may frequently engage in bailment relationships. A customer may bring a dress or suit to the business for alterations or repairs, thereby creating a mutual benefit bailment. In this situation, the business owner (bailee) has a duty to take reasonable care of the garment and return it to the owner or to a designated third party. The operator of a home-based typing service may borrow a neighbor's typewriter when the business machine malfunctions. In this bailment for the benefit of the bailee, the business owner (bailee) ordinarily has the duty to take reasonable care of the borrowed equipment.

Many home-based businesses today operate as bed-and-breakfast inns for travelers. As an innkeeper, the business owner should review the state statute relevant to limiting the innkeeper's strict liability for loss or damage to the guest's personal property. The state law may require the innkeeper provide a vault for the guest's valuables and also require that notification of the vault be placed in each guest room. Failure to comply with the statute may extend the innkeeper's liability relevant to the guest's personal property.

REDUCING YOUR RISKS

Specific steps the small business owner can take to reduce the risk of liability for failure to take proper care of bailment property include the following:

(1) Make certain that all employees understand that a legally recognized duty of care arises whenever an employee agrees to take temporary possession of a third party's personal property. As a bailee, the employee (and the business) can be liable if the property is lost or damaged.

(2) If the business rents items of personal property to customers, make certain the property is in good condition. If the property is defective and causes personal injury or property damage to the customer, the business may be liable.

(3) Make certain employees understand the importance of putting any items inadvertently left in the store by a customer in a safe place.

An involuntary bailment has been created, and the store may be liable if the goods are stolen by a third party.

(4) If the business plans to leave personal property in the possession of an innkeeper, be familiar with the state law limiting the innkeeper's liability regarding the bailment property.

(5) When shipping business items by common carrier, recognize the limited liability of the carrier and purchase additional insurance if necessary.

* KEY WORDS AND PHRASES

Bailee

Bailment

Bailment for Benefit of Bailee

Bailment for Benefit of Bailor

Bailor

Common Carrier

Innkeeper

Involuntary Bailment

Mislaid Property

Mutual Benefit Bailment

Personal Property

CHAPTER SUMMARY

Bailments

1. Types of Bailment

a. For Benefit of Bailor—The bailee receives no compensation or benefit for taking care of the bailment property.

b. For Benefit of Bailee—The bailee "borrows" the bailment property and uses the property in some manner for the bailee's own benefit.

c. For Mutual Benefit—The bailor compensates the bailee in some manner for the latter taking possession of the property. An example is when a customer takes a coat to the dry cleaners and pays the business for cleaning the garment.

2. Bailee's Duties Toward the Bailment Property

a. For Benefit of Bailor—Most courts today require the bailee to take reasonable care of the property.

b. For Benefit of Bailee—Most courts today require the bailee to take reasonable care of the property.

c. For Mutual Benefit—The bailee has the duty to take reasonable care of the property.

3. Involuntary Bailments

a. This type of bailment occurs when a customer inadvertently leaves personal property in a place of business.

b. The place of business where the property is left becomes an involuntary bailee and has the duty to take reasonable care of the property until the customer reclaims it.

4. Special Bailments

a. Innkeepers may limit their liability for guest's bailment property by complying with state laws.

b. As a general rule, common carriers are strictly liable for loss or damage to bailment property; there are narrow exceptions to the rule.

DISCUSSION QUESTIONS

1. Creation of a Bailment. Rick Retailer donates a computer to a local charity organization. Has a bailment been created? Why or why not?

2. Type of Bailment. Rick Retailer loans a ladder used in his store to Ed Entrepreneur, who is opening a new restaurant across the street and needs the ladder for hanging a banner in front of the new business. What type of bailment was created?

3. Bailee's Duty of Care. Assume in #2 that Ed forgets to return the ladder at the end of the day and leaves it in an alleyway, where it is stolen. Has Ed breached a duty owed to Rick? Explain.

4. <u>Bailee's Duty of Care</u>. Gordon Groom takes film from his wedding to a local photo shop for developing. The shop loses the film. Has the photo shop breached a duty to Gordon? Explain.

5. <u>Involuntary Bailment</u>. Cathy Customer accidently leaves her purse on the counter while shopping for clothes at the Klothing Korner. Within one minute, and before any store clerk sees the purse, Tom Thief steals it. Is Klothing Korner liable to Cathy? Why or why not? Assume the purse had been on the counter for thirty minutes and was spotted by a clerk who was too busy to put it in a safe place. Would your answer be any different? Explain.

Is It Ethical?

1. According to bailment law, the bailee may be liable for damages to bailment property even though the bailment was strictly for the benefit of the bailor. Assume that Harry Horticulturist leaves his prize orchid with Rick Retailer while Harry goes on a trip around the world. Rick has to work late several nights and forgets to water the orchid. As a result, the orchid dies. Harry returns from his vacation, learns the fate of his orchid and sues Rick. Is Harry's action ethical?

2. Rick Retailer loans his car to Ed Entrepreneur so the latter can make a delivery to a customer's home. Ed was in such a hurry to get the car that Rick did not have time to warn Ed that the back door of the car did not always shut properly. Ed loads the back seat with merchandise. At the first stoplight the back door swings open and all of the merchandise pours out onto the street. Ed sues Rick for failure to warn about the defective door. Is Ed's action ethical?

3. Ed Entrepreneur goes to the local wholesale distributor to purchase merchandise for the holiday season. While placing his order, Ed places his wallet on the order counter and inadvertently leaves it there. None of the clerks notice the wallet and twenty minutes later the wallet is stolen by a third party. Ed sues the wholesale distributor for failure to take reasonable care of his wallet. Is it ethical for Ed to sue?

4. State laws allow innkeepers to limit their liability for bailment property guests place in the hotel rooms. Assume Terrence Traveler, who speaks no English, does not understand the notice posted on the hotel room door advising him to place all valuables in the hotel safe. Terrence leaves an expensive VCR in the room and later returns to find it has been stolen. A court finds the hotel not liable because Terrence did not place the VCR in the safe. Is it ethical for the hotel to deny liability?

Discussion Case

Augustine v. Marriott Hotel

503 N.Y.S. 2d 498 (1986)

Facts:

The plaintiff, attending a professional seminar at defendant's hotel, placed his cashmere coat on a coat rack in the hotel lobby outside the meeting room. He left the meeting room at noon and found his coat was missing. The rack had been moved further down the lobby near an exit. Augustine sued the hotel for loss of the coat, claiming a bailment relationship had been created and therefore the hotel breached its duty to care for the coat. (The seminar sponsor had requested the coat rack).

Issue:

Was a bailment relationship created when the plaintiff placed his cashmere coat on the coat rack outside the meeting room?

Decision:

The court held that the plaintiff never entrusted his coat to the hotel and therefore a bailment relationship was not created.

Reason:

For a bailment to be created, the bailor must deliver the personal property to the bailee. In addition, the bailee must knowingly accept the possession and control of the property. In this case, the defendant hotel never knowingly accepted possession and control of the coat.

Discussion Questions

1. Assume the plaintiff had "checked" his coat with a hotel employee. Would the court have reached a different decision?

2. Do you think the hotel was negligent in placing the coat rack outside the meeting room?

3. Is it reasonable for a hotel guest to assume a coat would be safe on a rack in the public lobby of a hotel?

4. Is it fair to hold a small business liable for the loss of a customer's coat when the business voluntarily takes temporary possession of the coat but does not charge the customer for doing so?

CHAPTER 8

INSURING THE RISKS

CHAPTER OBJECTIVES

In this chapter you will learn to:

1. Understand the parties to an insurance policy.

2. Recognize who qualifies to take out an insurance policy based on having an insurable interest in the person or property being insured.

3. Know what contractual provisions are essential in an insurance policy for your small business.

4. Understand the various types of policies available and better determine the type of coverage appropriate for your business.

5. Appreciate the need to have a reputable and experienced insurance agent or broker representing your needs.

Risks of loss are an inevitable part of operating any small business today. A customer may claim illness from food served in a small restaurant, an employee may damage the company van while making a delivery, or the store may be seriously damaged when a severe storm sweeps the area. These are a few examples of the many risks facing today's entrepreneur. Although many risks are inevitable, the small business owner can reduce the potential loss through insurance covering the various types of risks.

This chapter will discuss the parties to an insurance policy, who can take out an insurance policy, contractual provisions in the typical insurance policy, and types of policies available to cover specific risks.

▶ "RED FLAG" SITUATIONS

Situation	Potential Problem
1. Your business regularly provides goods or services to the public	1. The risks of a negligence or product liability lawsuit increases with the expansion of your volume of business
2. You expand or improve the building in which your business is located	2. Your current property insurance coverage may offer inadequate protection if the building is damaged or destroyed
3. Employees of the business regularly drive vehicles while in the scope of employment	3. If the employee is engaged in an accident, inadequate insurance may result in liability for the assets of the business or the owner's personal assets
4. Employees are engaged in work-related activities that place the workers at risk for injuries or illnesses	4. Inadequate insurance for the employees may result in liability for the business or for the owner personally
5. You purchase an insurance policy without fully understanding all the terms of the policy	5. The coverage purchased may be inadequate or unnecessary

PARTIES TO THE POLICY

An insurance policy is based on contract law. The **insurer** (company offering the policy) offers insurance protection to the **insured** (policyholder) in exchange for the payment of a **premium**. In some policies, the insured is also the **beneficiary** (the party who will receive compensation in case of a loss). In other policies, the beneficiary may be a third party. Assume Rick Retailer takes out a life insurance payment with Isaac's Insurance Company. The policy provides that in the event of Rick's death his widow Anne will receive the policy proceeds. Anne is beneficiary of the policy. Since Anne did not contribute to the payment of the premiums, she is considered a third party donee beneficiary (Chapter 3, Contracts).

WHO QUALIFIES TO BUY A POLICY

Insurance law specifies who can buy a policy. In order to purchase an insurance policy, the insured must have an **insurable interest** in the person or property covered by the policy. An insurable interest means that the policyholder will suffer a loss if the insured person dies or the insured property is damaged or destroyed. For example, Moe's Manufacturing Co. may take out a life insurance policy on Edwina Executive, the company's chief executive officer. The manufacturing company has an insurable interest in Edwina because the company faces an actual loss in the event of the officer's death.

Assume that Rick Retailer also tries to purchase a life insurance policy on the President of the United States. Rick does not qualify to purchase the policy because his company will not suffer a direct pecuniary loss in the event of the President's death.

Rick also qualifies to purchase property insurance on the real property where the store is located, on the inventory, supplies, and vehicles used in the business operation. Rick qualifies because he faces pecuniary loss in case any of this property is damaged or destroyed.

PROVISIONS IN THE CONTRACT

Assume that Rick Retailer takes out a policy insuring against damage or loss of his newly renovated department store. In reviewing the contract, Rick will want to look for specific provisions:

(a) **Effective date of coverage**. The policy states the date coverage begins, which may be immediately or in the future. Between the time Rick pays the premium to the insurance agent and the policy is actually issued by the insurance company, Rick may request a binder to assure his coverage during this interim. The insured should review any type policy carefully to assure the effective date is properly shown.

(b) **Co-insurance clause**. The policy may require that the amount of Rick's policy is adequate to cover a specific percentage of the value of the property. For example, the policy may provide that the insurance company will pay the full face value of the policy in case of total loss only if Rick's policy adequately covers at least 80% of the value of the property. Rick will want to have his property appraised regularly to make certain his policy covers the required 80% value.

(c)   **Cancellation clause**. State statutes frequently limit the basis for which an insurance company can cancel a policy. Failure to comply with certain provisions of the contract may provide basis for cancellation.

(d)   **Arbitration clause**. Many insurance policies provide that in case of a dispute between the insured and insurer, the dispute will be referred to binding arbitration.

(e)   **Pre-existing condition**. This provision is frequently found in health and life insurance policies. It provides that the insurer will not cover loss due to a health condition existing at the time the policy is issued until a certain period of time elapses. Assume Fern of Fern's Florist has a heart condition and is hospitalized with an attack three days after she purchases a health insurance policy. The policy may provide the insurer will not compensate her for her heart-related hospitalizations for the first six months after the policy takes effect.

POLICIES ON THE MARKET

Today's newspapers and television programs are full of advertisements sponsored by the numerous insurance companies in this country. One of the most important decisions a small business owner makes is regarding the type and amount of insurance coverage needed. Depending on the size and type of business, the following types of coverage may be essential:

(1)   Property insurance. This insurance is essential for any small business owner. The insurance should adequately cover the value of the building and its furnishings, inventory, supplies, business vehicles and tools used in the business. An updated appraisal of the property is advisable if property values have significantly changed recently.

If the business owner vacates insured property, the insurance company should be immediately notified to assure policy coverage of the vacant building. Frequently a recently vacated building is vandalized without the insurer being notified of the vacancy. The insurer may well refuse to pay for damages because of the insured's failure to notify that the building was being vacated.

(2)   Health insurance. Employer-provided health insurance is a major factor for many employees in deciding where to work today. As mentioned previously, the health insurance policy may have a pre-existing condition clause. Many health policies today charge lower premiums for non-smokers and for employees enrolled in fitness programs. A major factor in a health insurance policy is the amount of the **deductible**, or the amount the insured must pay before the insurer begins payment. Many health insurance providers also offer major medical policies which cover the expenses related to serious illnesses or accidents.

(3)   Liability insurance. This type of insurance covers risks from claims by third parties for loses or damages sustained. Assume Clumsy Clyde slips

and falls in Fern's Florist and sues for $500,000. As a general rule, Fern's insurance company will defend the case and when necessary pay losses up to the amount of the policy.

In another instance assume one of Fern's employees slaps a customer. Again, Fern's insurer will handle the case and losses up to a certain amount. As a result of these lawsuits, Fern will find her premiums going up and at a certain point may not be able to get liability coverage for her business.

Because of these increases in premiums and the possibility of eventually losing coverage, the prudent small business owner makes certain the business is a safe place for customers and employees. In addition, the owner exercises care in selecting employees who will treat customers in a professional and respectful manner.

Small business owners are now being sued by non-smoking employees for illnesses resulting from exposure to other persons' smoking in the workplace. This accounts for many small businesses adopting a smoke-free work environment.

(4)   Life insurance. As mentioned earlier, a business will frequently take out a life insurance policy on a key employee. The policy may be a term life policy, with the coverage effective only during the time the premiums are paid.

(5)   Vehicle insurance. All vehicles involved in the operation of the small business need adequate insurance coverage. The policy can cover damage to the vehicle itself, damage to other vehicles, property damage and physical injuries to the driver, passengers and third parties. The amount of the deductible is a factor in determining the premium.

Selecting drivers for company vehicles is an important decision for the owner of a small business. Choosing mature drivers with safe driving records can reduce premiums as well as reduce the risks of accidents.

(6)   Title insurance. The purchaser of real property is advised to request a title insurance policy to assure the seller has clear title prior to selling the property. The title policy will list any exceptions to the seller's ownership. Examples of exceptions include easements granted to utility companies and mineral rights reserved by previous owners. Lending institutions today condition the loan on a title policy issued in the name of the new purchaser. If title to the property is challenged after the issuance of the policy, the title company will ordinarily go in and defend the title in the new owner's behalf.

Assume Enrique Entrepreneur decides to open a new restaurant and pay cash for an existing building. There is no lending institution involved to demand a title policy. Enrique should still insist on a title policy to assure the current owner has a fee simple absolute right of ownership (Chapter 6) in the property.

(7)   Workers' compensation insurance. State laws regulate workers' compensation insurance within the individual states. An employee covered

by workers' compensation insurance receives compensation for a job-related injury or illness even though the injury or illness is due to the worker's own negligence or that of another employee. In exchange for this assured compensation, the employee generally gives up the right to sue the employer. An increase in workers' compensation claims will increase the premiums the employer is required to pay.

Adequate insurance coverage is a necessity for today's small business. Understanding the types of policies available and the contractual terms of these policies is an important step in assuring adequate coverage. Working with a reputable and knowledgeable insurance agent or broker who is familiar with the needs of small businesses in the area is also essential. Many types of policies available through organizations or trade associations offer lower rates due to the large size of policyholders.

GOING GLOBAL

Conducting business in another country can create new risks for the small business owner. Competent advice from an insurer familiar with insurance laws in the host country is essential. Adequate insurance to cover shipment of goods abroad should be purchased in advance.

INSURING THE RISKS AND THE HOME–BASED BUSINESS

Adequate insurance coverage is essential for the home-based business. The owner should make certain the property insurance policy covers the business property as well as the residential property. Inventory, supplies and business tools are invaluable assets that need protection from loss.

Invitees and licensees may frequently visit the home-based business. The property insurance policy should cover claims by third parties injured on the premises. Liability insurance may also be essential to cover claims by third parties injured on the premises. Liability protection is also needed in the event a third party alleges injury from goods or services provided by the home-based business.

Adequate vehicle insurance is necessary if the business delivers goods to the customers. Making sure that only responsible drivers use the business vehicle can reduce the risk of a lawsuit due to a work-related accident.

The owner of a home-based business may obtain better insurance coverage and lower rates by joining with other members of an organization or trade association in obtaining group policies.

REDUCING YOUR RISKS

The small business owner can reduce the risks of loss due to inadequate insurance coverage in the following ways:

1. Become familiar with the types of insurance policies available and the essential contractual terms of a policy before purchasing any policy.

2. Make sure your property insurance policy adequately covers the value of your business property in case of a loss. A new appraisal of the business building may be advisable if property values have changed significantly.

3. Employ only responsible individuals with good driving records to use the business vehicles. Both business assets and the owner's personal assets may be at risk if the employee's negligent driving injures a third party.

4. Carry adequate liability insurance to cover claims by third parties alleging intentional torts or negligence against the business or its employees. Liability insurance should also offer protection from claims regarding the services or goods provided by the business.

5. Attend seminars and programs on insurance needs for your particular type of business. Business publications also frequently publish articles on the changing insurance needs of small businesses.

6. Work with a reputable insurance agent or broker who is familiar with the needs of small businesses in your area.

*KEY WORDS AND PHRASES

Arbitration Clause
Beneficiary
Binder
Cancellation Clause
Co-insurance Clause
Effective Date of Coverage

Insurable Interest
Insured
Insurer
Pre-existing Condition
Premium

CHAPTER SUMMARY

Insuring the Risks

1.	Parties to an Insurance Contract	a.	Insured
		b.	Insurer
		c.	Beneficiary
2.	Qualification to Purchase Insurance Based on Having an Insurable Interest	a.	Business will suffer pecuniary loss if property is damaged.
		b.	Business will suffer monetary loss if key executive or employee dies.
3.	Key Contractual Provisions in Insurance Policy	a.	Effective date of coverage
		b.	Co-insurance clause
		c.	Cancellation clause
		d.	Arbitration clause
		e.	Pre-existing condition
4.	Types of Policies	a.	Property insurance
		b.	Health insurance
		c.	Liability insurance
		d.	Life insurance
		e.	Vehicle insurance
		f.	Title insurance
		g.	Workers' compensation insurance

DISCUSSION QUESTIONS

1. <u>Parties to a Policy</u>. Sylvester Sly takes out a life insurance policy with Majestic Insurance Company. The policy provides that in case of Sylvester's death, his widow Sonia will receive $1,000,000. Identify the insured, insurer and beneficiary to the policy.

2. <u>Insurable Interest</u>. Sylvester feels very patriotic toward the White House in Washington, D.C. He decides to take out another $1,000,000 policy on that historical structure. Can he do so? Explain.

3. <u>Pre-existing Condition</u>. Rick Retailer has suffered from asthma for years. He takes out a health insurance policy with Majestic Insurance Company. The effective date of the policy is June 1. The policy's pre-existing condition clause provides that the company will not cover any pre-existing condition until the policy has been in effect for six months. On July 1 Rick is hospitalized with an asthma attack. His medical bills are $2000. Majestic refuses to pay. Rick claims breach of contract. Is Rick correct? Why or why not?

4.   <u>Liability Insurance</u>. Cathy Caterer's home-based business expands, forcing her to hire three employees. She assigns Larry Loud the job of taking the customer's orders when they come to the residential business. Betsy Bride comes in and orders a five-tier low-fat wedding cake sitting in a bed of carrots and parsley. (Betsy and her fiancé believe in healthy eating). Larry informs Betsy in the presence of other customers that her cake will look tacky and that only stupid people eat low-fat food. Betsy immediately goes to Ace Attorney and files a defamation lawsuit. Cathy checks and her insurance "...only covers property damage." Could she have purchased insurance to cover actions of her employees? If Cathy is a sole proprietorship, are her personal assets at risk?

5.   <u>Title Insurance</u>. Fern decides to expand her florist building. The owner of Greg's Garage next door offers to sell Fern 15 feet of his property for $1000. Fern decides to pay cash for the strip of land. Greg assures her no title insurance is necessary because the land has been in his family for several generations. Should Fern insist on a title policy? Explain.

IS IT ETHICAL?

1.   Bradford Broker, local insurance broker, learns that Ned Naive is opening a small hardware store. This is Ned's first business venture. Bradford rushes over and knowingly sells Ned more insurance than the hardware store needs. Is Bradford's action ethical? Assume Bradford needs money to pay for an operation for his son. Would your answer change?

2.   Ed Employee applies for health insurance through his employer's health plan. The application asks if Ed is a smoker. Knowing an affirmative answer will raise his premiums, Ed a chain-smoker at home, denies being a smoker. Understanding that lying on the application is illegal, Ed still answers in the negative. (He lives thirty miles away and feels no one will learn of his smoking at home). Is Ed's action ethical? If an increase in premiums would prevent Ed from buying health insurance for his wife and five children, would your answer change?

3.   A customer shopping in Rick's Retail Store slips and falls in the store. The fall is due to the 8 inch high heels she was wearing and not attributable to Rick's negligence. The customer sues. Rick's insurance company insists on settling out of court rather than expending the time and money to defend the suit. Is the insurance company's practice ethical? Does it encourage other frivolous claims?

4.   Ned Naive decides to move his hardware store to a new location. He forgets to inform Bradford Broker, his insurance agent, of the move. The vacant building where the store was previously located is vandalized and suffers $5000 in damages. Ned files his claim and Bradford points out a clause requiring Ned to notify the insurer if he vacates the premises. The company refuses to pay Ned's claim. Is the insurer's decision ethical? Explain.

5.   Sylvester Sly is trying to sell a piece of land that has been in his family for years. He knows Claudette Cousin is about to claim the land belongs to her side of the family and she will probably win her lawsuit. Sylvester decides to sell the land for cash. He encourages Ned Naive to buy the land for the future site of another hardware store. Sylvester assures Ned no title policy is needed. Is Sylvester's action ethical? Assuming Sylvester knew of no problem with the title, would your answer change?

DISCUSSION CASE

OSCO V. ST. PAUL FIRE AND MARINE INSURANCE CO.

656 N.E. 2d 548 (Ind. App. 1995)

Facts:

Defendant was in the business of hauling waste oil. The company was found liable for pollution damage and environmental contamination to two sites designated as Superfund sites. Liability was based on the Comprehensive Environmental Compensation and Liability Act (CERCLA). The insurance company sought a declaratory judgment holding that the pollution exclusion clauses in defendant's policies relieved the insurer of its duty to defend and indemnify. Several exclusion clauses provided the insurer was not liable for "...property damage arising out of the discharge, dispersal, release or escape of...contaminants or pollutants into or on land...; but this exclusion does not apply if such discharge...is sudden and accidental."

Defendant argued the exclusion clause did not apply because the discharge fell under the "sudden" category, claiming the word "sudden" means "unexpected" rather than "quick". The contamination had resulted from release of hazardous wastes over a period of years from waste oil stored in unlined lagoons and other methods of storage.

The trial court held for St. Paul relevant to the duty to indemnify and for defendant relevant to the insurer's duty to defend relevant to its CERCLA liability.

Issue:

Does the pollution exclusion clause relieve the insurance company of its duty to indemnify and its duty to defend the defendant?

Decision:

The Indiana Court of Appeals held the pollution exclusion clause relieved the insurance company of both its duty to indemnify and its duty to defend relevant to the CERCLA claims against defendant.

Reason:

The Court of Appeals held that the word "sudden" combines the idea of "unexpected" and "quick". The Court pointed out the damage resulted from oil storage in unlined lagoons and other areas that allowed environmental contamination over a period of years and therefore the damage was not "sudden."

Discussion Questions

1. Do you agree with the appellate court's decision?

2. In your opinion, what does the word "sudden" mean?

3. Do you think most business owners are familiar with the exclusion clauses of their insurance policies?

4. Is it fair for insurance companies to have exclusion clauses in policies? Give examples of other exclusion clauses typically found in health and life insurance policies.

5. Some health and life insurance policies are now excluding coverage for smoking-related illnesses and deaths. Is this ethical? Explain your answer.

CHAPTER 9

EMPLOYMENT LAW

CHAPTER OBJECTIVES

In this chapter you will learn to:

1. Recognize situations where an at-will employee can claim wrongful discharge even though there was no established duration of employment.

2. Identify situations which may lead to Title VII claims and defenses to these claims.

3. Identify the various forms of sexual harassment.

4. Understand the tests the courts apply in determining if a covenant not to compete will be upheld.

5. Understand who is disabled according to the Americans with Disabilities Act.

6. Identify potential legal problems in the interviewing and applications procedures of your business.

Businesses of all sizes are impacted by today's employment laws. The owner of a small retail store employing three workers may be sued by a disgruntled employee as quickly as a large corporation with hundreds of workers on its payroll. Employment law is constantly changing and redefining the rights and duties of employers and employees. For this reason, a small business owner will benefit from carefully monitoring these changes to make certain the owner is in compliance with the latest laws.

This chapter identifies certain "red flag" situations that may result in legal liability for employers. The current status of the "employment-at-will" doctrine is examined along with the consequences for wrongfully discharging an employee.

An overview of current employment discrimination laws and **sexual harassment** is presented. The court test for agreements not to compete is also examined. The chapter concludes with an overview of the new Americans with Disabilities Act.

 # "RED FLAG" SITUATIONS

Situation	Potential Problem
1. An employer tells an "at-will" worker he is no longer on the payroll even though the worker is doing a good job.	1. The employer may be liable for **wrongful discharge** even though the parties had never agreed on the duration of the job.
2. The owner of a small trucking company refuses to hire a competent male receptionist because the male truckers prefer an attractive female at the receptionist's desk.	2. The male applicant may have a valid sex discrimination claim.
3. A single female boss promises her male secretary a raise if he will escort her to certain social events.	3. The employee may claim sexual harassment.
4. A computer store owner requires her top salesman to sign a **covenant not to compete** in all the county for five years if he leaves her company.	4. The court may find the covenant unreasonable and not enforce it.
5. The owner of a small business refuses to make **reasonable accommodations** that would allow a competent hearing-impaired applicant to qualify for a job.	5. The disabled applicant may claim violation of the **Americans with Disabilities Act**.

EMPLOYMENT–AT–WILL: THE BOSS STILL HAS DUTIES

In many employment relationships, the employer and employee enter into a verbal or written contract specifying the duration of the relationship. The contract defines the rights and duties of each party and contract law applies when a dispute arises. An employment-at-will situation exists when there is no specific agreement between the employer and the employee regarding the duration of the employment relationship. In the past, courts held that an employer could terminate an at-will employee any time without reason or for the wrong reason. Recent court decisions, however, have held that discharging an at-will employee without valid cause can result in liability for the employer.

WRONGFUL DISCHARGE: THE EMPLOYEE CAN COME CHARGING BACK

As mentioned above, there has been an erosion of the employment-at-will doctrine, and courts may now hold the employer liable for wrongful discharge in an at-will relationship. The discharge may be considered wrongful based on the following reasons: the court finds the employer has breached an implied contract; the discharge violates a statute; or the discharge is against public policy.

Even in an at-will employment relationship, the court may find an implied contract existed. The implied contract may result from a verbal statement by the employer. Assume Rick Retailer tells Sam Salesman, an at-will employee, "Keep your sales up and the job is yours for as long as you want it." Sam's sales soar but Rick discharges him and gives the job to Rick, Jr. A court may find the verbal statement created an implied contract. Implied contracts may also be created by statements in personnel handbooks or procedure manuals distributed to employees.

The discharge of an at-will employee may also violate state or federal statutes. Numerous federal and state statutes prohibit employers from discharging an employee in retaliation for the employee's action in certain situations. Both federal and state whistle-blowing statutes protect employees from discharge when the employee reports wrongdoing on the employer's part. Employees who file discrimination complaints against employers are also protected from retaliatory discharge.

The discharge of an at-will employee may be against public policy. Assume Sam Salesman is back on the job and is summoned for jury duty. Rick Retailer decides Sam's jury duty is hurting sales and terminates Sam. Courts have held that terminating an employee for serving on a jury is against public policy since the employee was fulfilling his duty as a responsible citizen.

Discharging an employee for failure to follow unethical or illegal instructions is also against public policy. Assume Rick orders Sam to make certain fraudulent statements about the newer computer models and Sam refuses. Discharging Rick for failure to follow these instructions is against public policy.

Owners of small businesses may benefit from consulting with an attorney well qualified in employment law regarding the latest laws and court decisions relevant to discharge of at-will employees.

Any business owner may be vulnerable to a lawsuit when the owner discharges an employee who has recently been a whistle-blower. This potential liability applies whether the worker was an at-will employee or had a specific duration of employment. As the following case illustrates, jury awards may be quite large in such a case.

TEXAS DEPARTMENT OF HUMAN RESOURCES V. GREEN

Court of Appeals of Texas, 1993

855 S.W. 2d 136

Facts:

The plaintiff was employed as an architect for the defendant. While reviewing construction contracts between the department and private contractors, he discovered what he felt were irregularities on the part of the departmental procurement officers. After reporting his findings to his supervisors and feeling their responses were inadequate, plaintiff informed other departmental workers he was going to report to outside authorities.

The department reviewed his long-distance phone records for the past two years and determined one call was unauthorized and cost the employer 13 cents. The employer's surveillance also found he failed to attend one therapy session for a back injury. The plaintiff was fired for alleged abuse of sick leave, falsification of official DHS documents, and telephone misuse. Defendant also referred alleged violations to the district attorney's office.

Plaintiff sued based on the Texas Whistleblower Act, claiming the firing was retaliation on the defendant's part.

Issue:

Was the firing of the plaintiff a violation of the Texas Whistleblower Act, which protects public employees from retaliation?

Held:

The appellate court affirmed the lower court's decision for the plaintiff, holding the firing was retaliatory in nature and violated the Texas Whistleblower Act.

Reasoning:

The court held the department's attempt to prosecute based on an unauthorized thirteen cent telephone call and the unprecedented investigation of his sick leave indicated the firing was retaliatory action in violation of the Whistleblower Act.

Discussion Questions:

1.   Do you agree with the court's ruling?

2.   The jury awarded the plaintiff $3,459,832 in actual damages and $10,000,000 in punitive damages. Were these amounts excessive?

3.   Who ultimately pays for lawsuits against governmental agencies?

DISCRIMINATION LAWS AND SEXUAL HARASSMENT

Numerous federal and state laws protect employees from discrimination. **Title VII** of the U.S. Civil Rights Acts of 1964 prohibits discrimination based on sex, religion, race, color or national origin. The federal law applies to businesses that engage in interstate commerce and hire fifteen or more workers. The law forbids discrimination at any stage of the employment process, from interviewing to termination and retirement benefits.

Businesses charged with discrimination under Title VII may have several defenses; **bona fide occupational qualification** (BFOQ); business necessity; or seniority.

Assume Terry Thespian opens a small theatrical company and plans to hire twenty performers for a production of King Lear. Since members of the audience may come from different states (interstate commerce) and over fifteen employees are involved, Title VII applies. Alice Actress applies for the lead role but Terry refuses to hire her, claiming only a male is acceptable. Alice files a claim with the federal Equal Employment Opportunity Commission (EEOC), alleging sexual discrimination. The court may find that requiring a male for the lead role was a BFOQ—only a male was qualified for the role of King Lear.

An employer claiming a BFOQ defense must convince a court that the required job qualification relates directly to the ability of the employee to perform the job.

The **business necessity defense** applies when a particular qualification or test is essential to the employee's ability to perform a business function. For example, Bob Bookkeeper may require applicants qualify for a bookkeeping position by passing a math test. Alice Actress again files a sex discrimination claim, alleging the requirement favors males because more men in her city have taken math courses. A court may find that the test met the business necessity defense and Bob is not liable to Alice.

The seniority defense permits promotions and other benefits for certain employees due to the fact they have been employed for a longer period of time than other employees. For this defense to succeed, the employer must show the court there was no intent to discriminate and the seniority system is fair.

Title VII was amended by the **Pregnancy Discrimination Act** of 1978, which prohibits discrimination against women based on pregnancy or related conditions.

The **Age Discrimination in Employment Act** (ADEA) was passed in 1967 to protect applicants and employees from discrimination based on age. The Act applies to businesses engaged in interstate commerce with twenty or more employees. Small business owners are frequently surprised to learn that the ADEA protects workers as young as forty years of age and above.

As mentioned previously, Title VII of the Civil Rights Act and the ADEA apply only to businesses engaged in interstate commerce with a minimum number of employees. States have similar discrimination laws that may apply to smaller businesses involved solely in intrastate commerce, or business within the state. For this reason, an owner of a small business needs to be familiar with the discrimination laws in the owner's particular state.

Sexual harassment is covered by Title VII's prohibition on sex discrimination. Sexual harassment may be in the form of (1) actually requesting sexual favors of an employee in exchange for job benefits (**quid pro quo harassment**) or (2) sexually **hostile work environment**. An example of the latter situation is an employer permitting the posting of offensive cartoons or posters in the workplace.

Courts have held the employer liable for one employee's sexual harassment of another employee. In addition, an employer may be liable for a third party's sexual harassment of an employee if the employer knew or should have known about the situation and did nothing to stop the harassment.

Discrimination claims may result from questions asked while interviewing a prospective employee. Assume Rick Retailer asks Ella Employee if she plans to marry and have a family in the near future. Ella answers in the affirmative to both questions. Rick, deciding he does not want to spend time and money training an employee who may leave within the next two years, does not hire Ella. She may have a valid discrimination claim against Rick. Job application forms may also be discriminatory based on the questions they include.

Owners of small businesses can benefit from having competent counsel regularly review the company's job advertisements, application forms, and interview procedures. These consultation fees may be very small in comparison with damages paid to a plaintiff in a discrimination lawsuit.

 GOING GLOBAL A U.S. company that employs U.S. citizens in its foreign office or store can still be covered by Title VII in regard to the U.S. employees. The company is also subject to discrimination laws in the host country.

AGREEMENTS NOT TO COMPETE: REASONABLENESS IS THE KEY

Many contracts today contain covenants (agreements) not to compete. These covenants usually arise in one of two situations: (1) an employee agrees not to compete with the employer if the employee should leave her current position and (2) the seller of a business agrees not to open a new enterprise that competes with the purchaser's operations. At one time, the courts refused to enforce these covenants, holding they were illegal restraints of trade. Courts today enforce these covenants provided they meet the reasonableness test.

Assume Rick Retailer hires Sam Salesman, the top computer salesman in the area. The employment contract includes a covenant prohibiting Sam from competing with Rick's business if Sam should leave the store. The covenant provides Sam cannot compete by setting up his own store or working for a competitor for one year in the city where Rick's business is located.

Sam, seeing how much money can be made from computer sales, quits his job at Rick's and immediately sets up his own computer store across the street. Rick goes to Ace Attorney, who immediately sues Sam for breach of the covenant not to compete. The court will enforce the covenant if the restrictions are reasonable as to time and geographic location. The reasonableness test is a factual determination for a jury. In this situation, it is likely a jury will find both restrictions are reasonable and Sam cannot open his new business. If one or both restrictions is unreasonable, a court may "reform" the covenant and reduce the time limit or the geographic area.

Assume Rick Retailer decides to sell his business to Ed Entrepreneur. The sales price of $500,000 includes $100,000 paid for the goodwill (name and reputation) of the business. The sales contract includes a covenant where Rick agrees not to compete with Ed for ten years throughout the metropolitan area. A jury may find this longer time frame and more extensive geographic area also reasonable because Ed paid for the goodwill of the company. The value of a business's goodwill is greatly diminished if the former owner can immediately set up a competing business in the area.

Frequently an employee will decide to quit the present job and open a business in direct competition with the present employer. Before undertaking this enterprise, the employee should carefully review the current employment contract to determine if the new venture will violate a covenant not to compete.

Covenants not to compete impact both employers and employees. An employer needs to make certain the covenant meets the reasonableness test in order to be enforceable. A prospective employee needs to be sure the employee is not entering into a covenant that will interfere with a later goal of starting the employee's own business in the future.

THE AMERICANS WITH DISABILITIES ACT

The Americans with Disabilities Act (ADA) (42 U.S.C. Sections 12103-12118), became law in 1992. The ADA specifies the businesses subject to the Act and addresses employment discrimination against those who are disabled. A disability under the ADA is "(1) a physical or mental impairment that substantially limits one or more of the major life activities of such individuals; (2) a record of such impairment; or (3) being regarded as having such an impairment." Examples of disabilities covered include cancer, heart disease, cerebral palsy, paraplegia, and AIDS.

The ADA provides that if a disabled applicant is otherwise qualified for a job, the employer must make reasonable accommodations to enable the employee to perform the job.

Assume Ella Employee applies for a secretarial job at Rick Retailer's store. The job requires extensive time on the telephone and Ella has a hearing impairment. Ella is well qualified and an inexpensive amplifier can be attached to the telephone to alleviate her problem. Adding the amplifier is a "reasonable accommodation" Rick can make to enable Ella to perform the job.

According to the law, an interviewer cannot ask a prospective employee about disabilities or request the employee take a physical examination that is not required of other applicants. Although the job can be conditioned on all the applicants passing a physical exam, if the applicant fails the exam and is not hired, it must be shown the exam related to the ability to actually perform the job.

An employer is not required to hire a disabled applicant if so doing would directly threaten the health and safety of the applicant's co-workers. A prospective employer faced with this potential problem may benefit from a legal consultation prior to hiring or disqualifying the disabled applicant. The potential problem is twofold: (1) hiring an employee who harms co-workers may result in the employer being liable in negligence to the injured co-worker; (2) failing to hire a disabled applicant who does not meet the law's criteria of "direct threat" may result in liability to the applicant under the ADA.

It is impossible for any single textbook to completely cover all areas of potential employment liability for small business owners. Employment law is constantly changing and expanding; being aware of the latest regulations and court decisions is essential. Frequent attendance at seminars on employment law, reading the latest trade publications and regular consultations with competent legal counsel can reduce the risks for liability in this area of the law.

GOING GLOBAL

The ADA may also apply to U.S. employees working for a U.S. firm in a foreign country.

Employment Law and the Home–Based Business

The owner of a home-based business may face liability for the wrongful discharge of an at-will employee to the same extent as the business owner of a downtown retail store faces liability. A court may find the owner had created an implied contract by assuring the employee of a job so long as the employee performed in a satisfactory manner. Firing an employee for reporting unsafe working conditions may violate a whistle-blower's statute. Discharging an at-will employee because the worker had to serve on jury duty and miss several weeks of work is wrongful.

Many home-based businesses are exempt from certain federal employment discrimination laws because of the low number of workers employed. The business may still be liable for discrimination under state law. The business owner can therefore benefit from competent advice relevant to interviewing and hiring practices.

REDUCING YOUR RISKS

The small business owner can take the following steps to reduce the risk of liability due to claims by applicants and employees that the owner has violated employment laws:

1. Be careful as to any job assurances offered to at-will employees. A court may hold that a verbal statement or a personnel brochure has resulted in a contractual commitment to the employee.

2. Do not rely on the Bona Fide Occupational Qualification defense unless the discriminatory practice can be proven to be job-related.

3. Review covenants not to compete regularly to make certain they meet the reasonableness tests for your jurisdiction.

4. Provide regular training for human resource personnel in your business to assure they are familiar with the latest developments in employment law.

5. Do not ignore employee's complaints about sexual harassment on the part of other employees or third parties. The employer may become liable for failure to act on the complaints.

*KEY WORDS AND PHRASES

Americans with Disabilities Act
   (ADA)
Age Discrimination in
   Employment Act
Bona Fide Occupational
   Qualification (BFOQ)
Business Necessity Defense
Covenant Not to Compete
Employment-at-Will

Hostile Work Environment
Pregnancy Discrimination Act
Quid Pro Quo Harassment
Reasonable Accommodation
Sexual Harassment
Title VII
Wrongful Discharge

CHAPTER SUMMARY

Employment Law

1. Grounds for Wrongful Discharge
    Claims by an At-Will Employee

    a. Breach of implied contract
    b. Violation of statute
    c. Violation of public policy

2. Title VII Basis for Illegal
    Discrimination

    a. Discrimination based on sex
    b. Discrimination based on religion
    c. Discrimination based on race
    d. Discrimination based on color
    e. Discrimination based on national
        origin
    f. Discrimination based on age
    g. Discrimination based on preg-
        nancy

3. Defenses to Title VII Claims

    a. Bona fide occupational qualifica-
        tion
    b. Business necessity
    c. Seniority

4. Forms of Sexual Harassment

    a. Quid pro quo harassment
    b. Sexually hostile work environ-
        ment
    c. Harassment by other employees
        or third parties

5. Legal Requirements for Valid
    Covenants Not to Compete

    a. Reasonable as to time
    b. Reasonable as to geographic
        location

6. Disabilities Under the ADA
    a. Physical or mental impairment that substantially limits a major life activity
    b. Record of impairment
    c. Perceived as having such impairment.

7. Prohibited Interviewing Practices
    a. Inquiring about a disability
    b. Requiring a physical examination not required of other applicants.

DISCUSSION QUESTIONS

1. Wrongful Discharge. Rick Retailer's personnel manual provides all employees will have annual evaluations of their work performance. Any employee with an unsatisfactory evaluation will be counseled and given 90 days to improve the performance level and will then be reevaluated. Earnest Ed, an at-will employee, has had satisfactory evaluations for the past eight years. Due to a family illness, his performance rating dropped for the last evaluation. Three days after the evaluation, Rick fires Ed and replaces him with Rick, Jr. Ed sues for wrongful discharge. Does Ed have a valid claim? Why or why not?

2. Age Discrimination. Rick Retailer is hiring a new secretary. The first applicant is 21 years old and has no secretarial skills but is "willing to learn". The second applicant is 59 and highly skilled. Rick, presuming the second applicant will miss work due to age-related illnesses, hires the first applicant. (Rick's business is covered by Title VII). Does the second applicant have a valid complaint? Explain.

3. Americans with Disabilities Act. Assume the second applicant in #2 is 35 years old and is recovering from cancer. Rick, assuming a relapse, hires the first, lesser qualified applicant. Has Rick violated a law? Explain.

4. Covenants Not to Compete. Rick Retailer hires Super Salesman to join the sales staff. The written employment contract includes a covenant not to compete. The covenant provides that if Super leaves Rick's store, the salesman will not compete in the entire county for five years. Is the covenant enforceable? Why or why not?

5. Bona Fide Occupational Qualification. George's Gourmet Restaurant has expanded and now has 30 employees, including five chefs. George requires all applicants for chef positions pass a basic cooking test. Dorothy Disaster, an applicant, scorches the kitchen ceiling when her frying chicken flames up. She is denied the job and files a sexual discrimination claim against George. (A male chef was hired instead). Does George have a valid defense?

IS IT ETHICAL?

1.   Fern of Fern's Florist knows that Title VII of the Civil Rights Act applies to businesses engaged in interstate commerce with fifteen or more workers. Fern intentionally keeps her work force at fourteen to avoid Title VII. Is this practice ethical?

2.   Terry Tycoon owns XYZ television station. Terry understands that the Age Discrimination in Employment Act protects workers beginning at age forty. One day before her fortieth birthday, Terry fires Alice Anchorwoman because he wants a "younger face" at the anchor desk. Is this action ethical?

3.   Rick Retailer pays Super Salesman $400 per week with no commission. Due to a family illness, Super direly needs to make more money. He has an opportunity to go to work with a competing local chain store. Rick, reminding Super of the covenant not to compete in his employment contract, refuses to release him from the agreement. Is Rick's action ethical?

4.   Assume Super Salesman has an "at-will" employment contract with Rick Retailer. Needing money to pay family medical bills, Super applies for a job with a local retail chain. The prospective employer contacts Rick, who gives Super a poor reference rating even though Super has been a super employee. (Rick does not want to lose this valuable employee.) Is Rick's action ethical?

5.   Assume Rick Retailer has paid Super Salesman, an at-will employee, very well over the years. One week before Christmas, half of the sales staff becomes ill with the flu. At the same time, Super is offered a super job with a retail chain in the area and quits. Rick Retailer suffers substantial losses due to his reduced sales staff. Was Super's action ethical?

DISCUSSION CASE

C. THOMAS RYTHER V. KARE 11, AN NBC AFFILIATE; GANNETT CO., INC.

U.S. 8th Circuit Court of Appeals

84 F. 3d 1074 (1996)

Facts:

Plaintiff Ryther had been a sports anchor for defendant television station from December, 1979 until July, 1991. During that time he had entered into four three-year employment contracts with defendant. In 1991, at age 53, plaintiff was terminated when the station refused to renew his contract.

Beginning in the summer of 1988, his work assignments began to change. He was removed as host of a weekly show "Prep Sports Extra" and became co-anchor. In 1989, he was removed from the role of sports anchor on the six o'clock news and was assigned a recreational segment on the five-o'clock news. He was also excluded from promotion photos.

In March, 1991, plaintiff was informed his contract would not be renewed because he had failed in the market research.

Defendant claims the contract was not renewed based on a 1990 Gallup Survey. The Survey reported plaintiff had a 76% viewer recognition, second to a sportscaster at a competing station in the overall market of the Twin Cities. The Survey also reported plaintiff "underperformed" and was not a strong player for the station. Plaintiff claims that the overall market research was an indication of the station's failure to emphasize sports rather than an indication of his abilities. Plaintiff also claims the decision to dismiss him was made prior to the Gallup Survey and the decision was based on age discrimination, in violation of the federal age Discrimination in Employment Act (ADEA).

The jury verdict in the district court was in the plaintiff's behalf. Plaintiff was awarded $1,254,535 in back pay, future pay, attorney fees and liquidated damages. Defendant appeals.

Issue:

Was plaintiffs discharge based on age discrimination in violation of the federal Age Discrimination in Employment Act (ADEA) or did the employer have a legitimate reason for dismissal based on the market research?

Decision:

The Eighth Circuit Court of Appeals affirmed the district court's judgment for plaintiff.

Reason:

The Court of Appeals agreed with the district court's analysis that the jury could reasonably conclude defendant was engaged in age discrimination and its asserted reason for discharge was false.

Discussion Questions

1.   Do you agree with the court's decision?

2.   Should age be a Bona Fide Occupational Qualification for television newscasters if market surveys show the viewing public prefers younger faces on the television screen?

3.   The federal Age Discrimination in Employment Act protects employees and prospective employees beginning at the age of 40. Do you believe workers as young as 40 need protection from age discrimination?

CHAPTER 10

CONSUMER RIGHTS

CHAPTER OBJECTIVES

In this chapter you will learn to:

1. Recognize how a seller or lessor of goods or services can create an express warranty.

2. Recognize how implied warranties are created, including merchantability of food and beverage.

3. Determine when a warranty has been effectively disclaimed.

4. Identify activities in your business that are subject to federal and state consumer protection laws.

Until recently the law's attitude toward consumers in this country was "**caveat emptor**" or "let the buyer beware." That attitude has changed dramatically in recent years with the advent of consumerism. Today's **consumer** may rely on contract law, tort law, and numerous state and federal statutes and administrative regulations to enforce the consumer's legal rights.

This chapter identifies certain "red flag" situations which may result in consumer liability for the small business owner who sells or leases goods or services to a consumer. Legal grounds for consumer lawsuits are explained, including breach of warranties and violation of consumer protection laws.

▶ "RED FLAG" SITUATIONS

Situation	Potential Problem
1. Seafood gumbo served by a small cafe contains a crab shell.	1. The customer cracks her tooth on the shell and claims the cafe has breached an **implied warranty** by serving unfit food.
2. A small retail store sells an imported pre-packaged doll with easily removed buttons.	2. A customer's child swallows a button and the customer sues the local store, which had nothing to do with the manufacture or packaging of the doll.
3. A salesclerk in a small garden supply store recommends a pesticide for a home gardener's prized orchid.	3. The pesticide is inappropriate for orchids and the store owner is sued when the chemical destroys the flower.
4. A collection agency regularly calls a customer at midnight about a delinquent account.	4. The customer claims the agency has violated the **Fair Debt Collection Practices Act**.

LEGAL BASIS FOR THE CONSUMER TO SUE

As mentioned earlier, small businesses today face potential liability to consumers based on contract law, tort law, and statutory law, and violation of administrative regulations. A consumer is one who buys or leases goods or services for the buyer's own personal use, for use by the buyer's family, or use by the buyer's household.

In determining if the plaintiff qualifies as a consumer, the court looks at the use of the goods or services. Assume Paul Pix, a professional photographer, buys a new camera to use in his work. The camera is considered professional equipment and Paul would not qualify as a consumer in this transaction. On his son's fifteenth birthday,

Paul buys a camera from Carl's Camera Corner Store for Paul, Jr. to use on vacation. In this case, Paul is a consumer because the camera is purchased for family use. The camera purchased from Carl's for Paul Jr. takes only black and white pictures although Paul requested a camera that takes colored film. Paul may sue on his son's behalf claiming breach of contract.

Consumer Lawsuit Claiming Breach of Contract

When Paul sues Carl's Camera Corner he may claim breach of contract and allege the store breached a warranty (or guarantee) that accompanied the sale of the camera. A warranty may be expressed or implied. An **express warranty** is created when the seller makes a written or verbal factual assertion about the goods or services being provided. Assume Carl assured Paul the camera would take colored pictures. Carl's statement resulted in an express warranty.

Certain warranties are implied with the sale of goods. According to Article 2 of the Uniform Commercial Code (see Chapter 3), certain warranties automatically accompany the sale of goods unless the seller specifically disclaims the warranty. (Warranties are discussed more fully later in this chapter.)

Consumer Lawsuit Claiming Tort Liability

Assume the camera Paul purchased exploded in his son's hands. Paul may bring a tort case against the manufacturer, claiming either negligence or **strict product liability**.

As explained in Chapter 4, a negligence suit requires the plaintiff prove the following: (1) the defendant owed a duty to the plaintiff (2) the defendant breached that duty and (3) the breach was the proximate (foreseeable) cause of the injuries plaintiff suffered.

To succeed in the negligence suit, Paul will show that the manufacturer (1) had a duty to make a camera that would not explode (2) the manufacturer breached that duty by using an inferior material that would easily explode and (3) it was foreseeable that using the inferior material that would result in the camera exploding and injuring the user.

Consumers may also claim negligence in the design or packaging of a product; in failure to adequately warn of the dangers from misuse of the product; and failure to provide adequate instructions for assembling or using the product.

Another possible tort theory Paul may claim is strict product liability. To prevail under this theory, the plaintiff must prove (1) product was defective when it left the merchant seller (2) product was not altered in any way between the time it left the seller and reached the consumer (3) the plaintiff was injured due to the dangerous characteristic of the product and (4) in some states, product was unreasonably dangerous.

Owners of small businesses may be particularly vulnerable to strict product liability because every party in the distribution chain, from manufacturer to retailer, may be held liable. Assume Mark's Music Store sells imported pre-packaged whistles for children. The whistles are so small that a three-year-old child swallows one and chokes to death. Mark may be liable based on strict product liability even though he had nothing to do with the manufacture or packaging of the whistle. In many states, the retailer, distributer and wholesaler may be liable as well as the manufacturer. For this reason, Mark would benefit by making sure the products he sells are safe and by being certain the manufacturer will be available to reimburse him in case he is sued based on strict product liability or liability without fault.

Consumer Lawsuit Claiming Violation of a Statute

A consumer may bring a lawsuit alleging the defendant violated a state or federal consumer law or regulation. Assume Cathy Consumer purchased a stereo from Rick Retailer's electronics store. Cathy was a little short of cash at the time of the purchase and signed a promissory note agreeing to pay Rick $75 per month for 12 months. Cathy becomes even shorter on cash and misses a monthly payment. Rick turns the matter over to Callous' Collection Agency. Callous starts calling Cathy each evening at 11 p.m. demanding payment. Callous knows the late night phone calls awaken Cathy's small children and thinks this might make her pay sooner. Cathy becomes quite distressed and visits Ace Attorney, asking if she has any recourse against the nighttime phone calls.

Ace sues the collection agency for violation of the Fair Debt Collection Practices Act, a federal law that prohibits collection agencies from contacting the debtor late at night. The Act also prohibits the agency from contacting Cathy at work if her employer objects; from harassing or intimidating her; from contacting third parties about her debt except in limited situations; and contacting Cathy after she has notified the agency she refuses to pay the debt, unless the agency is advising her of its future action.

Many states now have their own debt collection practices statutes that apply to creditors as well as collection agencies. In many states Rick will be liable if he tries to collect the payment himself in a manner the state statute deems as unfair. Owners of small businesses can benefit from a review of the debt collection laws in their individual states.

Federal and state consumer protection laws are discussed more fully later in the chapter.

WARRANTIES THAT GO WITH THE SALE (EVEN WHEN NO GUARANTEE IS GIVEN)

As mentioned above, small businesses are often sued by consumers claiming breach of contract based on an express or implied warranty that accompanied the transaction. The express warranty is created by the seller or lessor in some manner.

Small businesses that are engaged in the sale of goods (movable, tangible items) are covered by Article 2 of the Uniform Commercial Code (UCC). The UCC specifies how a seller may create express warranties and which warranties are implied in every transaction for the sale of goods. The UCC has special rules for sellers who are **merchants**. A merchant is one who is in the business of selling a particular type of goods or holds himself out as an expert relevant to the goods being sold.

Express Warranties Under the UCC

According to the UCC, a seller of goods creates an express warranty in several ways: (1) by making a written or verbal factual assertion relevant to the goods (2) by a drawing or diagram of the goods (3) by using a descriptive word or phrase and (4) by showing a sample of the goods.

Assume Rick Retailer tells Cathy Consumer that a VCR in his store will play any brand of VHS tape. Cathy buys the VCR and then learns it will only play one expensive brand of VHS tape. Rick has breached an express warranty he made relevant to the tapes the machine will play.

The VCR that Cathy purchased is packaged in a box that shows the slot for inserting tapes in the front of the machine. Cathy looks at the box, noting the convenient location of the insert slot. Once Cathy gets the VCR home, she discovers the insert slot is located in the back of the machine, opposite the location of the control knobs. The express warranty created by the picture on the box was breached.

Cathy also purchases a wristwatch in Rick's store for her ten-year-old niece's birthday. Cathy, a safety-conscious consumer, selects a watch that is labeled "shatter-proof." The first time her niece wears the watch, the child lightly hits her wrist against a door. The watch immediately shatters, cutting the child severely. The express warranty created by the term "shatterproof" has been breached in this case.

Dejected over her problems at Rick's, Cathy decides to buy a new dress. She goes to Diedre's Design Shoppe, where Mr. Paul of Paris is showing his new fall collection. Mr. Paul holds a beautiful pure silk evening gown in front of Cathy. She immediately places an order for the gown in her size. Three weeks later the gown arrives. It is exactly like the sample Mr. Paul showed with one exception: the dress is made of polyester and not pure silk. Mr. Paul has breached the express warranty he created when he showed Cathy the sample of the pure silk dress.

The UCC allows a seller of goods to disclaim express warranties provided the disclaimer is clear and easy for the consumer to understand and there was no fraud on the seller's part. Frequently a written sales contract will state the seller disclaims all warranties not contained within the contract.

Implied Warranties Under the UCC

The UCC provides that certain warranties automatically become part of the sale unless they are specifically disclaimed. These implied warranties include (1) **warranty of merchantability** (2) implied **warranty of fitness for a particular purpose** and (3) implied warranty due to trade usage or course of dealing.

The implied warranty of merchantability accompanies sales by merchants. Goods are considered merchantable (1) if they are fit for their ordinary use (2) if fungible, all goods are of similar texture, size, shape and (3) they are considered acceptable within the trade.

Assume Cathy Consumer goes back to Diedre's Design Shoppe and buys an imported umbrella. The next day it rains and Cathy eagerly opens up her new umbrella and confidently walks into the shower. The umbrella is not water repellant and Cathy is immediately soaked. Diedre has breached the implied warranty of merchantability because the umbrella was not fit for its ordinary purpose.

Next Cathy goes to George's Gourmet Grocer and buys a pound of rice to prepare her famous rice pilaf. When Cathy opens the bag of rice, she finds some grains are three times as large as other grains, thus making it impossible for all the rice to cook in the same length of time. Fungible goods that are not of similar size are not merchantable.

A special problem may arise for the sellers of foods and beverages. Article 2 of the UCC applies to these sales whether the goods are consumed on the business premises (as in a cafe) or taken home. The implied warranty of merchantability applies, but the courts differ in determining if a food item or beverage is merchantable. Some courts follow the **reasonable expectation test** while others follow the **foreign-natural test**.

Assume Cathy Consumer goes to Rene's Restaurant and orders pecan pie. A pecan has not been completely shelled and Cathy cracks a took while eating the pie. She rushes over to Ace Attorney's office. Ace explains that she is in luck because the court in her jurisdiction follows the reasonable expectation test. If a jury determines it is reasonable for a consumer to expect the shells to be removed from the pecans in a pecan pie, Cathy will win her case.

If the court in Cathy's jurisdiction followed the foreign-natural test she would not be so fortunate. In that case, if the jury determined that shells were natural (rather than foreign) to pecans, Cathy would lose her case.

To disclaim the implied warranty of merchantability, the merchant seller must (1) specifically disclaim the warranty by using the word "merchantability" or (2) by using language such as "with all faults" or "as is" to inform the consumer of the disclaimer. The written disclaimer must be conspicuously placed in large letters.

The implied warranty of fitness for a particular purpose arises when the seller selects the goods for the consumer after the consumer informs the seller of the particular purpose for the goods. Assume Cathy Consumer tells a clerk at Rick's Retailer Store she is looking for wallpaper that will "stick" in a high humidity climate. The clerk recommends a particular brand, which Cathy buys. After the paper is hung, it immediately "unsticks" in the high humidity and falls to the floor. Rick's has breached the implied warranty of fitness for a particular purpose.

To disclaim this warranty, Rick's must either have a specific written disclaimer or use words indicating the goods are being sold "as is", "with all faults" or similar language.

The sale of commercial goods in a foreign country may be covered by the Convention on Contracts for the International Sale of Goods (CISG). The CISG includes provisions for express and implied warranties.

GOING GLOBAL

FEDERAL CONSUMER LAWS

In the past few years, Congress has passed numerous laws to protect the consumer in sales or lease transactions. Among the federal laws that impact small business owners are the following:

(1)   Federal Trade Commission Act (15 U.S.C. Sections 41-58)

False and deceptive advertising, bait-and-switch tactics and other deceptive trade practices are illegal under this Act. An advertisement that has the potential to deceive may be considered deceptive under the **Federal Trade Commission Act**. False claims as to a product's efficacy, ingredients, or origin are deceptive under the Act. Courts have held that withholding relevant information about a product or presenting a "half-truth" may also be deceptive.

(2)   Federal Trade Commission Regulation on Door - to - Door Sales

The FTC provides that whenever goods or services are sold door - to - door to the consumer's home, the purchaser has a right to cancel within three days of the transaction. Any money paid must be returned within ten business days.

(3)   Truth-in-Lending Act (15 U.S.C. Sections 1601-1693r)

Administered by the Federal Reserve Board, the **Truth-in-Lending Act** requires lenders and sellers to disclose all relevant terms of the credit sale or loan to the consumer. The Act also limits a credit card holder's liability to $50 in case the card is lost or stolen and card holder properly notifies the credit card issuer.

(4)   Equal Credit Opportunity Act (15 U.S.C. Sections 1691-1691f)

The **Equal Credit Opportunity Act** prohibits discrimination in the extension of credit based on religion, race, color, national origin, sex, age, marital status and on certain sources of income. Owners of small businesses can benefit from having an attorney review their credit application forms to assure compliance with this Act.

(5)   Fair Debt Collection Practices Act (15 U.S.C. Sections 1692-1692o) (Discussed above)

(6)   Fair Credit Reporting Act (15 U.S.C. Sections 1681-1681t)

The **Fair Credit Reporting Act** gives consumers the right to access the information in their credit reports and correct any erroneous information. A regular review of one's credit file can reveal errors and allow the consumer to correct those errors before the consumer is ready to make an expensive purchase on credit.

(7)   Telephone Consumer Protection Act (47 U.S.C. Section 227)

The **Telephone Consumer Protection Act** regulates telephone solicitations that use prerecorded voices, automatic dialing systems and ads transmitted by fax.

(8)   Used Motor Vehicle Registration Rule (16 C.F.R. Sections 455.1-455.5)

The Used Motor Vehicle Registration Rule regulates the sale of used cars and requires sellers to attach a "Buyer's Guide" to all used cars. The seller must show on the label if the car is being sold "as is" or with a warranty along with other required information.

STATE CONSUMER LAWS

All states now have consumer protection laws to protect consumers of goods and services within the state. In many instances, the state law may be more protective of the consumer than a comparable federal law.

GOING GLOBAL   Before selling or leasing goods or services in a foreign market, the small business owner should review relevant consumer protection laws in the host country. Many countries also regulate the advertising of goods and services through all forms of media.

Owners of small businesses can benefit from a regular review of the consumer protection laws in the state where the business is located. An individual state's laws addressing deceptive trade practices is of special interest to the owner. For example, the Deceptive Trade Practices Act in Texas, includes a long "laundry list" of specific activities that are considered deceptive. These activities include odometer rollbacks (which also violates federal law); claiming the sales item is "new" when it has been used; advertising "going out of business" sales merely to lure the customers into the store; and advertising goods without having an adequate supply or without indicating in the ad that supplies are limited.

As mentioned earlier, many states also have Fair Debt Collection Practices Acts that apply to business owners collecting their own debts. (The federal law applies to collection agencies).

CONSUMER RIGHTS AND THE HOME–BASED BUSINESS

Despite its small size, the home-based business is vulnerable to lawsuits by its customers. An express warranty is created when the owner of the home-based business makes a factual assertion about its goods or services; provides a sample or drawing of the goods or shows a sample. The implied warranties of merchantability and fitness also apply to the home-based business. For example, a caterer who provides a wedding cake impliedly warrants that the cake is fit for human consumption.

The home-based business is also subject to federal and state consumer protection laws. In many cases, the state laws are more restrictive than the federal laws.

REDUCING YOUR RISKS

Steps the owner of a small business can take to reduce the risk of a lawsuit by a consumer of goods or services include the following:

1. Familiarize all members of the sales staff with the manner in which they may create an express warranty through their words or actions.

2. Make certain the sales staff understands the potential liability when selecting goods for the consumer based on the consumer's specific needs.

3. Inspect inventory goods regularly to make sure they are merchantable, or fit for their ordinary purposes.

4. Purchase quality inventory from reputable manufacturers and distributors to reduce the risk of a strict product liability case.

5. Inform employees involved in debt collection practices of the proper procedure for collecting on unpaid accounts.

6. Make certain that business advertisements do not deceive or have the potential to deceive the buyer.

7. Review the company's credit application forms to assure compliance with the Equal Credit Opportunity Act.

---

* KEY WORDS AND PHRASES

Caveat Emptor

Consumer

Equal Credit Opportunity Act

Express Warranty

Fair Credit Reporting Act

Fair Debt Collection Practices Act

Federal Trade Commission Act

Foreign-Natural Test

Implied Warranty

Merchant

Reasonable Expectation Test

Strict Product Liability

Telephone Consumer Protection Act

Truth-in-Lending Act

Warranty of Fitness for a Particular Purpose

Warranty of Merchantability

CHAPTER SUMMARY

Consumer Rights

1.	Creation of Warranties: Express Warranties	a.	By written or verbal factual assertion
		b.	By drawing or diagram of the goods
		c.	By descriptive word or phrase
		d.	By showing a sample
2.	Creation of Implied Warranties	a.	Of fitness for a particular purpose
		b.	Of merchantability
		c.	Due to trade usage or course of dealing
3.	Tests for Merchantability of Food and Beverage	a.	Reasonable expectation test
		b.	Foreign-natural test
4.	Disclaimers of Warranties	a.	By specific language
		b.	By words such as "with all faults" or "as is"
5.	Federal Consumer Laws	a.	Federal Trade Commission Act
		b.	Door-to-Door Sales Regulation
		c.	Truth-in-Lending Act
		d.	Equal Credit Opportunity Act
		e.	Fair Debt Collection Practices Act
		f.	Fair Credit Reporting Act
		g.	Telephone Consumer Protection Act
		h.	Used Motor Vehicle Registration Rule

DISCUSSION QUESTIONS

1. <u>Express Warranty</u>. Cathy Consumer goes to Fern's Florist to purchase a dozen roses for a party Cathy is having the following day. Cathy asks when the roses were picked and if they will still be fresh for her party. Fern assures Cathy the roses were picked from the florist's own flower bed less than an hour earlier and they will remain fresh for "at least forty-eight hours." The roses were actually shipped in three days earlier and they are wilted by party time. Did Fern breach any warranties? Explain.

2. <u>Implied Warranty</u>. Cathy Consumer goes to Bobbie's Boutique and purchases a beautiful parasol. When the next rain comes, Cathy eagerly rushes out,

confident her parasol will protect her. Within thirty seconds, Cathy is soaking wet. She claims Bobbie's has breached the implied warranty of merchantability. Is Cathy correct?

3. Merchantability of Food. Juan Diner goes to Rosalinda's Restaurant for dinner. Juan bites into a bone chip in a meatball and breaks a tooth. The courts in the jurisdiction follow the foreign-natural test. Is Rosalinda liable?

4. Deceptive Advertising. Fern's Florist runs an advertisement in the local newspaper for "Dutch Tulips". The tulips were actually grown in the florist's nursery and are not from Holland. Is this false advertising? Why or why not?

5. Credit Card Liability. Stephanie Student, nineteen years old, loses her credit card in the mail. Terri Thief finds it and charges $500 for clothing on the card. Is Stephanie liable for the full $500 debt? Explain.

Is It Ethical?

1. Sid Shopper owes $3500 to Ed's Electronics. Sid has not made a payment in three months because all of his extra money is going toward payments on his nifty new sports car. Ed turns the bill over to Cal's Collection Agency. Cal has a new employee who does not know Sid has informed the agency of his refusal to pay. The new employee calls Sid, who then sues Cal's for violation of the Fair Debt Collection Practices Act. Is Sid's action ethical?

2. Cathy Consumer buys a blow dryer at Dan's Drug Store. The dryer is defective and severely shocks Cathy while she is drying her hair. The dryer was manufactured by Metro Manufacturing, one the largest manufacturers in the country. In Cathy's jurisdiction, the retailer can be liable as well as the manufacturer for the defective product based on strict liability. Cathy sues Dan's rather than Metro because of an old family feud with Dan. Is Cathy's action ethical?

3. Assume in #2 that Cathy, along with several thousand other consumers, sues Metro Manufacturing because of the defective dryers. Metro immediately files for bankruptcy, thereby preventing the claimants from proceeding with their lawsuits. Is Metro's action ethical? If payment of the lawsuits would force Metro to close down and lay off 2000 workers, would your answer be different?

4. Juan Diner breaks his tooth when he bites down on a pecan shell in a piece of pecan pie at Rosalinda's Restaurant. The courts in Juan's jurisdiction follow the foreign-natural test and therefore Rosalinda's is not legally liable. The restaurant has insurance that would cover this type of incident. Fearing her premiums will go up, Rosalinda refuses to file a claim. Juan has to pay his $2000 dental bill. Is Rosalinda's action ethical?

5. The Federal Trade Commission permits advertisers to use certain "mock-ups" in their advertisements, such as using shaving cream to represent ice cream in a television ad. Even if the "mock-up" is legal, is it ethical?

6. Assume a pesticide is banned in this country for health reasons. The producer has a large stockpile of the product and begins selling the product in a developing country where the sale is permissible. Is the practice ethical?

DISCUSSION CASE

WIENER V. BLOOMFIELD

901 F. Supp. 771 (S.D.N.Y. 1995)

Facts:

A company retained defendant to collect $1,019.76 which the company claimed plaintiff owed the company for servicing her home fuel oil tank. The plaintiff lived in Westchester County, New York and defendant had an office in the Bronx. A series of letters defendant sent to plaintiff form the basis for this lawsuit.

In a letter of March 1, 1995, defendant identified himself as the company's representative to collect the $1,019.76. The letter threatened to "proceed to prepare for litigation" if plaintiff didn't respond within ten days and also stated the plaintiff had 30 days to dispute the debt. In a letter of March 27, the defendant set an April 6 deadline for plaintiff's response and threatened immediate litigation if plaintiff failed to respond by the deadline. The letter was accompanied by documents labeled "Summons," "Verified Complaint," "Summons and Complaint: Service Pursuant to CPLR 312-a" and "Acknowledgment of Receipt of Summons and Complaint." The documents were captioned to indicate the parties to the suit. Plaintiff did not respond to the communications and did not inform defendant or the company that she disputed the debt.

On April 24, plaintiff's complaint in this lawsuit was filed. Plaintiff claims defendant's letters violated the Fair Debt Collections Practices Act (the Act).

Issue:

Did defendant's letters violate the Fair Debt Collection Practices Act by using conflicting deadlines, threatening to do what cannot legally be done and by misrepresenting documents sent to plaintiff as legal process?

Decision:

The court held for the plaintiff and awarded her $350 on her complaint.

Reasons:

The court held that the defendant violated the Act in the following ways:

(1)   The use of a conflicting date in the letter of March overshadowed the Act's debt validation period. A violation occurs when conflicting deadlines overshadow the Act's requirement for notice of the consumer's right to 30 days in which to dispute the debt. The March 1 letter stated plaintiff had 30 days to dispute the debt but also said she must respond within ten days and cited a deadline of March 11, after which defendant would proceed to prepare for litigation.

(2)   The March 27 letter threatened to file suit in the County of the Bronx, which was improper venue for the case. The Act provides venue shall be where the consumer resides or where the contract, if written, is signed.

(3)   The Act was violated by sending a summons and complaint that conveyed the impression legal proceedings had been instituted against the plaintiff. This action violates the Act's prohibition on the use of documents that simulate they have been authorized by a court.

Discussion Questions

1.   Why was the creditor not liable for the actions of the collection agent?

2.   Do you agree with the provisions of the Fair Debt Collections Practices Act regarding conflicting deadlines, threatening to do that which one cannot legally do and misrepresenting documents as legal process?

3.   Many states have laws on debt collection practices that are more consumer-oriented than the federal law. Do you believe most small business owners are familiar with the debt collection laws in their own states?

CHAPTER 11

FORMS OF BUSINESS ORGANIZATIONS

CHAPTER OBJECTIVES

In this chapter you will learn to:

1. Identify the various forms of business organizations.

2. Understand factors to consider when selecting the appropriate form for your business.

3. Identify sources of information to assist you in selecting the appropriate form of business organization.

Determining what form of business organization to establish is one of the first decisions facing anyone considering setting up a small business. Many prospective entrepreneurs are surprised to learn the number of options available even for the small business enterprise. The main forms available include operating as a **sole proprietorship**, a **partnership**, a corporation, or a **limited liability company**. The choice as to which form of business to establish can carry with it numerous legal and financial consequences for the owner.

This chapter will list certain "red flag" situations that may arise as a result of choosing a specific form of business operation. Advantages and disadvantages of the sole proprietorship and partnership are analyzed. The legal and financial ramifications of incorporation are discussed. The chapter concludes with suggested sources of advice that may be helpful in deciding the proper form of business organization.

▶ "RED FLAG" SITUATIONS

Situation	Potential Problem
1. A customer slips and falls on the greasy floor of a grocery store operated as a sole proprietorship.	1. The customer wins a negligence suit and can collect from the proprietor's personal assets if necessary to satisfy the judgement.
2. One partner contributes twice as much capital and works twice as hard as the other partner in a **general partnership**.	2. If the partners did not specify how profits are to be divided, all partners share equally despite the capital contribution and work load.
3. One **general partner** is away for a month and the other partner negligently serves rancid food in the cafe.	3. The "absent" general partner may be named as the sole defendant in a negligence suit by a customer who becomes ill from the food.
4. The owners of a small corporation regularly use the business's airplane for family trips and negligently injure an airport worker on the runway while taking off on a family outing.	4. The plaintiff injured in the accident may "pierce the corporate veil" and recover from the personal assets of the business owners.

WHETHER TO GO IT ALONE OR JOIN A FRIEND: PROPRIETORSHIPS AND PARTNERSHIPS

In deciding which form of business organization to establish, the owner can benefit from carefully analyzing the advantages and disadvantages of each form.

Frequently the owner of a small business is initially undecided as to whether to set up a sole proprietorship or bring in a friend or relative and establish a partnership. A careful analysis of the advantages and disadvantages of each form is essential to assure the best decision is made.

Many small businesses start out as a sole proprietorship. Advantages of this form of organization include the following:

(1) Ease of organization. A sole proprietorship is essentially created when the owner decides to start up. No formal legal documents are required for its creation, although the business must comply with local registration requirements.

(2) Inexpensive to create. Certain forms of business organizations are statutory in nature (a specific statute permits it to exist) and must therefore pay a fee to the state for the permit. A sole proprietorship is not a statutory form of organization and the owner does not have to pay an organization fee to the state.

(3) Ease of operation. Detailed records of board meetings, shareholder meetings and certain other aspects of the business operations are not required under state statute for a sole proprietorship.

(4) The owner keeps all of the net profits. A major advantage of the sole proprietorship is the fact that the owner does not have to share profits with other shareholders or partners.

(5) The owner is the boss. The sole proprietor can make all of the decisions relevant to the business, including when to work and when to close.

Disadvantages of the sole proprietorship include:

(1) The owner's personal assets are at risk if the business cannot pay a debt or judgement. This disadvantage is especially important if the sole proprietorship is engaged in a type of business that may lead to negligence or strict liability lawsuits.

(2) The owner may have difficulty in raising capital for the business based solely on the owner's creditworthiness.

(3) The sole proprietor must carry the entire work load herself.

(4) The owner must rely entirely on her own business talents and expertise.

Sole Proprietorship or Partnership?

Assume Barbara Baker has become quite famous in her neighborhood for her delicious fat-free almond tarts and apple strudels. Encouraged by her friends, Barbara decides to set up a business and sell the pastries out of her kitchen. Her operation will include delivery service to her customer's homes. Barbara's next major decision is determining which form of business organization is appropriate for her business.

Barbara's neighbor Larry Loud, foreseeing great profits in the pastry business, encourages her to set up a partnership. Naturally Larry offers to be Barbara's partner in the endeavor.

The definition of a partnership is found in the Uniform Partnership Act (UPA), which has been adopted by all of the states except Louisiana. According to the UPA, a partnership is "...an association of two or more persons to carry on as co-owners a business for profit."

The two major types of partnerships are general partnerships and **limited partnerships**. In a general partnership, all of the partners are general partners with unlimited personal liability.

A limited partnership is statutory in nature, and a copy of the agreement must be filed in the proper state office. There must be at least one general partner (with unlimited personal liability). As a general rule, the liability of a **limited partner** is limited to the amount the limited partner has invested in the partnership. A limited partner may lose this limited liability, however, by actively participating in the management of the business.

Advantages of a partnership include the following:

(1)   More available start-up capital. It may be easier for the business to raise capital since the lender will be looking at the creditworthiness of more than one owner.

(2)   Combined skills. The partnership can benefit from the talent and expertise of more than one person.

(3)   Shared workload. The time spent working in the business can be shared with the other owners.

Disadvantages of a partnership include:

(1)   Potential personal liability for the action of another partner. There exists joint and several liability for each general partner if a plaintiff injured by the business brings a tort case. This means the plaintiff can join all the general partners as defendants or "sever" off one general partner and name only that partner. The partner named in the lawsuit can seek contributions from the other general partners to pay the total judgment if the business does not have adequate funds.

(2)   Joint liability for partnership debts. If a creditor sues the partnership, all partners are jointly liable. If only one partner is solvent, that partner must pay the entire judgement and then try to collect from the others.

(3)   UPA's "gap filling" provisions. If the partners do not specify certain terms in the partnership agreement, the UPA will "fill in the gaps" in a manner that may not be agreeable to all parties.

Absent a specific agreement among the partners, the UPA provides all profits will be shared equally in a general partnership. Assume Barbara contributed $10,000 to the partnership and Larry $500. If the partnership realizes a profit of $20,000, Larry will receive $10,000 absent an agreement as to distribution of profits.

The UPA provides no partner is entitled to a salary absent a specific agreement. Although Barbara works 14 hours per day in her kitchen, she receives no salary unless the partners agreed to her salary.

Numerous other "gaps" are filled in by the UPA if the partners do not provide otherwise. If a person decides to establish a partnership, that individual may prefer to work with an individual who is not a relative or a close friend. Any type of personal disagreement with one of the latter may carry over to the business operations with a devastating effect on profits.

Tax consequences may be a major consideration for Barbara in determining what form of business organization to establish. In both sole proprietorships and partnerships the profits or losses of the business are shown on the owner's individual tax returns. Since many small businesses operate at a loss in the beginning, she may wish to show the loss on her own personal income tax return.

A major disadvantage of a sole proprietorship or partnership is the potential personal liability for an owner. This is especially critical if the small business is engaged in any type of activity that may lead to legal liability. In Barbara's situation, she is preparing food to be eaten by the public. A customer who becomes ill may claim negligence in preparing the food or may claim breach of warranty of merchantability.

In addition, Barbara will offer delivery service. If her employee negligently hits a pedestrian while making a delivery, Barbara may face personal liability for the tort.

In considering a partnership arrangement, Barbara will need to carefully evaluate the advantages and disadvantages of forming a partnership with Larry Loud. Assume Larry comes into Barbara's kitchen when Cathy Customer is picking up pastries. Cathy complains about the price of the pastries and Larry loudly informs her that the price is higher because Barbara uses pure ingredients. Larry goes on to say that Dahlia's Delicacy Shoppe uses powdered milk and artificial sweetener in its "all natural" pastries.

Learning of the statement, Dahlia immediately sues the partnership for defamation of her business reputation. As a result of Larry's statement, both he and Barbara face personal liability if the partnership cannot pay the judgement.

CORPORATIONS DON'T HAVE TO BE BIG

The third major form of business organization available to small businesses is the corporation. Many small business owners erroneously assume that incorporation is only available for large business enterprises with extensive assets. In many states today, only one person is required to incorporate.

Advantages of incorporation include the following:

(1) Limited personal liability. As a general rule, the liability of an incorporator is limited to the amount of her capital investment in the corporation. Assume Barbara Baker forms a corporation to operate her pastry business. If a customer slips and falls in Barbara's kitchen and sues for negligence, the general rule is that the plaintiff can only recover from the corporation's assets.

An exception to the limited liability rule exists when a plaintiff can "**pierce the corporate veil**" and recover from the owner's personal assets. The courts allow the plaintiff to pierce the corporate veil in the following situations:

(a) The owner uses the corporation as an "alter ego." This frequently occurs when an owner commingles personal and corporate funds or uses the corporation's assets for personal purposes.

(b) The corporation is undercapitalized, indicating to the court the owner had no intention of establishing a serious business operation.

Assume Barbara incorporates and then takes a month's vacation in Paris. She charges all expenses to the bakery but conducts no business activities during the trip. The travel agency sends the bakery a bill for $3,000 for the first-class round trip airfare to Paris. Barbara refuses the pay, claiming the bakery has only $300 in assets. The travel agency may be able to "pierce the corporate veil" and recover from Barbara's personal assets.

(2) Perpetual existence. A corporation continues to exist even though one of its incorporators dies or becomes incapacitated.

(3) More available capital. The capital contributions of more than one owner may enhance the business's opportunity for loans.

(4) Combined expertise. The different owners can bring different skills and talents to the business.

(5) Delegation of workloads. The corporation owners may share the work among themselves or delegate to employees.

Disadvantages of incorporating include:

(1) Incorporation fees. As mentioned earlier, corporations are statutory creatures that exist because a state law authorizes their existence. Each state requires the corporation to pay a fee in order to receive its corporate charter. Attorney and accountant fees are also frequently incurred in establishing a corporation.

(2) Detailed record keeping. In order to receive the benefits of corporate existence, state laws require corporations to maintain careful records of directors' meetings, shareholder meetings, and other activities of the business.

(3) Required meetings. State corporation laws also require the business to hold shareholder meetings at least once a year.

Limited Liability Companies

Most states have passed legislation authorizing the formation of a limited liability company (LLC). The LLC is a statutory creature comprised of members rather than shareholders. The LLC offers limited personal liability to its owners and is taxed as a partnership.

SOURCES OF ADVICE TO DETERMINE THE RIGHT FORM

As mentioned earlier, one of the first critical decisions for the owner of a small business is determining the proper form of business organization to establish. The choice can have significant legal and financial consequences. Seeking competent professional advice prior to making the decision can prevent serious problems later. Sources of professional advice include the following:

(1) An attorney well qualified in commercial law for small businesses. The laws in this country are becoming increasingly complex. It is therefore impossible for any one attorney to be totally familiar with every area of the law. A small business owner can benefit from a legal consultation with an attorney familiar with the various forms of business organizations for small enterprises. The fee paid for a consultation prior to forming a small business can be inconsequential in comparison with a large judgement the owner may have to personally pay if the business is later sued.

(2) An accountant familiar with the various forms of business organizations and their potential tax consequences.

Before entering into any partnership agreement, the businessperson should request the proposed agreement be put in writing. The written agreement should then be reviewed by the individual's own attorney to make certain all rights and duties are clearly defined.

The requirements for establishing a particular form of business organization may be quite different in a foreign country. The small business owner should seek competent legal advice in advance. Many foreign governments require a business in the host country be at least 51% owned by nationals.

GOING GLOBAL

FORMS OF BUSINESS ORGANIZATIONS AND THE HOME-BASED BUSINESS

Deciding the proper form of business organization is as critical for the home-based business as for the large department store operating in a shopping mall.

The legal and tax consequences of the sole proprietorship, partnership and corporation should be evaluated in relationship to the risk factors and the personal financial status of the owner of a home-based business.

If the products or services provided have the potential to harm a customer or user, the owner should carefully consider the limited liability afforded by a corporation. If numerous customers or clients come to the premises of the home-based business, the liability issue may also be critical.

The sources of information discussed above are also available to owners of home-based businesses and should be utilized to the fullest extent possible.

REDUCING YOUR RISKS

The small business owner can take the following steps to reduce the risk of liability in the event a creditor, customer or other third party sues the business:

1. Analyze the risk factors in your business and determine if you can benefit from a form of business operation that protects your personal assets in case the business is sued.

2. Carefully consider anyone who may become your general partner. You may be personally liable for actions or inactions of that partner.

3. Have your own attorney review any partnership agreement before you sign to make certain your interests are fully protected.

4. Make sure your corporate assets are not used for personal purposes; otherwise a party suing the corporation may pierce the corporate veil and recover from your personal assets.

5. Seek competent advice from a lawyer and an accountant before deciding what form of business operation to adopt. The accountant's advice relevant to tax consequences may be a major factor in determining the best form of business organization for you.

---

*KEY WORDS AND PHRASES

Corporation	Limited Partnership
General Partner	Limited Personal Liability
General Partnership	Partnership
Limited Liability Company	Pierce the Corporate Veil
Limited Partner	Sole Proprietorship

CHAPTER SUMMARY

Forms of Business Organizations

1.	Forms of Business Organizations	a.	Sole proprietorship
		b.	General partnership
		c.	Limited partnership
		d.	Corporation
		e.	Limited liability company
2.	Factors to Consider in Selecting a Form of Business Organization	a.	Need to limit personal liability of owner(s)
		b.	Tax consequences
		c.	Ease and cost of formation
		d.	Required formality of operation
		e.	Ability to raise capital
		f.	Available expertise among owners
3.	Sources of Information	a.	Attorneys and accountants
		b.	Seminars
		c.	Business centers in colleges and universities

DISCUSSION QUESTIONS

1. <u>Sole proprietorship</u>. Hans Hatmaker operates a fine men's haberdashery as a sole proprietorship. One day Dan Dash dashes in to buy a top hat for an evening gala. While dashing around, Dan slips on a coffee spill on the Italian tile floor. The coffee was spilled several hours earlier but Hans was too busy to mop it up. Dan breaks his leg and sues Hans for $500,000. Unfortunately, the business assets total $300,000. If the court awards Dan the full amount, does he have recourse against Hans for the remaining $200,000? Explain.

2. <u>Assume in #1 that Hans had formed a limited partnership with Dora Dunne as a limited partner</u>. Dora had invested $1,000 in the partnership; her net worth is over $1,000,000. How much of Dora's money is at risk?

3. <u>Assume in #1 that Hans and Dora Dunne are general partners in the business</u>. Dora has been in Europe for six months prior to the accident. If Hans is personally unable to pay any of the judgement, how much is Dora's total potential personal liability?

4. <u>Rick Retailer incorporates his retail business</u>. The corporation buys a company car and company recreation vehicle for travel to trade shows. Rick uses both vehicles regularly for family trips and family vacations. He frequently dips into the corporate funds to pay for his daughter's college tuition. Dan

Dash dashes into Rick's store and slips on a skateboard Rick's youngest child left in the store aisle. Dan breaks his other leg and sues the corporation for $1,000,000. The court awards him the full amount. Unfortunately, the corporation has only $1,000 in assets due to Rick's use of the funds for family purposes. Does Dan have any recourse against Rick? Explain.

5. <u>Sharon Senior will soon graduate with a degree in business administration</u>. She is considering opening a new computer software company. She will write her own programs, which will be used by financial planners in predicting how money funds will do in the coming months. What form of business operation is best for Sharon? (Assume she has limited capital for investment). Why?

IS IT ETHICAL?

1. Many businesses choose to incorporate in order to protect the owners' personal assets in the event a lawsuit is brought against the corporation. Is it ethical to incorporate for this reason?

2. Belinda and Brad form a general partnership and open a boutique shop. Brad works in the store eighteen hours a day during the first month, while Belinda spends her time at the health spa working out. At the end of the month Brad asks for his salary. Belinda points out that there was no provision for salary in the partnership agreement. She also reminds him that according to the Uniform Partnership Act, in the absence of a specific provision, no partner is automatically entitled to a salary. Belinda then refuses to agree to a salary for Brad. Is Belinda's action ethical?

3. Belinda contributed $1,000 to the formation of the general partnership in #2 and Brad contributed $50,000. The partnership agreement was silent as to distribution of profits. The boutique realized a net profit of $20,000 the first year. Belinda insisted she receive half of the profits, pointing out the UPA provides that in the absence of a specific provision, profits are shared equally. Is Belinda's action ethical?

4. Dan Dash is shopping in Pamela's Pet Shop, Inc. and slips and falls on a gerbil running around the floor. Dan is seriously injured and sues for $200,000. The court awards Dan the full amount; however, the business has assets of only $1,000. Pamela is an independently wealthy millionaire. Dan is unable to work and recovers only $1,000. Pamela congratulates herself for incorporating and thereby avoiding personal liability for Dan's injury. Is Pamela performing in an ethical manner?

5. Pamela (in #4 above) realizes the pet shop is losing so much money she will have to close it soon. She takes a four-week trip to Africa to look over exotic pets that local pet shops may be importing. The travel agency sends the $20,000 bill to the shop. Due to its limited assets, the agency is only paid $1,000 of the bill. Was Pamela's action in taking the trip ethical?

DISCUSSION CASE

```
┌─────────────────────────────────────────────────────┐
│                                                       │
│       PARAMOUNT PETROLEUM CORP. V.                    │
│           TAYLOR RENTAL CENTER                        │
│                                                       │
│              712 S.W. 2d 534                          │
│                                                       │
│        Court of Appeals of Texas (1986)               │
│                                                       │
└─────────────────────────────────────────────────────┘
```

Facts:

Plaintiff Taylor Rental Center rented equipment four times for use on a seagoing vessel called the *M/V Courtney D.* After receiving the first request, plaintiff called the number provided to confirm authority for the order. The answerer identified the business as "Paramount" and told Taylor to send invoices to the company's Houston post office box. A later rental request came from a captain who indicated he represented Paramount Steamship Co. Invoices were sent to the same address and equipment was to be used on the same vessel. Invoices were not paid.

Plaintiff was informed Paramount Steamship was apparently no longer in business and then turned to Paramount Petroleum for payment, claiming if it was a different corporation from Paramount Steamship, it was a partner and therefore liable on Paramount Steamship's debt.

The trial court held for plaintiff and defendant appeals.

Issue:

Did a partnership by estoppel exist between Paramount Petroleum Corp. and Paramount Steamship, thereby making Paramount Petroleum liable on the debts of Paramount Steamship?

Decision:

The Court of Appeals affirmed the lower court's decision that a partnership by estoppel existed.

Reasons:

The appellate court pointed out that a partnership by estoppel requires (a) representation by the party being charged that the party was a partner and (b) reliance on the part of the party providing the credit on the presumption that a partnership did exist.

The court found that Paramount Petroleum represented itself as a partner by its identification over the telephone as "Paramount," and by permitting Petroleum Steamship to use its office. In addition, the court found that Taylor relied on the representation.

Discussion Questions

1. In your opinion, was Taylor justified in relying on the assumption that a partnership existed between Paramount Steamship and Paramount Petroleum?

2. Would you say that partnership by estoppel is based on apparent authority?

3. Describe how two independent accountants sharing an office may create the appearance of a partnership.

CHAPTER 12

GOING GLOBAL

CHAPTER OBJECTIVES

In this chapter you will learn to:

1. Recognize the various sources of international law that may impact the operation of a small business.

2. Understand the special legal doctrines of comity, sovereign immunity and act of state and their impact on international business.

3. Identify international contracts that may come under the Convention on Contracts for the International Sale of Goods (CISG) and identify how the CISG impacts those contracts.

4. Identify sources of assistance for small businesses entering the international market for the first time.

An increasing number of small businesses are entering the global marketplace for the first time. Today's entrepreneur may export goods or services across a US. border into Canada or Mexico, across an ocean to a Pacific Rim country, or to new consumers in a former Eastern Bloc country. These same entrepreneurs may import goods from abroad for resale in the U.S. market. Whether the business is exporting or importing, the owner can benefit from a basic understanding of certain aspects of international commercial law.

This chapter examines the various sources of international law and special legal doctrines that impact the U.S. entrepreneur. The applicability of the Convention on Contracts for the International Sales of Goods and the **Foreign Corrupt Practices Act** on U.S. entrepreneurs is explained. The chapter concludes by identifying various sources of assistance for small business owners entering the global market for the first time.

▶ ## "RED FLAG" SITUATIONS

Situation	Potential Problem
1. An international sales contract fails to specify how a dispute will be settled.	1. The U.S. buyer/seller may face litigation in an unfriendly foreign court.
2. An international sales contract fails to "spell out" all the terms of the contract.	2. If the **Convention on Contracts for the International Sale of Goods (CISG)** applies, it may "fill in the gaps" with terms unsatisfactory to the U.S. business.
3. A U.S. seller agrees to sell on credit to an unknown foreign buyer.	3. If the buyer refuses to pay, the seller may have no viable recourse.
4. A U.S. buyer pays in advance for imported goods.	4. If the goods are not delivered, the buyer may have no viable recourse.
5. A U.S. company's overseas assets are confiscated by an unfriendly foreign government.	5. According to the **doctrine of sovereign immunity**, the U.S. company may have no viable recourse against the foreign government.
6. A U.S. entrepreneur pays a foreign official for "help" in getting a contract with the foreign government.	6. The entrepreneur may face criminal charges for violating the U.S. Foreign Corrupt Practices Act.

SOURCES OF INTERNATIONAL LAW

International law is comprised of laws, both written and unwritten, that are observed by independent countries.

International law evolves from various sources just as domestic law stems from different sources (Chapter 1). The sources of international law include custom; treaties; conventions; and international organizations. When a custom is recognized and practiced internationally over an extended period of time, it can become a part of international law. For example, the U.S. Supreme Court ruled in 1900 that Spanish fishing boats fishing along the Cuban coast were exempt from **confiscation** by the U.S. Navy even though the Spanish-American War had begun. The Court relied on international custom that a country's fishing boats were exempt from confiscation by the enemy (The Paquette Habana, 175 U.S. 677).

Treaties comprise another source of international law. A treaty is a formally adopted agreement between two or more countries. The North American Free Trade Agreement (NAFTA) is an example of a recent treaty entered into by the U.S.

International organizations, such as the United Nations and the International Monetary Fund, are sources of international law. These organizations pass rules and resolutions that govern the relevant activities of the member nations.

International conferences sponsored by international organizations frequently result in international laws. For example, the U.N.-sponsored Convention on Contracts for the International Sale of Goods (CISG) adopted rules that govern the international sale of commercial goods.

A major problem relevant to international law relates to enforcement. If a domestic law is violated, the court can enforce the law through sanctions against the defendant. If a country violates an international law, the situation is different: the violator is a sovereign which cannot be imprisoned or forced to pay a fine. Possible recourses against the violating country include boycotts, severance of diplomatic relations or declaration of war.

SPECIAL LEGAL DOCTRINES

Several special legal doctrines are applicable to international disputes. These doctrines are referred to as **comity**, the doctrine of sovereign immunity and the **act of state doctrine**.

Comity

The doctrine of comity is based on respect for another country's laws and judicial holdings. For example, U.S. courts will acknowledge laws of another country if those laws do not violate U.S. law or policy.

Assume Rick Retailer orders $5,000 worth of silk dresses in green and red from Beatrice's British Finery of London to sell during the Christmas season. The trusting Rick sends his payment in advance but the dresses never arrive. When Beatrice refuses to refund his money, Rick retains Ace Attorney and sues in a U.S. court.

The court finds Beatrice is liable for breach of contract and Rick is entitled to his $5000 back. Since it was foreseeable the dresses were needed for the holiday season, Rick is also awarded $2000 consequential damages for his lost profits.

The problem Rick and Ace now face is collection of the $7000 from a defendant whose assets are all located in London. Based on the principle of comity, a British court may defer to the U.S. court's decision and enforce the judgement in London provided the judgement is consistent with British law.

Sovereign Immunity

The doctrine of sovereign immunity is based on the concept that the sovereign (government) cannot be sued without its permission. In the U.S., a plaintiff cannot sue a governmental entity without its permission. For example, the Federal Tort Claims Act specifies when and how a plaintiff can bring a tort claim against the federal government.

International law recognizes the doctrine of sovereign immunity, which prohibits a plaintiff from suing a foreign nation without the latter's permission. An exception to this rule allows U.S. businesses to sue foreign nations in certain situations without the defendant's permission. The Foreign Sovereign Immunities Act (28 U.S.C. Sections 1602-1611) was passed by Congress in 1976. The Act provides that a defendant nation is not exempt from U.S. court jurisdiction when the cause of action involves a commercial activity that has a direct effect in the U.S.

Assume that Moe Manufacturer, a U.S. entrepreneur, enters into a contract with Zorroland to supply the new country with 500 of Moe's Miracle Mowers every month for two years. Moe specially manufactures 12,000 of the mowers to accommodate the especially tall and tough grasses of Zorroland. After two months the country informs Moe the contract is off.

Ace Attorney represents Moe and sues Zorroland in a U.S. court for breach of contract. The defendant pleads the doctrine of sovereign immunity as its defense. Ace convinces the court that the Foreign Sovereign Immunities Act applies since the dispute involved a commercial contract that has a direct effect in the U.S.

Act of State Doctrine

The act of state doctrine provides that the courts of one country should not determine the legality of actions taken by another country within the latters' borders.

Assume Moe sets up a large manufacturing plant in Zorroland, investing several million dollars in its operations. One morning Moe reads in the newspaper that Zorroland has just confiscated all foreign-owned assets within its borders. Knowing that "confiscation" refers to the taking of private property for illegal reasons and without fair compensation, Moe rushes over to Ace Attorney's office.

Ace informs Moe that even if he sues Zorroland in a U.S. court, the judge may rule that the act of state doctrine applies and prevent the U.S. court from addressing the legality of Zorroland's confiscation of Moe's property.

THE CONVENTION ON CONTRACTS FOR THE INTERNATIONAL SALE OF GOODS

As mentioned earlier, the United Nations' Convention on Contracts for the International Sale of Goods (CISG) is a source of international law governing certain international sales transactions. The CISG's application to the international sale of goods is similar in many ways to the Uniform Commercial Code's application to domestic sales of goods. If the CISG applies, it will "fill in the gaps" and apply its own rules to the contract if the parties have not provided otherwise. The CISG may apply to international contracts for the sale of commercial goods if both parties are from countries that are signatories to the Convention. The CISG does not apply to the sale of consumer goods or the sale of services. Even though the CISG can apply to a particular contract, the parties may specify another law will apply instead.

Based on the fact the CISG requires the terms in the acceptance "mirror" the terms in the offer, U.S. business owners should carefully review contract forms they plan to use.

The CISG considers an offer irrevocable if the offeror verbally states it is irrevocable or if the offeree reasonably believes it is irrevocable and relies on that belief. In addition, the CISG does not require a contract be written to be enforceable.

According to the CISG, an acceptance is not effective until actually received by the offeror. The offeror's power to revoke the offer is terminated, however, when the offeree sends the acceptance.

The above examples illustrate some ways in which the CISG differs from the Uniform Commercial Code. A U.S. business considering entering an international transaction for the first time can benefit from a legal consultation prior to entering into the contract to assure that the contract does in fact contain all the terms and conditions the owner wants included. As mentioned earlier, if certain terms are omitted and the CISG applies, the results under the convention may be different from what the contracting parties intended.

A party to an international contract may wish to include other special provisions in the contract relevant to the choice of law and **forum** (court) in case a dispute arises. For example, a contract between Moe Manufacturer and Francoise of Paris may provide that a French court will hear any disputes and that U.S. law will apply. The contract may also provide which language will apply in interpreting the contract in case of a dispute. If the contract provides for arbitration in case of a dispute, the official language for arbitration may also be designated in the contract. An attorney familiar with the laws and court systems in the parties' countries can offer valuable advice in drafting the contract.

SOURCES OF ASSISTANCE

A small U.S. business entering the international market for the first time may be unfamiliar with the various sources of information and assistance available.

As mentioned earlier, competent legal counsel familiar with international commercial law is essential in negotiating and drafting the contract.

In addition, legal counsel can familiarize the entrepreneur with the Foreign Corrupt Practices Act. This federal law prohibits U.S. businesses (including their officers, shareholders and employees) from paying foreign officials in order to get or keep business for the U.S. company. Violation of this Act carries heavy criminal penalties.

Legal counsel can also advise the entrepreneur on the various methods of conducting business in another country and the potential legal liability of each method. For example, assume Moe Manufacturer sells his products abroad through a foreign distributor. The latter usually takes title to the goods and bears the loss if the items do not resell. In addition, Moe is usually not legally liable for the torts of the foreign distributor. If Moe decides to sell through a sales representative in another country, an agency relationship may result and Moe becomes legally liable for the actions of the sales representative committed within the scope of employment.

The names of other sources of information relevant to international transactions include the following:

(1)   Government agencies and universities

Governmental agencies and university centers for small business development are major sources of assistance for businesses entering the global market for the first time:

    (a)   The U.S. Department of Commerce in Washington, D.C. provides numerous publications on conducting business abroad. Examples include: <u>A Basic Guide to Exporting</u>; <u>International Business Practices</u>; and <u>The Export Trading Guidebook</u> (For sale through the Superintendent of Documents, U.S. Government Printing Office, Washington, D.C. 20402).

    (b)   The U.S. Small Business Administration is another possible source of information. The address of the nearest SBA office is usually available in the local telephone directory. Publications include <u>Exporter's Guide to Federal Resources for Small Businesses</u> (For sale through the Superintendent of Documents, U.S. Government Printing Office, Washington, D.C. 20402).

    (c)   Many colleges and universities offer information and advice through their centers for small business development. An example is <u>Trade Secrets: The Export Answer Book: Answers to the Most Commonly Asked International Trade Questions</u>: by Julie

Ann Clowes and Sarah McCue. Published by the Michigan Small Business Development Center, Wayne State University, Detroit, Michigan, 1995.

(d) Businesses planning to advertise in Canada can obtain current material on Canada's advertising laws by contacting the following government office:

Consumer and Corporate Affairs Canada
Bureau of Competition Policy
Marketing Practice Branch
Place du Portage
Phase II, 5th Floor
Hull, Quebec, K1A 0C9
Phone: 819-997-4282

The Bureau will review a proposed advertisement and provide an Advisory Opinion to assure its compliance with the relevant Canadian laws.

(e) Many countries have Consulate offices in cities throughout the U.S. These offices can offer information relevant to the business environment in the home country. Consulate addresses are usually listed in metropolitan telephone directories.

(2) Organizations

Examples of organizations providing assistance include the following:

(a) The International Chamber of Commerce offers numerous publications and services. For example, the Chamber maintains a roster of arbitrators available for arbitrating international commercial disputes.

(b) Publications issued by the United Nations (New York) include World Statistics in Brief; Development Forum; and General Business Guide.

(c) Businesses planning to advertise in the United Kingdom can contact the Advertising Standards Authority (ASA) for guidelines on non-broadcast advertisements to assure the ad's compliance with the British Codes of Advertising and Sales Promotion.

Address: The Advertising Standards Authority
2 Torrington Place
London WC1E 7HW
Phone: 0171-580-5555
Fax: 0170-631-3051

(3) Other Publications

(a) A series of publications on "Doing Business in (various countries)" is published by Price, Waterhouse, World Firm Limited, Toronto. These publications include an overview of the geographic, social, cultural, financial, economical, political and legal environment of a country. Many local libraries maintain copies of these publications.

(b) Numerous U.S. and international journals and magazines address global business practices. Examples include Nation's Business; Business Week; Newsweek; Forbes; Business International; International Financial Management; and U.S. News and World Report.

(c) Newspapers carrying regular columns on international business include The Wall Street Journal; The New York Times; The Asian Wall Street Journal; and The London Times.

(4) Computer Searches

Many small businesses today have access to computer online information retrieval systems that may offer extensive information on international business. Examples include:

(a) "SBA: Small Business Administration Home Page"

(b) "Bureau of Export Administration"

(c) "International Trade Commission"

(d) "The State Department"

(e) "NAFTA Online"

INTERNATIONAL LAW AND THE HOME–BASED BUSINESS

As more home-based businesses enter the global marketplace, they may be impacted by the same legal problems that affect other small businesses. The home-based business is subject to the legal concept of comity, the act of state doctrine and the doctrine of sovereign immunity. The Convention on Contracts for the International Sale of Goods may apply if the home-based business is involved in a contract to sell commercial goods and the other party is in a country which is signatory to the Convention. The home-based business can also be impacted by the choice of language, law or forum in the contract. In addition, the business may be liable for the actions of a sales representative selling its goods or services abroad. The business is also subject to the Foreign Corrupt Practices Act.

The home-based business can benefit from a legal consultation prior to entering into an international contract. The same sources of information available to other small businesses can enable the owner of a home-based business to become better informed about business opportunities and risks in other countries.

REDUCING YOUR RISKS

The owner of a small business can reduce the risks of a dispute relevant to an international transaction by following these recommendations:

1. When dealing with a foreign buyer or seller for the first time, confirm the other party's reliability and creditworthiness.

2. If you are selling goods abroad, make certain the transaction does not violate U.S. Customs regulations which may

   (a) ban the export of the goods themselves or

   (b) prohibit sales to the buyer's country

3. When investing in another country, obtain adequate insurance in case your property is taken over by the foreign government.

4. If your contract is covered by the CISG, make certain all relevant terms are included; otherwise, the CISG may fill in the terms in a manner that is unfavorable to your company.

5. Consult with an attorney familiar with the laws in the host country prior to entering into the international contract. The attorney may recommend choice of law and choice of forum clauses in the contract.

6. Become familiar with methods of payment, such as letters of credit, which reduce the risks to parties selling goods to a foreign buyer.

---

*KEY WORDS AND PHRASES

Act of State Doctrine
Comity
Confiscation
Convention on Contracts for the
International Sale of Goods
(CISG)

Doctrine of Sovereign Immunity
Forum
Foreign Corrupt Practices Act
Treaty

CHAPTER SUMMARY

Going Global

1. Sources of International Law

    a. Custom
    b. Treaties
    c. International organizations
    d. International conferences

2. Special Legal Doctrines

    a. Doctrine of comity
    b. Doctrine of sovereign immunity
    c. Act of State doctrine

3. When the CISG Applies

    a. Sale of goods and
    b. Sale is for commercial purpose and
    c. Parties are from different countries that have ratified the CISG

4. Special Provisions of the CISG

    a. "Fill in the gap" rules
    b. Mirror image rule
    c. Irrevocability of offer
    d. When acceptance is effective

5. Sources of Assistance

    a. Government agencies
    b. Universities
    c. International organizations
    d. Publications
    e. Computer Searches

DISCUSSION QUESTIONS

1. <u>Sources of International Law</u>. Do international laws have to be in writing to be recognized by the international community? Explain your answer.

2. <u>Sovereign Immunity</u>. Fred Farmer contracts to sell 1000 tons of wheat to the new country of Zorroland. Fred sends the wheat but is never paid. He files suit in U.S. District Court of breach of contract. The defendant country claims that based on the doctrine of sovereign immunity, Fred cannot sue without Zorroland's permission. Is the defendant correct? Why or why not?

3. <u>CISG Writing Requirements</u>. Cathy Caterer verbally agrees to buy 50 pounds of pure Dutch chocolate from an Amsterdam company at a price of $15 per pound. (Cathy's customers have very expensive taste). Cathy finds she can obtain the chocolate from a German seller at $12 per pound. She cancels the Dutch order and the seller claims breach of contract. The contract is

covered by the CISG. Cathy argues that the CISG's Statute of Frauds requires the contract be in writing. Is Cathy correct?

4. <u>Acceptance and the CISG</u>. Assume that in #3 Cathy calls the Dutch seller to cancel her offer to buy the chocolate ten minutes after the seller wires its acceptance. (Cathy receives the wire five minutes after her call revoking the contract). The seller sues for breach of contract, claiming Cathy's revocation was ineffective. Is the seller correct? Explain.

5. <u>Choice of Forum</u>. Cathy orders 50 yards of white silk from Beatrice's British Finery of London for use in decorating bridal tables at wedding receptions Cathy caters. The contract provides if a dispute arises, a British court will hear the case. Cathy claims the fabric sent was polyester rather than silk and sues for breach of contract in a U.S. federal court. Beatrice's attorney claims only a British court can hear the case. Is the attorney correct?

Is It Ethical?

1. Ned Naive builds a hardware store in the new country of Zorroland. Business does so well that the Minister of Trade in Zorroland convinces the President the business should be taken over by the host country. Ned awakens one morning to learn his business has been confiscated with no payment provisions for Ned. Is the confiscation ethical? Would your answer change if you learned the proceeds from the confiscated business were applied to low-income housing in the country?

2. Moe's Manufacturing Company is doing very well exporting its farm equipment to Zorroland. Moe learns that the U.S. government may ban exports to Zorroland because of the country's child labor policies. Moe lobbies members of Congress to vote against the ban. Is Moe's practice ethical? Assume Moe's business will close without the sales to Zorroland and twenty employees will lose their jobs. Does this change your answer?

3. Moe decides to close his U.S. plant and set up manufacturing operations in Zorroland, where there are no environmental regulations to worry about. Is Moe's practice ethical? Explain.

4. Some countries allow its citizens to claim commercial briberies paid to foreign officials as tax deductible expenses. Does this policy encourage bribery? Is it ethical?

5. Roberta Restauranteur opens a small cafe in Zorroland. The host country has no health regulations requiring restaurant dishes be washed in water of a minimum temperature for sanitation reasons. (Roberta's restaurant in the U.S. must comply with these regulations). Roberta decides to forego buying a hot water heater for the cafe and runs the used dishes under tepid tap water. Even though this practice is legal, is it ethical?

Discussion Case

Republic of Argentina v. Weltover, Inc.

112 S.Ct. 2160 (1992)

Facts:

The Republic of Argentina and its central bank, Banco Central (referred to as Argentina here) issued bonds called "Bonods." The bonds were to be repaid in U.S. dollars in several locations, including New York City. Plaintiff bondholders are a Swiss bank and two Panamanian corporations.

Argentina determined it lacked enough foreign exchange to pay off the Bonods as they matured and unilaterally extended the payment date and offered bondholders substitute instruments.

Plaintiffs insisted on repayment in New York and refused to accept the rescheduling. Plaintiffs sued, claiming breach of contract. Plaintiffs assert the defendant's actions come under the Foreign Sovereign Immunities Act and are therefore subject to the jurisdiction of the U.S. courts.

Issue:

Was Argentina's bond default an act "in connection with a commercial activity" that had a "direct effect in the United States" therefore subjecting defendants to the jurisdiction of U.S. courts under the Foreign Sovereign Immunities Act?

Decision:

The U.S. Supreme Court unanimously upheld the District Court's assertion of jurisdiction under the FSIA.

Reason:

The Supreme Court held that the issuance of the bonds was a "commercial activity" under the FSIA. The court further held that the rescheduling of dates of maturity was an action "in connection with" the commercial activity and the unilateral rescheduling also had a "direct effect in the U.S." In summary, the court's finding that the bond default was an act taken "in connection with a commercial activity" having a "direct effect in the U.S." subjects defendant to the jurisdiction of the U.S. courts.

Discussion Questions

1. Why did Congress pass the Foreign Sovereign Immunities Act?

2. Do you agree that Argentina should be subject to the jurisdiction of the U.S. court in this case?

3. Describe a transaction between a U.S. business and a foreign government that may come under the Foreign Sovereign Immunities Act.

PART III

COMMONSENSE APPROACHES TO AVOID LAWSUITS

CHAPTER 13

KEEPING UP WITH THE LAW

CHAPTER OBJECTIVES

In this chapter you will learn to:

1. Understand the importance of keeping up with changes in the law.

2. Identify sources of legal information that impact the operation of small businesses.

3. Appreciate the benefits of joining organizations and trade associations that provide relevant legal information to their members.

4. Understand the importance of practicing preventative law by consulting with a competent attorney prior to taking action that may result in a lawsuit.

5. Identify and assemble information that can be helpful in a legal consultation.

As discussed in previous chapters, domestic and international laws come from many sources. A new domestic law may evolve in the following situations: a judge holds social and business hosts liable for the drunk driving of their guests; the U.S. Congress passes a federal law relevant to telemarketing practices; or a state administrative agency adopts a new rule regulating the disposal of hazardous waste within the state.

GOING GLOBAL Examples of how international laws evolve include the following: the President of the U.S., with the approval of the Senate, enters into a trade agreement with another country; the United Nations-sponsored World Court rules that a country has violated international law; or members of an international convention adopt new rules regulating fishing practices in international waters.

Owners of small businesses need to be aware of any changes in domestic or international law that may impact their business practices. This chapter discusses ways in which a business owner can keep up with the continuous changes in law. Sources of legal information available in most localities are discussed. Examples of organizations that provide relevant legal information are listed. The chapter concludes with suggestions on seeking professional legal help.

▶ "RED FLAG" SITUATIONS

Situation	Potential Problem
1. The media announces the state legislature has just passed sweeping new consumer protection laws	1. The new law may impose new restrictions on the ads you run or your debt collection practices
2. The person responsible for hiring in your business has not attended a professional seminar in years	2. Your business may be violating state or federal employment hiring practices
3. A customers loudly protests the tobacco smoke in your restaurant	3. You may be in noncompliance with a local or state smoking ordinance
4. You do not know any attorneys in your area who handle small business matters	4. Waiting until your business is sued may be too late for finding a competent attorney
5. Your company decides to import goods without consulting with the proper agencies	5. Importation of the goods may violate U.S. Customs laws

WHERE TO LOOK IT UP

A trip to the local library or through cyberspace on a personal computer may be a quick way to identify new laws or changes in existing laws that impact small businesses.

Most local libraries subscribe to business newspapers and periodicals that cover commercial law. These publications may be general in nature, such as The Wall Street Journal and Business Week. Examples of specialized publications include Self-Employed America; National Cattlemen; and Lodging Hospitality Magazine. Many newspapers and periodicals are now accessible through various computer services.

Monitoring proposed new laws or proposed changes in existing laws offers two advantages: (1) the entrepreneur may have the opportunity to comment on the proposal and suggest changes before adoption of the law and (2) the small business owner can prepare in advance for any adaptions or changes the new law may require. For example, many cities and states have proposed new and stricter laws regulating smoking in public places. A small business owner currently renovating his restaurant may make sure his remodeled business will comply with the proposed law and thereby avoid expensive renovations in the future.

Business newspapers and periodicals that discuss new laws usually highlight proposed laws pending in Congress or the state legislatures. The Code of Federal Regulations (C.F.R.), an official document published by the U.S. Government Printing Office daily, includes new regulations proposed by the various federal agencies. Frequently a proposed regulation will be followed by an address where interested parties can send comments. Many business publications monitor the C.F.R. carefully and alert business owners of the proposals and where to send comments.

Proposed state laws are printed in an official publication by the state. Again, business owners can review the proposal and will frequently have the opportunity to comment in advance.

Many library holdings are now available through computer on-line services. By accessing the U.S. Congress Law Library on computer, the small business owner can retrieve copies of federal laws, international treaties and federal government regulations.

JOIN! JOIN! JOIN!

Most owners of small businesses share one common problem: not enough time to get everything done each day. The owner must therefore prioritize activities to assure the most important activities receive his attention first. Joining and participating in a business organization or association frequently is low on the priority list and may even be considered a frivolous social activity. On the contrary, the information disseminated through a business organization may be invaluable to its members.

Organizations such as the Chamber of Commerce have professional staffs that can monitor proposed changes in state and federal laws and alert members well in advance. Seminars are offered to explain how small businesses can comply with the new laws. For example, organizations throughout the U.S. hosted seminars to explain the Americans with Disabilities Act to members.

Local chapters of organizations often invite attorneys, accountants and other professionals to speak to its members on the impact of new laws.

The publications distributed by these organizations are another source of valuable information.

WHEN A LEGAL CONSULTATION PAYS OFF

The health care industry has focused on "preventative medicine" in recent years, advising patients on certain practices relative to diet and lifestyle that may prevent illnesses.

This emphasis on "preventative law" may reduce the risk of a small business owner being party to a lawsuit. One of the major steps toward avoiding a future lawsuit is consulting an attorney before a decision is made or action taken. For example, seeking legal advice as to the courts' current ruling on employee dismissals before firing an employee may prevent a wrongful discharge suit later.

GOING GLOBAL  Confirming in advance that the importation of goods from a foreign seller is legal can avoid later problems if the goods are banned for import by U.S. Customs or business transactions with parties from the seller's home country are currently illegal.

Many attorneys are "board certified" by their state bar associations in special areas of the law, such as bankruptcy, commercial law, and international law. The certification indicates the attorney has taken extra courses and passed a special examination on the subject matter. A client with a particular legal problem or question may benefit from consulting with an attorney who is a specialist in that area of the law. The first consultation visit to an attorney's office may be free. A prospective client should not hesitate to ask in advance if this is the situation and how much the attorney will charge for time spent on the telephone with clients. The client can cut costs by having all information easily retrievable before beginning the phone conversation.

The more relevant information an attorney has about a problem or potential problem, the better she can serve the client. It is therefore important for the business owner to have all necessary papers organized and ready to review with the attorney. Preparing a "chronology of events" leading up to the situation that is the subject matter of the consultation is beneficial in two ways: (1) it helps the client organize his thoughts and triggers the remembrance of certain previously forgotten details and (2) it enables the attorney to review the situation more quickly and start asking pertinent questions.

As mentioned earlier, the dollars spent on a legal consultation before a problem arises may be extremely small compared to the legal fees involved in a lawsuit later.

SOURCES OF LAW AND THE HOME–BASED BUSINESS

The home-based business must also comply with new laws and changes in existing laws. Keeping up with the latest laws is essential in order for the home-based entrepreneur to avoid legal liability. For example, the home caterer must comply with the state's new laws regulating the preparation and handling of food sold to the public. The home-based florist needs to be aware of current federal laws relative to the importation of exotic flowers from foreign countries. The owner of a home-based business can also benefit from reading current articles in the local library or from a computer retrieval service. Joining business organizations and associations may offer an additional advantage to the owner of a home-based business: other local businesses become aware of the services or goods she provides and may refer future customers her way.

The advantages of a legal consultation in advance of taking action can be equally beneficial to the small business owner. Being prepared prior to the consultation is important to enable the attorney to better understand the situation and offer the best advice possible.

REDUCING YOUR RISKS

The owner of a small business can reduce the risks of being sued for violation of an unknown law by following these recommendations:

1. Become familiar with the various sources of legal information that may impact your business and learn how to retrieve this information.

2. Join professional organizations and subscribe to these publications that provide relevant information.

3. Meet with a competent attorney and discuss your business operations before you have a legal problem. The attorney may identify potential problem areas and offer advice that will prevent a future lawsuit.

4. Seek competent counsel before entering into any international transactions to assure compliance with domestic and international laws.

CHAPTER SUMMARY

Keeping Up With the Law

1. Reasons to keep up with the law
   a. Recent changes may result in new areas of potential liability
   b. The courts generally do not recognize ignorance of the law as a valid defense

2. Sources of legal information
   a. Libraries
   b. Newspapers and periodicals
   c. Governmental publications
   d. Computer searches

3. Benefits of joining business organizastions
   a. Access to professional staffs who monitor changes in the law
   b. Opportunity to attend seminars on how to comply with new laws
   c. Access to relevant publications

4. Reasons for legal consultation prior to being sued
   a. Difficulty in finding competent counsel on short notice if business has no previous contact with an attorney
   b. Attorney may identify potential problems in the business and recommend solutions in advance of a lawsuit

5. Need to maintain adequate records
   a. Helps business owner prepare chronology of events in case of lawsuit
   b. Enables the attorney to better serve the client

DISCUSSION QUESTIONS

1. <u>Sources of Information</u>. Ned Naive is contemplating opening a pizza parlor in a residential neighborhood. He plans to have a live rock band playing in the evenings on the outdoor patio. Where can Ned go to determine if his business will break any laws?

2. <u>Business Organizations</u>. Ned Naive is invited to join a reputable local business association but feels he is too busy. What are the advantages of joining?

3. <u>Competent Counsel</u>. Ned decides he needs legal counsel prior to opening his new business. Denise Divorcee advises Ned to go to the divorce attorney who represented her in a recent divorce. What advice would you offer Ned relevant to finding an attorney?

4. <u>Maintaining Records</u>. Rick Retailer is advised by one of his store clerks that Clumsy Customer slipped and fell while shopping. What information regarding the fall should the store obtain? Should there be a set policy already in place regarding store accidents?

Is It Ethical?

1. Sylvester Sly opens an upscale restaurant with some of his lottery winnings. He attends a seminar on the state's new environmental regulations and learns of new requirements for restaurants disposing of their used cooking oil. Sylvester knows that Carl, owner of Carl's Cafe, is unaware of the new requirements and may be heavily fined in the near future. Sylvester decides not to inform his competitor of the new requirements. Is Sylvester's decision ethical? Assume Sylvester knew Carl had wanted to attend the seminar but had to be with his hospitalized son. Would your answer be different?

2. Sylvester Sly resents the competition from Carl's Cafe and anonymously calls the state regulatory agency and reports Carl's violation of the new state environmental regulation on used cooking oil. Is Sylvester's action ethical?

3. Rick Retailer regularly reads trade publications to learn about proposed laws that may impact his business. He learns the state legislature is proposing a new fire code that will require Rick to spend approximately $10,000 in order for his store to meet the new code. Rick lobbies against the proposed legislation. (Statistics indicate the new code will enhance the safety of commercial buildings.) Is Rick's action ethical?

4. Ned Naive is preparing to open a new business. He decides to visit Ace Attorney for advice on any permits he may need and the legality of the name of his new business. Ace spends an hour advising Ned about the business and then sends Ned a bill for $150. Ned complains that Ace should not have charged since Ace did no paperwork for him. Was Ace's billing ethical?

5. Frequently members of state legislatures and the U.S. Congress wait on public opinion before determining how they will vote on a proposed bill. Is this an ethical approach? Explain.

Sources for Keeping Up with the Law

As Chapter 13 points out, keeping up with the law as it currently pertains to small businesses is an important factor in avoiding the risk of a lawsuit. The owner of a small business may be surprised to find the amount of information available through computer searches.

Among the legal resources available are the following:

1. The Better Business Bureau Services for Consumers and Businesses are available at http://www.bbb.org/services. Topics covered include Scam Alerts; Business Advisory Service Publications; Alternative Dispute Resolution; Better Business Bureau Code of Advertising; CARU Guidelines for Childrens Advertising and Standards for Charitable Solicitation. Additional topics are Americans with Disabilities Act; Marketplace Ethics; Membership Information; and Business Advice and Information.

2. A list of legal resources available on the World Wide Web is available at http://www.usc.edu/dept/law-lib/legal/titlest. This service of the University of Southern California Law Library provides a menu of primary legal resources that are available on the Internet. These resources include federal and state statutes, case law, and regulations.

Among the legal resources available are the United States Code; Copyright Act; Patent Act; Trademark Act of the U.S.; Uniform Commercial Code; Code of Federal Regulations; Federal Register; and U.S. Supreme Court Opinions.

3. Opinions of the U.S. Supreme Court are also available through Cornell Law School at http://www.law.cornell/edu/syllabi.

4. Opinions from the federal Circuit Courts of Appeals are also available. For example, the Villanova Center for Information Law and Policy of http://www.law.vill.edu provides opinions from the Ninth Circuit.

5. One source of international law is the U.S. House of Representatives Internet Law Library at http://www.law.house.gov.

The above list shows the extensive amount of legal information currently available via computers. Owners of small businesses need to keep in mind that laws change regularly and the court in one jurisdiction may apply the law differently than the court in another jurisdiction. It is therefore important to seek competent legal counsel whenever a legal question arises.

CHAPTER 14

THE ASSET OF ETHICS

CHAPTER OBJECTIVES

In this chapter you will learn to:

1.   Recognize ethics as an asset of a small business.

2.   Understand the various sources of ethics.

3.   Identify situations in your own business that may present an ethical dilemma for you or your employees.

4.   Analyze the potential consequences of a decision that is legal but unethical.

5.   Recognize ways in which ethical practices can become a part of your business practices.

Ask the owner of a small business to list the assets of the business and the owner will probably include real property (land, building, permanent fixtures); tangible personal property (inventory, supplies, furnishings, etc.); and intangible personal property (trademarks, patents, accounts receivable, goodwill, etc.). One of the most important assets to any business is frequently overlooked: the asset of ethics.

This chapter discusses the definition of ethics and its sources. Examples of ethical dilemmas regarding personnel matters that a small business may face are discussed and the consequences of the owner's decision are analyzed. The chapter concludes with recommendations for establishing ethical practices in your own business.

▶ "RED FLAG" SITUATIONS

Situation	Potential Problem
1. Your billing clerk accuses a foreign buyer of cheating by refusing to pay interest	1. The charging of interest may be considered unethical in the buyer's home country
2. Knowing that the selling of goods is legal seven days a week in your state, you insist on closing a deal with a foreign buyer on a particular day	2. The potential buyer may reject your offer because the buyer's religion forbids conducting business on that day
3. Your company has never established an office policy on proper use of office supplies.	3. Employees may assume it is permissible to take office supplies home
4. Your business has never adopted a code of ethics	4. New employees may not recognize that certain business practices are unethical and can harm the reputation of the business
5. New employees are not counseled on the company's philosophy	5. Unethical practices may become prevalent throughout the business

CAN "ETHICS" BE DEFINED?

Ask five business owners to define "ethics" and it is quite likely each answer, though somewhat different, will be similar. Each owner will probably agree "ethics" is based on determining what is the "right" thing to do.

Although all five business owners agree on the basic definition of the term "ethics," opinions may differ greatly as to what is "right" or "wrong" behavior. Assume a store owner is asked "Is it right to sell goods on credit and charge the customer 6% interest?" Many business owners and customers would agree that this is a "right" business practice. In some areas of the world, however, charging any interest for the lending of money is considered morally wrong and is forbidden. Determining whether an action is right or wrong is based on the individual's personal code of ethics. Sources of one's code of ethics may include family; educators; peers; community; co-workers; employers and religion. The following hypothetical situation illustrates the role religion and philosophy played in two businessmen's decisions.

Assume Mr. Woo owns an import/export business. He follows the teachings of the philosopher Confucius, who was born in China in 551 B.C. Mr. Woo is considering the purchase of frozen chocolate candies from Fred's Foods, a small U.S. company specializing in frozen foods. Mr. Woo is also negotiating to sell shrimp to Fred for use in Fred's frozen seafood dinners.

Fred, a religious man, tells Mr. Woo about his company's newest popular chocolate candy, "Slim Licks." An ad is shown to Mr. Woo, depicting very slim men, women and children eating Slim Licks. Mr. Woo is aware of the growing concern among his own customers over fat.

There is no requirement in Mr. Woo's country that the candy's wrapper list the fat content. Mr. Woo muses aloud that "Slim Licks" chocolate must be low in fat content because of the name and the slim models used in the tape.

Fred realizes Mr. Woo does not understand chocolate may be high in fat. Since Mr. Woo did not specifically ask him about the fat in chocolate, Fred can merely remain quiet and close the sale.

Fred, however, remembers the "Golden Rule," and imagines himself in Mr. Woo's place. He responds immediately and informs Mr. Woo of the fat content, knowing he will in all likelihood lose this sale. Fred's religious background reminds him that he would want Mr. Woo to inform him if the situation were reversed. Mr. Woo thanks Fred for the information, cancels the chocolate order and immediately places a larger order for Fred's no-fat blueberry muffins.

On another occasion, Fred is considering the large purchase of a species of small shrimp from Mr. Woo for frozen T.V. dinners and the former remarks that these should cook quickly in the customers' microwave ovens. Mr. Woo hears the comment and remembers that the small shrimp toughened when he microwaved them at home. Should Mr. Woo advise Fred or remain silent and close this deal?

Mr. Woo reflects on his lesson in Confucianism, which emphasized reciprocity or not treating others in a way one does not wish to be treated himself. As a result of this, Mr. Woo came to the same decision regarding withholding of information which Fred had concluded.

In the above examples, Mr. Woo and Fred each applied his personal code of ethics to an important business decision.

Many business owners do not realize that an unethical act may be completely legal. If the unethical act is also illegal, sanctions can be imposed on the wrongdoer. For example, insider trading is a violation of the federal securities laws and can result in harsh punishments which are established in the federal statutes. A toy manufacturer who carelessly designs and sells unsafe toys faces monetary damages when a jury determines the company's performance was negligent. In these cases, a source of law has declared "wrong" action is also "illegal" and the defendant must face the penalties imposed by the law. These legal sanctions provide tangible reasons for avoiding unethical practices.

What if the "wrong" behavior does not violate an existing law, and is therefore legal? Does the wrongdoer increase his risks of future lawsuits? Is there a victim of this action? The following examples present such a situation.

How a Personal Code of Ethics Can Influence a Personnel Decision

Rick's Chance to Unload Larry Loser

Rick Retailer is facing a real dilemma. His most vocal and difficult employee, Larry Loser, has been late for work a dozen times this month and company policy dictates dismissal. Rick knows Larry will immediately contact his attorney and challenge the action in court.

While Rick is deciding Larry's future, Larry applies for a job with a competing retail chain. The competitor's human resource manager calls and asks for Rick's opinion of Larry.

Rick can praise Larry in glowing terms and win on two fronts: his most troublesome employee is gone, plus the competition will have a new liability.

If the competition complains later about Rick's recommendation, he can always defend himself on the grounds that Larry's performance must have changed dramatically in the new job situation.

No fines, prison sentence, or jury awards hinge on Rick's action, so why not send Larry off with accolades?

Analyzing the term "ethics," the question arises as to whether Rick's action is "right". Is it fair to knowingly misrepresent an employee's qualifications in order to rid Rick's company of a troublemaker? Even if Rick's action is not right, are there any adverse consequences for Rick and his company?

A few of the potential consequences of Rick's actions may be:

(1)   Rick's credibility with the competitor's human resource manager may be damaged if there is any suspicion of the motivation behind the glowing report.

(2)   Larry brags to his former co-workers about the strong recommendation. Knowing of Larry's poor record, they also lose respect for Rick and the company.

(3)   Other employees decide to follow in Larry's footsteps: by becoming too troublesome, Rick will supply them with strong recommendations to also be rid of them.

(4)   Rick has compromised his own professional standards once; the next time a similar situation arises it may be easier to convince himself the ends (his own company's welfare) justify the means (misrepresenting an employee's qualifications). A future "wrong" action may be illegal as well as unethical.

(5)   Rick's Retail Store may become the target of the same type of intentional misrepresentations by other companies in the future who want to "dump" trouble-making employees.

Rick's Opportunity to Deter Sam Salesman's Departure

Another dilemma faces Rick Retailer. His top salesman, Sam, has just asked Rick for a letter of recommendation for a special scholarship at the college of business at the local university. Sam had to quit college after his freshman year for financial reasons and has always wanted to return and complete the program. He has just learned of the scholarship and must have the recommendation by the next morning in order to qualify.

Sam has been the top salesman in the company for the last five years and continues to generate more revenue for the business. His departure will in all likelihood cost the company quite a bit of revenue for next year.

Rick understands how much the scholarship will mean to Sam. At the same time the retailer realizes the impact Sam's departure will have on the store's income. Rick considers the alternatives he has:

(1)   Rick can "misplace" the scholarship form or claim he misunderstood the deadline and stall until the time for filing has passed.

(2)   He can fill out the form in such a "lukewarm" manner that the university will in all likelihood turn down the application.

(3)   He can fill out the recommendation form in an honest and timely manner, assuring Sam's chance of getting the scholarship.

Neither of the first two alternatives are illegal, but are they ethical? What are the possible consequences of each decision?

Rick may try to justify the first alternative by arguing that by preventing Sam's admission into college, the company will continue to realize profit from Sam's sales talents. Rick is trying to rationalize this decision by arguing that more people will benefit from Sam staying with the store: by the company making more profits. Rick will have more money to pay all of the employees and more money for his own family. At the same time, Rick recognizes that thwarting Sam's efforts to get more education is not the "right" thing to do.

The consequences of a "lukewarm" recommendation will probably be the same as not filling out the form at all: in both instances Sam will be denied the scholarship and the short-term results will probably benefit Rick and the company. Again, Rick realizes that following the second alternative is not the "right" thing to do.

Analyzing the alternatives more carefully, Rick realizes that even though the first two alternatives may benefit him and the company initially, the long-term consequences may be quite detrimental:

(1)   Once Sam realizes that Rick has intentionally blocked his educational opportunities, he will lose any sense of loyalty to the company and start looking for another job.

(2)   Sam will probably let other employees in the company know of Rick's tactics and other employees may follow Sam in leaving the store.

(3)   The next time Rick is encountered with a similar situation, he will probably find it easier to look out for his best interests at the expense of an employee's welfare.

If Rick chooses the third alternative and assists Sam in getting the scholarship, the long-term benefits can be extensive:

(1)   Sam will recognize that Rick is sacrificing his own financial gain in order to help an employee with his educational goals.

(2)   Other employees will appreciate Rick's interest in the welfare of his employees and employee morale and loyalty will be enhanced.

In addition, Rick may be able to turn the potential dilemma into a "win-win" situation. By adjusting Sam's work schedule, the salesman may be able to attend classes and also work part-time. In addition, after Sam graduates he may rejoin the store and bring new expertise to the business. Rick realizes he will be better off having someone with Sam's talents and energy working for Rick's Retail Store rather than having Sam work for a competitor.

ESTABLISHING ETHICAL BEHAVIOR IN YOUR BUSINESS

As this chapter points out, owners of small business face ethical issues on a daily basis. Frequently an action or inaction may be legal but unethical. To assist you and your business in recognizing and addressing ethical issues, the following recommendations can help:

(1)   Determine if there is a code of ethics for your profession, trade, or type of business. If so, study the code and acquaint your employees with it.

(2)   Develop a code of ethics for your individual business. Suggested formats can be found from the many books available on business ethics today and from reviewing other companies' codes.

(3) Provide each new employee with a copy of the code of ethics and explain it carefully.

(4) Review and update the code regularly to make certain it is addressing new ethical issues evolving in your area of business.

THE ASSET OF ETHICS AND THE HOME–BASED BUSINESS

The owner of a home-based business encounters the same ethical issues as those facing the owner of a retail store in the mall. The home-based entrepreneur makes ethical decisions daily in promoting and selling the business goods or services. Providing references for superior and inferior employees raise ethical issues. The business owner operating out of the home may have more opportunities to use business assets for personal benefit. There is also more opportunity to claim business deductions for assets used personally.

The same sources determine the ethics of the small business owner and the same need for ethical guidelines applies.

REDUCING YOUR RISKS

The owner of a small business can reduce the risks of having the business engage in unethical business practices by following these recommendations:

1. Make certain all employees who deal with customers or clients from other cultures understand the cultural differences in business-related matters.

2. Understand any ethical standards adopted by your trade or profession and how they impact your own business.

3. Adopt a code of ethics for your individual business and make certain employees understand and follow it.

4. Recognize that frequently laws are passed to address unethical behavior and make certain your business is not performing unethically. (The U.S. Foreign Corrupt Practices Act was passed because so many U.S. businesses were paying bribes to foreign officials).

5. Make certain new employees understand and follow the company's code of ethics.

CHAPTER SUMMARY

The Asset of Ethics

1. Why Ethics is a Business Asset
   a. Enhances reputation of the business.
   b. Attracts good employees.
   c. Enhances reputation of entire trade or profession.
   d. Increases value of company as part of the goodwill.

2. Sources of Ethics
   a. Family
   b. Religion
   c. Peers
   d. Community
   e. Co-workers
   f. Employers
   g. Educators

3. Examples of Ethical Dilemmas in Your Business
   a. Recommendation for inferior employee.
   b. Recommendation for superior employee.
   c. Determining how much to tell foreign buyer about your goods or services.
   d. Determining whether to relocate your business to another country with cheaper labor and fewer regulations.

4. Potential Consequences of Unethical Decisions
   a. Harms reputation of business.
   b. Lowers morale of employees.
   c. May make it easier to make an illegal decision in the future.

5. How to Incorporate Ethics into Your Business
   a. Adopt a practical code of ethics for your business.
   b. Acquaint all employees with the code.
   c. Select employees with personal code of ethics compatible with that of the business.

DISCUSSION QUESTIONS ON ETHICAL ISSUES

1.   <u>Definitions of Ethics</u>. In interviewing an applicant for a sales job in his store, Rick Retailer asks for the applicant's definition of ethical behavior. The applicant replies, "Ethical behavior is doing what is right." Do you agree? Can there be more than one correct answer?

2.   <u>Sources of Ethics</u>. What do you consider to be the primary sources for your personal code of ethics? Are these sources the same as your peers?

3.   <u>Ethics of Selling Certain Goods</u>. Clara's Candy Company decides to sell a candy bar that is a high-fat, high-cholesterol, high-calorie product with no nutritional value. Children will love it. Is it ethical to market such a product? Assume that if this product does not sell, Clara must close her business and lay off 20 employees. Does this change your answer?

4.   <u>Ethics of Selling Certain Goods</u>. Clara decides to sell her candy in Zorroland, where there are no labeling requirements and the candy will sell extremely well. The parents of the children will have no way of knowing the candy has no nutritional value. Is Clara's practice ethical?

5.   <u>Ethics in the Workplace</u>. Sam Salesman gets a little bored at work and enjoys playing games on the office computer. He purchases a software program that will "pop up" when Sam's boss comes in the office. The program shows a balance sheet and will lead the boss to think Sam has been working rather than playing games. Is Sam's practice ethical?

CHAPTER 15

MAKING FRIENDS, NOT ADVERSARIES

The news media regularly reports on lawsuits brought against U.S. businesses of all sizes. If the plaintiff wins, the court may award huge sums of money in compensatory and punitive damages. A foreign plaintiff may choose to sue a U.S. business in a U.S. court rather than sue in a foreign court due to the possibility of these large awards.

The owner of a small business may wonder if anything can be done to avoid these potentially devastating lawsuits. Although it is impossible to completely avoid the possibility of lawsuits, a few simple steps may reduce the risks of being sued. This chapter discusses the importance of being a "customer friendly" business and the advantages of treating all the stakeholders with respect. The chapter concludes with a discussion of the need to look upon customers as long-term investments.

▶ ## "RED FLAG" SITUATIONS

Situation	Potential Problem
1. A customer comes in with a perceived or real complaint about goods or services he has brought and a clerk rudely tells him nothing can be done.	1. The customer immediately feels defensive and starts thinking about litigation.
2. An employee calls in to say she is ill and cannot work and a new supervisor accuses her of laziness and fires her over the phone.	2. The longtime employee is dismayed and files a wrongful discharge lawsuit.
3. A waiter fails to tell the chef a customer requests no spice in her foods and then proceeds to serve the spicy food rather than admit his mistake.	3. The customer may become seriously ill and ultimately sue for negligence.

4. A long time customer comes in to say he will be a few days late in a payment because of a family emergency and the business manager immediately calls the customer a deadbeat in the presence of others.

4. The customer closes the account as fast as possible and then considers suing for slander.

A BUSINESS SHOULD BE "CUSTOMER FRIENDLY"

"No one likes to sue a friend." This adage can apply to business as well as personal relationships. In the past, the relationship between a business owner and his customers or clients was much more personal and friendly than today. A few years ago a customer could walk into the local hardware store or restaurant and be greeted by name. The business owner frequently inquired about the customer's family. The "customer friendly" business was prevalent throughout the U.S.

Today, with the advent of fast-food chains and discount stores, a customer may shop for months in an establishment without the owner or any clerk ever knowing his name. The customer can experience the same sense of anonymity in small businesses that he finds in huge national chain stores. If this customer has a problem, he is much more likely to sue a business he considers a "stranger" than a business that is "customer friendly" to him.

A small business owner may assure his business is more "customer friendly" by following these suggestions:

1. Have enough employees to adequately take care of the needs of the customers. The few dollars saved by cutting back on staff can be quickly lost if customers have to wait too long. Time is valuable to everyone today, and those customers will not only take their business elsewhere but will feel less tolerant if a problem arises with goods or services purchased from that business.

2. Make certain employees know HOW to treat customers. Today's society is so accustomed to television dialogue where everyone speaks in "sound bites" that new employees may not recognize the value of a phrase as simple as "thank you for your business."

3. Train employees to recognize potential problems and report them to management as soon as possible. If a customer slips and falls in a store aisle, a lawsuit may be averted if the manager immediately appears and shows genuine concern. Even if the customer's six inch high heels caused the fall, she may be tempted to sue if she feels management is not concerned over her injury.

4. The attitude "the customer is always right" may be more important today than ever before. Assume a customer returns a new VCR, claiming it doesn't work. Rather than accusing the customer of failing to read the instructions (which was the case), a careful demonstration and

a sympathetic comment on the complexity of today's electronics can go a long way toward assuring that customer leaves the store happy.

5. Be sure the employees fully understand the goods or services being offered. Assume a customer asks a clerk in a computer store to select the right size disk for a personal computer. The clerk selects the wrong size, the customer cannot finish a document that night and misses a contractual deadline. The frustrated customer may seriously consider a lawsuit against the store on breach of implied warranty of fitness for a particular purpose.

Assuring the customer is satisfied with the sales product and the customer service of a small business can help in two ways: (1) that customer is likely to return for all his future needs and (2) that customer is less likely to file a lawsuit in case a problem does arise in the future.

TREATING THE STAKEHOLDERS WITH RESPECT

Owners of small businesses may not realize how many different parties have a stake in the success or failure of the business. These stakeholders may include corporate shareholders; employees; suppliers; creditors; customers; the local community; taxing entities; and professionals that serve the business (attorneys, accountants, real estate brokers, etc.).

Each of these stakeholders may at some time be a potential plaintiff in a lawsuit against the business. For example, certain shareholders may claim corporate funds are mismanaged; a dismissed employee may sue for wrongful discharge; suppliers and other creditors may claim failure to pay or late payments; the local community may allege a zoning violation; the county tax collector may reappraise the business building and threaten to sue if the owner does not pay the increased taxes; and a local accountant may claim the business owner did not pay the full amount due for an audit.

Entrepreneurs frequently forget that other parties have a vital interest in the success of the business. Respecting the needs of each of these stakeholders may avert many potential disagreements. Regularly communicating with a stakeholder as to the aspects of the business that affect that stakeholder is beneficial to both parties.

For example, a clear explanation of how business income has been spent may reassure shareholders that the funds are not being mismanaged. Explaining to an employee that she was temporarily laid off due to an unexpected slump in sales may discourage any ideas of a wrongful discharge lawsuit on her part.

CUSTOMERS ARE LONG–TERM INVESTMENTS

The success or failure of a business is frequently measured today by the income or loss shown on the last quarterly statement. Small businesses that prove to be most successful think on a long-term basis rather than focusing on the next quarter alone. A long-term investment that is frequently overlooked has nothing to do with capital improvements or inventory; instead it focuses on customer relations.

Investing time and effort in cultivating a first-time customer into a long-term customer can be one of the soundest investments a small business makes. The following simple actions may be helpful:

1. Introduce the new customer to other staff who can serve the customer in the future and make sure they understand any special needs or requirements of that customer.

2. Follow up on major purchases from a new customer. Check to make sure the customer is satisfied and has no problems with the new car or electronic equipment.

3. Show the customer you still appreciate him in the future by notifying him of special sales.

4. Have new customers fill out evaluation cards to let the business know of improvements it needs to make.

MAKING FRIENDS FOR YOUR HOME–BASED BUSINESS

The need to be "customer friendly" applies to the home-based business as well as to the business located in a downtown building. Customers today frequently expect more personalized service from the home-based business than from the retail store in the malls. These customers are therefore especially disappointed when the business owner operating out of her home is perceived as disinterested in the customer's welfare. The suggestions for making downtown stores "customer friendly" apply equally to home-based businesses, including the need to have enough employees to adequately care for customer needs. Communicating with stakeholders and treating customers as long-term investments are also vitally important for the home-based business.

DISCUSSION QUESTIONS

This chapter has focused on the importance of the owner of a small business in establishing and maintaining a friendly relationship with customers and clients.

To enhance the business owner's understanding of how to have a positive relationship with customers and clients, it may be helpful to "put on the other hat" at this time. As a customer and client, answer the following questions relevant to your own recent business experiences:

1. When was the last time you were frustrated in dealing with a business? What caused your frustration?

2. Have you experienced any of the following situations recently?

a. Rudeness of employees toward the customer.

b. Incomplete or inaccurate answers to your questions about a product or service.

c. Perception that the employees were disinterested in your needs as a consumer.

d. Concern about the cleanliness or safety of the business premises.

e. Feeling that the customer is perceived as an interruption in the employee's work schedule.

f. Frustration over being left holding the telephone for a long period of time when calling a business.

g. Frustration over not receiving a return call after leaving your name and phone number with a business.

h. Feeling that the employee or owner will tell you whatever is necessary to get you out of the way.

3. Have you ever considered bringing a lawsuit against a business? If so, why?

4. Has a business you deal with ever made an honest mistake that could have lead to a lawsuit? If so, would you be less prone to sue that business if you have a good relationship with the owner and employees?

5. If you currently own a small business, how do you think your own customers or clients would answer these questions relevant to their experiences with your business?

APPENDIX A

THE CONSTITUTION OF THE UNITED STATES (EXCERPTS)

ARTICLE I

Section 1. All legislative Powers herein granted shall be vested in a Congress of the United States, which shall consist of a Senate and House of Representatives.

Section 2. The House of Representatives shall be composed of Members chosen every second Year by the People of the several States, and the Electors in each State shall have the Qualifications requisite for Electors of the most numerous Branch of the State Legislature.

No Person shall be a Representative who shall not have attained to the Age of twenty five Years, and been seven Years a Citizen of the United States, and who shall not, when elected, be an Inhabitant of that State in which he shall be chosen.

Representatives and direct Taxes shall be apportioned among the several States which may be included within this Union, according to their respective Numbers, which shall be determined by adding to the whole Number of free Persons, including those bound to Service for a Term of Years, and excluding Indians not taxed, three fifths of all other Persons. The actual Enumeration shall be made within three Years after the first Meeting of the Congress of the United States, and within every subsequent Term of ten Years, in such Manner as they shall by Law direct. The Number of Representatives shall not exceed one for every thirty Thousand, but each State shall have at Least one Representative; and until such enumeration shall be made, the State of New Hampshire shall be entitled to chuse three, Massachusetts eight, Rhode Island and Providence Plantations one, Connecticut five, New York six, New Jersey four, Pennsylvania eight, Delaware one, Maryland six, Virginia ten, North Carolina five, South Carolina five, and Georgia three.

When vacancies happen in the Representation from any State, the Executive Authority thereof shall issue Writs of Election to fill such Vacancies.

The House of Representatives shall chuse their Speaker and other Officers; and shall have the sole Power of Impeachment.

Section 3. The Senate of the United States shall be composed of two Senators from each State, chosen by the Legislature thereof, for six Years; and each Senator shall have one Vote.

Immediately after they shall be assembled in Consequence of the first Election, they shall be divided as equally as may be into three Classes. The Seats of the Senators of the first Class shall be vacated at the Expiration of the second Year, of the second Class at the Expiration of the fourth Year, and of the third Class at the Expiration of the sixth Year, so that one third may be chosen every second Year; and if Vacancies happen by Resignation, or otherwise, during the Recess of the Legislature of any State, the Executive thereof may make temporary Appointments until the next Meeting of the Legislature, which shall then fill such Vacancies.

No Person shall be a Senator who shall not have attained to the Age of thirty Years, and been nine Years a Citizen of the United States, and who shall not, when elected, be an Inhabitant of that State for which he shall be chosen.

The Vice President of the United States shall be President of the Senate, but shall have no Vote, unless they be equally divided.

The Senate shall chuse their other Officers, and also a President pro tempore, in the Absence of the Vice President, or when he shall exercise the Office of President of the United States.

The Senate shall have the sole Power to try all Impeachments. When sitting for that Purpose, they shall be on Oath or Affirmation. When the President of the United States is tried, the Chief Justice shall preside: And no Person shall be convicted without the Concurrence of two thirds of the Members present.

Judgment in Cases of Impeachment shall not extend further than to removal from Office, and disqualification to hold and enjoy any Office of honor, Trust, or Profit under the United States: but the Party convicted shall nevertheless be liable and subject to Indictment, Trial, Judgment, and Punishment, according to Law.

Section 4. The Times, Places and Manner of holding Elections for Senators and Representatives, shall be prescribed in each State by the Legislature thereof; but the Congress may at any time by Law make or alter such Regulations, except as to the Places of chusing Senators.

The Congress shall assemble at least once in every Year, and such Meeting shall be on the first Monday in December, unless they shall by Law appoint a different Day.

Section 5. Each House shall be the Judge of the Elections, Returns, and Qualifications of its own Members, and a Majority of each shall constitute a Quorum to do Business; but a smaller Number may adjourn from day to day, and may be authorized to compel the Attendance of absent Members, in such Manner, and under such Penalties as each House may provide.

Each House may determine the Rules of its Proceedings, punish its Members for disorderly Behavior, and, with the Concurrence of two thirds, expel a Member.

Each House shall keep a Journal of its Proceedings, and from time to time publish the same, excepting such Parts as may in their Judgment require Secrecy; and the Yeas and Nays of the Members of either House on any question shall, at the Desire of one fifth of those Present, be entered on the Journal.

Neither House, during the Session of Congress, shall, without the Consent of the other, adjourn for more than three days, nor to any other Place than that in which the two Houses shall be sitting.

Section 6. The Senators and Representatives shall receive a Compensation for their Services, to be ascertained by Law, and paid out of the Treasury of the United States. They shall in all Cases, except Treason, Felony and Breach of the Peace, be privileged from Arrest during their Attendance at the Session of their respective Houses, and in going to and returning from the same; and for any Speech or Debate in either House, they shall not be questioned in any other Place.

No Senator or Representative shall, during the Time for which he was elected, be appointed to any civil Office under the Authority of the United States, which shall have been created, or the Emoluments whereof shall have been increased during such time; and no Person holding any Office under the United States, shall be a Member of either House during his Continuance in Office.

Section 7. All Bills for raising Revenue shall originate in the House of Representatives; but the Senate may propose or concur with Amendments as on other Bills.

Every Bill which shall have passed the House of Representatives and the Senate, shall, before it become a Law, be presented to the President of the United States; If he approve he shall sign it, but if not he shall return it, with his Objections to the House in which it shall have originated, who shall enter the Objections at large on their Journal, and proceed to reconsider it. If after such Reconsideration two thirds of that House shall agree to pass the Bill, it shall be sent together with the Objections, to the other House, by which it shall likewise be reconsidered, and if approved by two thirds of that House, it shall become a Law. But in all such Cases the Votes of both Houses shall be determined by Yeas and Nays, and the Names of the Persons voting for and against the Bill shall be entered on the Journal of each House respectively. If any Bill shall not be returned by the President within ten Days (Sundays excepted) after it shall have been presented to him, the Same shall be a Law, in like Manner as if he had signed it, unless the Congress by their Adjournment prevent its Return in which Case it shall not be a Law.

Every Order, Resolution, or Vote, to which the Concurrence of the Senate and House of Representatives may be necessary (except on a question of Adjournment) shall be presented to the President of the United States; and before the Same shall take Effect, shall be approved by him, or being disapproved by him, shall be repassed by two thirds of the Senate and House of Representatives, according to the Rules and Limitations prescribed in the Case of a Bill.

Section 8. The Congress shall have Power To lay and collect Taxes, Duties, Imposts and Excises, to pay the Debts and provide for the common Defence and general Welfare of the United States; but all Duties, Imposts and Excises shall be uniform throughout the United States;

To borrow Money on the credit of the United States;

To regulate Commerce with foreign Nations, and among the several States, and with the Indian Tribes;

To establish an uniform Rule of Naturalization, and uniform Laws on the subject of Bankruptcies throughout the United States;

To coin Money, regulate the Value thereof, and of foreign Coin, and fix the Standard of Weights and Measures;

To provide for the Punishment of counterfeiting the Securities and current Coin of the United States;

To establish Post Offices and post Roads;

To promote the Progress of Science and useful Arts, by securing for limited Times to Authors and Inventors the exclusive Right to their respective Writings and Discoveries;

To constitute Tribunals inferior to the supreme Court;

To define and punish Piracies and Felonies committed on the high Seas, and Offenses against the Law of Nations;

To declare War, grant Letters of Marque and Reprisal, and make Rules concerning Captures on Land and Water;

To raise and support Armies, but no Appropriation of Money to that Use shall be for a longer Term than two Years;

To provide and maintain a Navy;

To make Rules for the Government and Regulation of the land and naval Forces;

To provide for calling forth the Militia to execute the Laws of the Union, suppress Insurrections and repel Invasions;

To provide for organizing, arming, and disciplining, the Militia, and for governing such Part of them as may be employed in the Service of the United States, reserving to the States respectively, the Appointment of the Officers, and the Authority of training the Militia according to the discipline prescribed by Congress;

To exercise exclusive Legislation in all Cases whatsoever, over such District (not exceeding ten Miles square) as may, by Cession of particular States, and the Acceptance of Congress, become the Seat of the Government of the United States, and to exercise like Authority over all Places purchased by the Consent of the Legislature of the State in which the Same shall be, for the Erection of Forts, Magazines, Arsenals, dock-Yards, and other needful Buildings;—And

To make all Laws which shall be necessary and proper for carrying into Execution the foregoing Powers, and all other Powers vested by this Constitution in the Government of the United States, or in any Department or Officer thereof.

Section 9. The Migration or Importation of such Persons as any of the States now existing shall think proper to admit, shall not be prohibited by the Congress prior to the Year one thousand eight hundred and eight, but a Tax or duty may be imposed on such Importation, not exceeding ten dollars for each Person.

The privilege of the Writ of Habeas Corpus shall not be suspended, unless when in Cases of Rebellion or Invasion the public Safety may require it.

No Bill of Attainder or ex post facto Law shall be passed.

No Capitation, or other direct, Tax shall be laid, unless in Proportion to the Census or Enumeration herein before directed to be taken.

No Tax or Duty shall be laid on Articles exported from any State.

No Preference shall be given by any Regulation of Commerce or Revenue to the Ports of one State over those of another: nor shall Vessels bound to, or from, one State be obliged to enter, clear, or pay Duties in another.

No Money shall be drawn from the Treasury, but in Consequence of Appropriations made by Law; and a regular Statement and Account of the Receipts and Expenditures of all public Money shall be published from time to time.

No Title of Nobility shall be granted by the United States: And no Person holding any Office of Profit or Trust under them, shall, without the Consent of the Congress, accept of any present, Emolument, Office, or Title, of any kind whatever, from any King, Prince, or foreign State.

Section 10. No State shall enter into any Treaty, Alliance, or Confederation; grant Letters of Marque and Reprisal; coin Money; emit Bills of Credit; make any Thing but gold and silver Coin a Tender in Payment of Debts; pass any Bill of Attainder, ex post facto Law, or Law impairing the Obligation of Contracts, or grant any Title of Nobility.

No State shall, without the Consent of the Congress, lay any Imposts or Duties on Imports or Exports, except what may be absolutely necessary for executing its inspection Laws: and the net Produce of all Duties and Imposts, laid by any State on Imports or Exports, shall be for the Use of the Treasury of the United States; and all such Laws shall be subject to the Revision and Controul of the Congress.

No State shall, without the Consent of Congress, lay any Duty of Tonnage, keep Troops, or Ships of War in time of Peace, enter into any Agreement or Compact with another State, or with a foreign Power, or engage in War, unless actually invaded, or in such imminent Danger as will not admit of delay.

ARTICLE II

Section 1. The executive Power shall be vested in a President of the United States of America. He shall hold his Office during the Term of four Years, and, together with the Vice President, chosen for the same Term, be elected, as follows:

Each State shall appoint, in such Manner as the Legislature thereof may direct, a Number of Electors, equal to the whole Number of Senators and Representatives to which the State may be entitled in the Congress; but no Senator or Representative, or Person holding an Office of Trust or Profit under the United States, shall be appointed an Elector.

The Electors shall meet in their respective States, and vote by Ballot for two Persons, of whom one at least shall not be an Inhabitant of the same State with themselves. And they shall make a List of all the Persons voted for, and of the Number of Votes for each; which List they shall sign and certify, and transmit sealed to the Seat of the Government of the United States, directed to the President of the Senate. The President of the Senate shall, in the Presence of the Senate and House of Representatives, open all the Certificates, and the Votes shall then be counted. The Person having the greatest Number of Votes shall be the President, if such Number be a Majority of the whole Number of Electors appointed; and if there be more than one who have such Majority, and have an equal Number of Votes, then the House of Representatives shall immediately chuse by Ballot one of them for President; and if no Person have a Majority, then from the five highest on the List the said House shall in like Manner chuse the President. But in chusing the President, the Votes shall be taken by States, the Representation from each State having one Vote; A quorum for this Purpose shall consist of a Member or Members from two thirds of the States, and a Majority of all the States shall be necessary to a Choice. In every Case, after the Choice of the President, the Person having the greater Number of Votes of the Electors shall be the Vice President. But if there should remain two or more who have equal Votes, the Senate shall chuse from them by Ballot the Vice President.

The Congress may determine the Time of chusing the Electors, and the Day on which they shall give their Votes; which

Day shall be the same throughout the United States.

No person except a natural born Citizen, or a Citizen of the United States, at the time of the Adoption of this Constitution, shall be eligible to the Office of President; neither shall any Person be eligible to that Office who shall not have attained to the Age of thirty five Years, and been fourteen Years a Resident within the United States.

In Case of the Removal of the President from Office, or of his Death, Resignation or Inability to discharge the Powers and Duties of the said Office, the same shall devolve on the Vice President, and the Congress may by Law provide for the Case of Removal, Death, Resignation or Inability, both of the President and Vice President, declaring what Officer shall then act as President, and such Officer shall act accordingly, until the Disability be removed, or a President shall be elected.

The President shall, at stated Times, receive for his Services, a Compensation, which shall neither be increased nor diminished during the Period for which he shall have been elected, and he shall not receive within that Period any other Emolument from the United States, or any of them.

Before he enter on the Execution of his Office, he shall take the following Oath or Affirmation: "I do solemnly swear (or affirm) that I will faithfully execute the Office of President of the United States, and will to the best of my Ability, preserve, protect and defend the Constitution of the United States."

Section 2. The President shall be Commander in Chief of the Army and Navy of the United States, and of the Militia of the several States, when called into the actual Service of the United States; he may require the Opinion, in writing, of the principal Officer in each of the executive Departments, upon any Subject relating to the Duties of their respective Offices, and he shall have Power to grant Reprieves and Pardons for Offenses against the United States, except in Cases of Impeachment.

He shall have Power, by and with the Advice and Consent of the Senate to make Treaties, provided two thirds of the Senators present concur; and he shall nominate, and by and with the Advice and Consent of the Senate, shall appoint Ambassadors, other public Ministers and Consuls, Judges of the supreme Court, and all other Officers of the United States, whose Appointments are not herein otherwise provided for, and which shall be established by Law; but the Congress may by Law vest the Appointment of such inferior Officers, as they think proper, in the President alone, in the Courts of Law, or in the Heads of Departments.

The President shall have Power to fill up all Vacancies that may happen during the Recess of the Senate, by granting Commissions which shall expire at the End of their next Session.

Section 3. He shall from time to time give to the Congress Information of the State of the Union, and recommend to their Consideration such Measures as he shall judge necessary and expedient; he may, on extraordinary Occasions, convene both Houses, or either of them, and in Case of Disagreement between them, with Respect to the Time of Adjournment, he may adjourn them to such Time as he shall think proper; he shall receive Ambassadors and other public Ministers; he shall take Care that the Laws be faithfully executed, and shall Commission all the Officers of the United States.

Section 4. The President, Vice President and all civil Officers of the United States, shall be removed from Office on Impeachment for, and Conviction of, Treason, Bribery, or other high Crimes and Misdemeanors.

ARTICLE III

Section 1. The judicial Power of the United States, shall be vested in one supreme Court, and in such inferior Courts as the Congress may from time to time ordain and establish. The Judges, both of the supreme and inferior Courts, shall hold their Offices during good Behaviour, and shall, at stated Times, receive for their Services a Compensation, which shall not be diminished during their Continuance in Office.

Section 2. The judicial Power shall extend to all Cases, in Law and Equity, arising under this Constitution, the Laws of the United States, and Treaties made, or which shall be made, under their Authority;—to all Cases affecting Ambassadors, other public Ministers and Consuls;—to all Cases of admiralty and maritime Jurisdiction;—to Controversies to which the United States shall be a Party;—to Controversies between two or more States;—between a State and Citizens of another State;—between Citizens of different States;—between Citizens of the same State claiming Lands under Grants of different States, and between a State, or the Citizens thereof, and foreign States, Citizens or Subjects.

In all Cases affecting Ambassadors, other public Ministers and Consuls, and those in which a State shall be a Party, the supreme Court shall have original Jurisdiction. In all the other Cases before mentioned, the supreme Court shall have appellate Jurisdiction, both as to Law and Fact, with such Exceptions, and under such Regulations as the Congress shall make.

The Trial of all Crimes, except in Cases of Impeachment, shall be by Jury; and such Trial shall be held in the State where the said Crimes shall have been committed; but when not committed within any State, the Trial shall be at such Place or Places as the Congress may by Law have directed.

Section 3.   Treason against the United States, shall consist only in levying War against them, or, in adhering to their Enemies, giving them Aid and Comfort. No Person shall be convicted of Treason unless on the Testimony of two Witnesses to the same overt Act, or on Confession in open Court.

The Congress shall have Power to declare the Punishment of Treason, but no Attainder of Treason shall work Corruption of Blood, or Forfeiture except during the Life of the Person attainted.

Amendment I [1791]

Congress shall make no law respecting an establishment of religion, or prohibiting the free exercise thereof; or abridging the freedom of speech, or of the press; or the right of the people peaceably to assembly, and to petition the Government for a redress of grievances.

Amendment XIV [1868]

Section 1.   All persons born or naturalized in the United States, and subject to the jurisdiction thereof, are citizens of the United States and of the State wherein they reside. No State shall make or enforce any law which shall abridge the privileges or immunities of citizens of the United States; nor shall any State deprive any person of life, liberty, or property, without due process of law; nor deny to any person within its jurisdiction the equal protection of the laws.

Section 2.   Representatives shall be apportioned among the several States according to their respective numbers, counting the whole number of persons in each State, excluding Indians not taxed. But when the right to vote at any election for the choice of electors for President and Vice President of the United States, Representatives in Congress, the Executive and Judicial officers of a State, or the members of the Legislature thereof, is denied to any of the male inhabitants of such State, being twenty-one years of age, and citizens of the United States, or in any way abridged, except for participation in rebellion, or other crime, the basis of representation therein shall be reduced in the proportion which the number of such male citizens shall bear to the whole number of male citizens twenty-one years of age in such State.

Section 3.   No person shall be a Senator or Representative in Congress, or elector of President and Vice President, or hold any office, civil or military, under the United States, or under any State, who having previously taken an oath, as a member of Congress, or as an officer of the United States, or as a member of any State legislature, or as an executive or judicial officer of any State, to support the Constitution of the United States, shall have engaged in insurrection or rebellion against the same, or given aid or comfort to the enemies thereof. But Congress may by a vote of two-thirds of each House, remove such disability.

Section 4.   The validity of the public debt of the United States, authorized by law, including debts incurred for payment of pensions and bounties for services in suppressing insurrection or rebellion, shall not be questioned. But neither the United States nor any State shall assume or pay any debt or obligation incurred in aid of insurrection or rebellion against the United States, or any claim for the loss or emancipation of any slave; but all such debts, obligations and claims shall be held illegal and void.

Section 5.   The Congress shall have power to enforce, by appropriate legislation, the provisions of this article.

APPENDIX B

THE UNIFORM COMMERCIAL CODE (EXCERPTS)

§ 2—101. Short Title.

This Article shall be known and may be cited as Uniform Commercial Code—Sales.

§ 2—104. Definitions: "Merchant"; "Between Merchants"; "Financing Agency".

(1) "Merchant" means a person who deals in goods of the kind or otherwise by his occupation holds himself out as having knowledge or skill peculiar to the practices or goods involved in the transaction or to whom such knowledge or skill may be attributed by his employment of an agent or broker or other intermediary who by his occupation holds himself out as having such knowledge or skill.

(2) "Financing agency" means a bank, finance company or other person who in the ordinary course of business makes advances against goods or documents of title or who by arrangement with either the seller or the buyer intervenes in ordinary course to make or collect payment due or claimed under the contract for sale, as by purchasing or paying the seller's draft or making advances against it or by merely taking it for collection whether or not documents of title accompany the draft. "Financing agency" includes also a bank or other person who similarly intervenes between persons who are in the position of seller and buyer in respect to the goods (Section 2—707).

(3) "Between merchants" means in any transaction with respect to which both parties are chargeable with the knowledge or skill of merchants.

§ 2—105. Definitions: Transferability; "Goods"; "Future" Goods; "Lot"; "Commercial Unit".

(1) "Goods" means all things (including specially manufactured goods) which are movable at the time of identification to the contract for sale other than the money in which the price is to be paid, investment securities (Article 8) and things in action. "Goods" also includes the unborn young of animals and growing crops and other identified things attached to realty as described in the section on goods to be severed from realty (Section 2—107).

(2) Goods must be both existing and identified before any interest in them can pass. Goods which are not both existing and identified are "future" goods. A purported present sale of future goods or of any interest therein operates as a contract to sell.

(3) There may be a sale of a part interest in existing identified goods.

(4) An undivided share in an identified bulk of fungible goods is sufficiently identified to be sold although the quantity of the bulk is not determined. Any agreed proportion of such a bulk or any quantity thereof agreed upon by number, weight or other measure may to the extent of the seller's interest in the bulk be sold to the buyer who then becomes an owner in common.

(5) "Lot" means a parcel or a single article which is the subject matter of a separate sale or delivery, whether or not it is sufficient to perform the contract.

(6) "Commercial unit" means such a unit of goods as by commercial usage is a single

whole for purposes of sale and division of which materially impairs its character or value on the market or in use. A commercial unit may be a single article (as a machine) or a set of articles (as a suite of furniture or an assortment of sizes) or a quantity (as a bale, gross, or carload) or any other unit treated in use or in the relevant market as a single whole.

§ 2—201. Formal Requirements; Statute of Frauds.

(1) Except as otherwise provided in this section a contract for the sale of goods for the price of $500 or more is not enforceable by way of action or defense unless there is some writing sufficient to indicate that a contract for sale has been made between the parties and signed by the party against whom enforcement is sought or by his authorized agent or broker. A writing is not insufficient because it omits or incorrectly states a term agreed upon but the contract is not enforceable under this paragraph beyond the quantity of goods shown in such writing.

(2) Between merchants if within a reasonable time a writing in confirmation of the contract and sufficient against the sender is received and the party receiving it has reason to know its contents, it satisfies the requirements of subsection (1) against such party unless written notice of objection to its contents is given within ten days after it is received.

(3) A contract which does not satisfy the requirements of subsection (1) but which is valid in other respects is enforceable

(a) if the goods are to be specially manufactured for the buyer and are not suitable for sale to others in the ordinary course of the seller's business and the seller, before notice of repudiation is received and under circumstances which reasonably indicate that the goods are for the buyer, has made either a substantial beginning of their manufacture or commitments for their procurement; or

(b) if the party against whom enforcement is sought admits in his pleading, testimony or otherwise in court that a contract for sale was made, but the contract is not enforceable under this provision beyond the quantity of goods admitted; or

(c) with respect to goods for which payment has been made and accepted or which have been received and accepted (Sec. 2—606).

§ 2—204. Formation in General.

(1) A contract for sale of goods may be made in any manner sufficient to show agreement, including conduct by both parties which recognizes the existence of such a contract.

(2) An agreement sufficient to constitute a contract for sale may be found even though the moment of its making is undetermined.

(3) Even though one or more terms are left open a contract for sale does not fail for indefiniteness if the parties have intended to make a contract and there is a reasonably certain basis for giving an appropriate remedy.

§ 2—205. Firm Offers.

An offer by a merchant to buy or sell goods in a signed writing which by its terms gives assurance that it will be held open is not revocable, for lack of consideration, during the time stated or if no time is stated for a reasonable time, but in no event may such period of irrevocability exceed three months; but any such term of assurance on a form supplied by the offeree must be separately signed by the offeror.

§ 2—206. Offer and Acceptance in Formation of Contract.

(1) Unless otherwise unambiguously indicated by the language or circumstances

(a) an offer to make a contract shall be construed as inviting acceptance in any manner and by any medium reasonable in the circumstances;

(b) an order or other offer to buy goods for prompt or current shipment shall be construed as inviting acceptance either by a prompt promise to ship or by the prompt or current shipment of conforming or nonconforming goods, but such a shipment of nonconforming goods does not constitute an acceptance if the seller seasonably notifies the buyer that the shipment is offered only as an accommodation to the buyer.

(2) Where the beginning of a requested performance is a reasonable mode of acceptance an offeror who is not notified of acceptance

within a reasonable time may treat the offer as having lapsed before acceptance.

§ 2—207. Additional Terms in Acceptance or Confirmation.

(1) A definite and seasonable expression of acceptance or a written confirmation which is sent within a reasonable time operates as an acceptance even though it states terms additional to or different from those offered or agreed upon, unless acceptance is expressly made conditional on assent to the additional or different terms.

(2) The additional terms are to be construed as proposals for addition to the contract. Between merchants such terms become part of the contract unless:

(a) the offer expressly limits acceptance to the terms of the offer;

(b) they materially alter it; or

(c) notification of objection to them has already been given or is given within a reasonable time after notice of them is received.

(3) Conduct by both parties which recognizes the existence of a contract is sufficient to establish a contract for sale although the writings of the parties do not otherwise establish a contract. In such case the terms of the particular contract consist of those terms on which the writings of the parties agree, together with any supplementary terms incorporated under any other provisions of this Act.

§ 2—305. Open Price Term.

(1) The parties if they so intend can conclude a contract for sale even though the price is not settled. In such a case the price is a reasonable price at the time for delivery if

(a) nothing is said as to price; or

(b) the price is left to be agreed by the parties and they fail to agree; or

(c) the price is to be fixed in terms of some agreed market or other standard as set or recorded by a third person or agency and it is not so set or recorded.

(2) A price to be fixed by the seller or by the buyer means a price for him to fix in good faith.

(3) When a price left to be fixed otherwise than by agreement of the parties fails to be fixed through fault of one party the other

may at his option treat the contract as cancelled or himself fix a reasonable price.

(4) Where, however, the parties intend not to be bound unless the price be fixed or agreed and it is not fixed or agreed there is no contract. In such a case the buyer must return any goods already received or if unable so to do must pay their reasonable value at the time of delivery and the seller must return any portion of the price paid on account.

§ 2—312. Warranty of Title and Against Infringement; Buyer's Obligation Against Infringement.

(1) Subject to subsection (2) there is in a contract for sale a warranty by the seller that

(a) the title conveyed shall be good, and its transfer rightful; and

(b) the goods shall be delivered free from any security interest or other lien or encumbrance of which the buyer at the time of contracting has no knowledge.

(2) A warranty under subsection (1) will be excluded or modified only by specific language or by circumstances which give the buyer reason to know that the person selling does not claim title in himself or that he is purporting to sell only such right or title as he or a third person may have.

(3) Unless otherwise agreed a seller who is a merchant regularly dealing in goods of the kind warrants that the goods shall be delivered free of the rightful claim of any third person by way of infringement or the like but a buyer who furnishes specifications to the seller must hold the seller harmless against any such claim which arises out of compliance with the specifications.

§ 2—313. Express Warranties by Affirmation, Promise, Description, Sample.

(1) Express warranties by the seller are created as follows:

(a) Any affirmation of fact or promise made by the seller to the buyer which relates to the goods and becomes part of the basis of the bargain creates an express warranty that the goods shall conform to the affirmation or promise.

(b) Any description of the goods which is made part of the basis of the bargain creates an express warranty that the goods shall conform to the description.

(c) Any sample or model which is made part of the basis of the bargain creates an express warranty that the whole of the goods shall conform to the sample or model.

(2) It is not necessary to the creation of an express warranty that the seller use formal words such as "warrant" or "guarantee" or that he have a specific intention to make a warranty, but an affirmation merely of the value of the goods or a statement purporting to be merely the seller's opinion or commendation of the goods does not create a warranty.

§ 2—314. Implied Warranty: Merchantability; Usage of Trade.

(1) Unless excluded or modified (Section 2—316), a warranty that the goods shall be merchantable is implied in a contract for their sale if the seller is a merchant with respect to goods of that kind. Under this section the serving for value of food or drink to be consumed either on the premises or elsewhere is a sale.

(2) Goods to be merchantable must be at least such as

(a) pass without objection in the trade under the contract description; and

(b) in the case of fungible goods, are of fair average quality within the description; and

(c) are fit for the ordinary purposes for which such goods are used; and

(d) run, within the variations permitted by the agreement, of even kind, quality and quantity within each unit and among all units involved; and

(e) are adequately contained, packaged, and labeled as the agreement may require; and

(f) conform to the promises or affirmations of fact made on the container or label if any.

(3) Unless excluded or modified (Section 2—316) other implied warranties may arise from course of dealing or usage of trade.

§ 2—315. Implied Warranty: Fitness for Particular Purpose.

Where the seller at the time of contracting has reason to know any particular purpose for which the goods are required and that the buyer is relying on the seller's skill or judgment to select or furnish suitable goods, there is unless excluded or modified under the next section an implied warranty that the goods shall be fit for such purpose.

§ 2—316. Exclusion or Modification of Warranties.

(1) Words or conduct relevant to the creation of an express warranty and words or conduct tending to negate or limit warranty shall be construed wherever reasonable as consistent with each other; but subject to the provisions of this Article on parol or extrinsic evidence (Section 2—202) negation or limitation is inoperative to the extent that such construction is unreasonable.

(2) Subject to subsection (3), to exclude or modify the implied warranty of merchantability or any part of it the language must mention merchantability and in case of a writing must be conspicuous, and to exclude or modify any implied warranty of fitness the exclusion must be by a writing and conspicuous. Language to exclude all implied warranties of fitness is sufficient if it states, for example, that "There are no warranties which extend beyond the description on the face hereof."

(3) Notwithstanding subsection (2)

(a) unless the circumstances indicate otherwise, all implied warranties are excluded by expressions like "as is", "with all faults" or other language which in common understanding calls the buyer's attention to the exclusion of warranties and makes plain that there is no implied warranty; and

(b) when the buyer before entering into the contract has examined the goods or the sample or model as fully as he desired or has refused to examine the goods there is no implied warranty with regard to defects which an examination ought in the circumstances to have revealed to him; and

(c) an implied warranty can also be excluded or modified by course of dealing or course of performance or usage of trade.

(4) Remedies for breach of warranty can be limited in accordance with the provisions of this Article on liquidation or limitation of damages and on contractual modification of remedy (Sections 2—718 and 2—719).

APPENDIX C

RESTATEMENT (SECOND) OF TORTS (EXCERPTS)

Section 402A. Special liability of seller of product for physical harm to user or consumer.

(1) One who sells any product in a defective condition unreasonably dangerous to the consumer or to his property is subject to liability for physical harm thereby caused to the ultimate user or consumer, or to his property, if

(a) the seller is engaged in the business of selling usch a product, and

(b) it is expected to and does reach the user or consumer without substantial change in the condition in which it is sold.

(2) The rule stated in Subsection (1) applies although

(a) the seller has exercised all possible care in the preparation and sale of his product, and

(b) the user or consumer has not bought the product from or entered into any contractual relation with the seller.

GLOSSARY

A

Act of state doctrine Doctrine of international law providing that as a general rule the courts of one country will not determine the legality of public actions taken by another country within the latter's own borders.

Actual authority In agency law, the authority based on what a principal expressly or impliedly authorizes an agent to do.

Administrative law Law based on regulations handed down by federal, state, county and city regulatory agencies.

Adverse possession Statutory means of acquiring ownership of real property by using the property without the owner's permission for a specified period of time.

Age Discrimination in Employment Act (ADEA) Federal law protecting job applicants and employees from discrimination based on age.

Agent One who represents another party (the principal) in dealing with third parties.

Alternative dispute resolution Means of settling a dispute in a manner other than litigation. Examples include negotiation, mediation and arbitration.

Americans with Disabilities Act Federal law addressing employment discrimination against disabled applicants and employees. Act requires employers to provide reasonable accommodations for an otherwise qualified employee.

Answer Defendant's response to the plaintiff's complaint in a lawsuit.

Apparent authority In agency law, the authority based on what a third party reasonably believes an agent is authorized to do.

Appeal Action of the party losing a lawsuit who seeks to have the adverse decision overturned by a higher court.

Arbitration Means of dispute resolution where a third party arbitrator hears the dispute and makes a binding determination on the matter.

Arbitration clause Clause in a contract providing that in case of a dispute the parties will refer the dispute to binding arbitration.

Assault Intentional tort where defendant's act causes plaintiff to experience reasonable fear of imminent physical harm.

B

Bailee   Party taking temporary possession of bailment property.

Bailment   Relationship based on bailor's transfer of temporary possession of personal property to bailee.

Bailment for benefit of bailee   Bailment arising when bailee "borrows" bailor's personal property and uses it solely for bailee's own benefit.

Bailment for benefit of bailor   Bailment arising when bailee takes temporary possession of bailor's personal property for the benefit of the bailor.

Bailor   Owner of personal property who transfers temporary possession to the bailee.

Battery   Intentional tort based on defendant or an extension of defendant offensively touching plaintiff without plaintiff's consent.

Beneficiary   For insurance purposes, the party who will receive compensation from an insurance policy in case of a loss.

Bilateral contract   Contract based on mutual exchange of promises between the offeror and the offeree.

Binder   Insurance company's agreement to assure insured's coverage between time premium is paid and the time the policy is issued.

Bona fide occupational qualification (BFOQ)   Defense to a Title VII employment discrimination complaint based on qualifications required by employer in order for employee to perform a job.

Business invitees   Customers and prospective customers who visit a business that is open to the public.

Business necessity defense   Defense to a Title VII employment discrimination complaint applicable when a particular qualification or test is essential to the employee's ability to perform a business function.

C

Cancellation clause   Clause in an insurance policy relevant to insurer's right to cancel policy.

Capacity   The legal power to enter into a valid contract. Lack of capacity may be due to minority of age, being under the influence of alcohol or drugs or due to insanity.

Caveat emptor   Term meaning "let the buyer beware."

Civil law   Category of law including wrongs committed against a private party. In contrast, criminal law addresses wrongs committed against society as a whole.

Civil law system   Legal systems based on written statutes as the primary source of law.

Co-insurance clause   Clause in an insurance policy requiring the policy to cover a specific percentage of the value of the property.

Common carrier   Carrier in the business of transporting goods for the public.

Common law   Refers to laws based on a judge's decision; frequently referred to as "judge-made law."

Common law system   The legal system which is primarily based on judicial decisions. The United States follows the common law system, which originated in England.

Comparative negligence   Defense available in a negligence case based on plaintiff's own negligence contributing to injuries plaintiff suffered. Plaintiff's award is reduced based on the degree of plaintiff's contributory negligence.

Compensatory damages   Amount paid to the plaintiff for damages actually suffered.

Complaint   Document filed by plaintiff's attorney in a civil lawsuit or by a prosecutor in a criminal case establishing the court's jurisdiction, the complaint against the defendant, and, in a civil suit, the damages sought.

Condition precedent   A specific condition that must be met before a party is obligated to perform on a contract.

Condition subsequent   A condition that will relieve a party from a contractual obligation if the condition occurs subsequent to entering into the contract.

Confiscation   Taking of private property by a governmental entity without fair compensation or for an improper purpose.

Confusion   Means of acquiring ownership of personal property when one owner's fungible goods are mixed with another's fungible goods.

Consequential damages   Damages that "flow from" or result from the defendant's failure to comply with the terms of a contract or from defendant's improper action.

Consideration   The legal detriment a party must generally give in order to enforce a contract against another party.

Constitutional law   Refers to area of law based on federal or state constitutions.

Consumer   One who buys or leases goods or services for personal use or use by one's family or household.

Contributory negligence   Defense available in a negligence cased based on plaintiff's own negligence contributing to plaintiff's injuries. If a court adopts the doctrine of contributory negligence, the plaintiff is barred from recovering any damages.

Convention on Contracts for the International Sale of Goods (CISG)   International convention sponsored by the United Nations that addresses the international sale of commercial goods.

Copyright   Intellectual property right available to creators of certain intellectual endeavors such as books, software programs, videos and music giving the holder the exclusive right to use or sell the protected material for a specified period of time.

Corporation   Statutorily authorized form of business operation that is an entity separate and apart from its shareholders.

Countersuit   Defendant's answer to a lawsuit whereby defendant responds by suing the plaintiff.

Covenant not to compete   Agreement where one party agrees not to compete with another party within a certain geographic area for a specified length of time.

D

Damages   Monetary award plaintiff receives in a civil lawsuit.

Deed   Document conveying ownership of real property.

Defamation   Intentional tort based on defendant's false statement that is harmful to plaintiff's reputation and is published to at least one other person.

Default judgement   Judgement for one party based on the other party's failure to answer the Complaint.

Deposition   Verbal questions one party's attorney asks of another party or of witnesses to a lawsuit. Questions and responses are transcribed and become part of the official court record.

Discovery   Process of gathering of evidence to be presented at trial.

Disclosed principal   In agency law, the category of principal that is based on fact the third party knows of the agency relationship and also knows the identity of the principal.

Doctrine of sovereign immunity   Legal doctrine holding that a sovereign or government cannot be sued without its permission.

Donative intent   Donor's intent to convey property to donee in the form of a gift.

Donee   Recipient of a gift.

Donor   Party conveying a gift.

Duress   In contract law, threat of harm that forces one party to enter into a contract with another party.

E

Effective date of coverage   Relevant to insurance law, the date insurance protection begins.

Employee   One who works for and under the close supervision of another (the employer).

Eminent domain   Governmental means of purchasing real property from private party when the property is to be used for a public purpose and fair compensation is paid.

Employee-at-will   Employment relationship where there is no specific agreement between parties regarding the duration of employment.

Equal Credit Opportunity Act   Federal law prohibiting discrimination in the extension of credit.

Exculpatory clause   A "hold harmless" clause where one party agrees not to hold the other party liable for damages the first party may suffer as a result of the second party's action.

Executed contract   A contract which has been fully performed by all parties.

Executory contract   A contract where one or both parties has not fully performed all contractual duties.

Express authority   In agency law, the authority based on what the principal expressly authorizes the agent to do.

Express warranty   Factual assertion expressly given by seller or lessor relevant to goods or services.

F

Fair Credit Reporting Act   Federal law providing consumers with the right to access information in their credit reports and correct erroneous information.

Fair Debt Collection Practices Act   Federal law prohibiting collection agencies from engaging in unfair or harassing collection methods.

False imprisonment   Intentional tort where the defendant deprives the plaintiff of the right of freedom of movement.

Federal Trade Commission Act   Federal consumer protection law that includes regulations on deceptive advertising and door-to-door sales.

Fee simple absolute   Highest form of ownership of real property which allows the owner to use or dispose of the property as the owner chooses.

Fee simple defeasible   Ownership of real property conditioned on the present owner using the property in the manner required by a former owner.

Fixtures   Items that were previously considered personal property which are now included as part of the real property with which they are associated.

Foreign Corrupt Practices Act   Federal law prohibiting U.S. businesses and individuals from payment of bribes to foreign officials (or candidates for foreign office) in order to benefit the U.S. company. Violation carries heavy criminal penalties.

Foreign-natural test   Test courts impose to determine if foods and beverages are merchantable. If the cause of plaintiff's injury naturally occurs in the food or beverage, the product is considered merchantable and the merchant is not liable.

Forum   Term referring to the court which hears a case.

Fraud   Intentional tort involving defendant's intentionally making a false or misleading material assertion which plaintiff reasonably relies on and thereby suffers damages.

G

Gift causa mortis   Conditional gift made based on donor's belief that death is imminent.

Gift inter vivos   Unconditional gift made during donor's life (and not made in contemplation of imminent death).

General partner   Co-owner of a partnership who faces unlimited personal liability for the debts of the partnership.

General partnership   Form of for-profit business co-owned by two or more general partners.

H

Hostile work environment   In sexual harassment claims, refers to a workplace where employer permits sexually offensive environment to exist.

I

Implied authority   In agency law, the authority based on what an agent reasonably believes is necessary to carry out the agent's express duties.

Implied warranty   A guarantee that impliedly accompanies a sale or lease even though the seller or lessor has made no express guarantee.

Impracticability   Grounds for excusing a party from contractual performance due to an unforeseen circumstance or event.

Intellectual property   Intangible property based on one's creative endeavors. Examples include inventions, books, and business trademarks.

In personam jurisdiction   A court's jurisdiction over a person involved in a lawsuit.

In rem jurisdiction   A court's jurisdiction over property involved in a lawsuit.

Intentional torts   Category of tort where defendant actually intended the action that resulted in harm to plaintiff's personal or property rights.

Interstate Commerce Clause   Article I, Section 8 of the U.S. Constitution granting Congress the power to regulate commerce "with foreign Nations, and among the several States, and with the Indian tribes."

Intestate   Refers to an individual dying without a valid will.

Insurable interest   In order to take out an insurance policy, a party must have an insurable interest in, or stand to incur an actual loss, if harm comes to the insured property or person.

Insured   Party who is the holder of an insurance policy.

Insurer   Company offering the insurance policy.

Interrogatories   Written questions one party to a lawsuit serves on the other and which become part of the official court record.

Intestate   Refers to when a person dies without leaving a valid will.

Invasion of privacy   Intentional tort involving public dissemination of private information or "placing a person in a false light." An example of the latter is appropriating a celebrity's likeness in an advertisement without the celebrity's permission.

J

Joint tenancy   Form of co-ownership of real property providing that upon the death of one joint tenant, the deceased's property goes to the remaining joint tenant(s).

Jurisdiction   Refers to the power of the court to hear a case.

L

Law   A rule handed down by a person or group with authority for which noncompliance results in sanctions or punishment.

Libel   Written statement that is false, harmful to plaintiff's reputation and published to at least one other person.

Limited liability company   Statutorily authorized form of business operation offering limited personal liability to owners and is taxed as a partnership.

Limited partner   Partner in a limited partnership whose liability is generally limited to the amount invested in the partnership.

Limited partnership   Statutorily authorized form of business operation composed of at least one general partner in addition to the limited partner(s).

Limited personal liability   Refers to the liability of a limited partner or a corporate shareholder whose liability is limited to the amount invested in the business.

M

Malice   In tort law, refers to defendant making a defamatory statement, either knowingly or with reckless disregard for the truth.

Material breach   Contractual breach where defendant's performance is so inferior that the plaintiff receives little or no benefit.

Mediation   Means of alternative dispute resolution where a third party mediator attempts to help the parties resolve their dispute.

Merchant   One who is in the business of selling a particular type of goods or who holds oneself out as an expert in dealing with that type of goods.

Mislaid property   Personal property that the owner places in a specific place and inadvertently leaves it in that place.

Mistake   In contract law, a unilateral or bilateral error or misunderstanding involving a material aspect of a contract.

Mortgage   Contract between a lender and borrower providing the lender (mortgagee) can foreclose on the collateral property under certain circumstances.

Mortgagee   Party who lends money or extends credit and takes a collateral interest in the property used to secure the loan or credit.

Mortgagor   Party who borrows money and executes a mortgage to secure the loan.

Mutual benefit bailment   Bailment situation where both bailor and bailee receive some type of benefit.

N

Necessaries   Goods or services required to maintain one's standard of living. In contract law, a minor must pay the reasonable value for necessaries purchased or leased.

Negligence   Unintentional tort based on defendant's breach of a duty owed to plaintiff. As a general rule, plaintiff must prove the breach was the actual and foreseeable cause of the injury plaintiff suffered.

Negligence per se   Theory applied in negligence cases when defendant violates a statute which was passed to protect persons such as plaintiff from type of injury plaintiff suffered.

Negotiation   Means of alternative dispute resolution where parties attempt to resolve the dispute between themselves.

P

Partially disclosed principal   In agency law, the type of principal where the third party knows an agency relationship exists but does not know the identity of the principal.

Patent   Legal right granting inventors of new products, designs or processes the exclusive right to use or sell the subject matter of the patent for a specified period of time.

Personal property   All property not classified as real property. Personal property is movable and may be tangible or intangible.

Pierce the corporate veil   In corporation law, refers to the action where a plaintiff can recover from a corporate shareholder's personal assets if the corporation cannot pay the judgement.

Pre-existing condition   In insurance law, refers to a health condition existing at the time the insured takes out a health or life insurance policy.

Pregnancy Discrimination Act of 1978   Federal law prohibiting employment discrimination against women based on pregnancy or related conditions.

Premium   Money paid by the insured to the insurer in exchange for insurance coverage.

Principal   In agency law, one who authorizes another party (the agent) to act on the first party's behalf in dealing with third parties.

Promissory estoppel   A legal doctrine that allows a party to enforce a contract even though that party gave no consideration.

Punitive damages   Damages awarded by a court to either punish the defendant for what the court considers outrageous behavior or to serve as a deterrent to future wrongdoers.

Q

Quid pro quo harassment   Sexual harassment in the form of the employer requesting sexual favors of an employee in exchange for job benefits.

R

Ratify   In agency law, the principal's action in agreeing to assume responsibility for a previously unauthorized contract entered into by an agent on the principal's behalf.

Real property   Category of property that includes the surface and subsurface of the land, growing crops and plants, certain airspace above and items of personal property that are classified as "fixtures".

Reasonable accommodation   Refers to degree of workplace accommodation required of an employer or a prospective employer to enable a disabled employee or prospective employee to perform a job. For example, reasonable accommodation for a hearing impaired employee may include placing a special device on a telephone.

Reasonable expectation test   Test courts impose in determining if foods or beverages are merchantable. The test is based on what the jury or court determines a consumer would reasonably expect relevant to contents and quality.

Res ipsa loquitur   Legal theory applied in negligence cases when an injury is caused by an object that was in the exclusive control of the defendant and which does not ordinarily cause injury in the absence of negligence. Application of the theory raises a rebuttable presumption that the defendant was negligent.

Respondent superior   Latin term meaning "let the master respond." The term is applied when an employer is held liable for an employee's torts that were committed within the scope of employment.

Revocation   The offeror's termination of a contractual offer.

S

Scope of employment   In agency law, refers to actions (including torts) committed by an employee when the employee's activity was related to the furtherance of the employer's interest.

Sexual harassment   In employment law, a situation where sexual favors are requested of an employee in exchange for job benefits or the employee is forced to work in a sexually hostile (offensive) work environment.

Slander   Defamatory statement that is spoken by the defendant and is published to at least one third party.

Sole proprietorship   Form of business operation where one individual solely owns the business and the business is not considered a separate entity. The sole proprietor faces unlimited personal liability for the debts of the business.

Sovereign immunity   Doctrine of international law based on the concept that a sovereign (government) cannot be sued without its permission.

Specific performance   Court remedy where the court orders the defendant to perform a specific act.

Statute of frauds   Written law requiring that certain contracts must be in writing to be enforceable.

Statutory law   Refers to a written law passed by a law-making body such as a state legislature or the federal Congress.

Strict liability   Tort liability imposed despite the fact the defendant did not intend the harmful act and was not negligent. This type of liability is also referred to as "liability without fault."

Strict product liability   No-fault liability imposed on sellers of goods when the goods (1) are considered defective when they leave the merchant seller (2) are not altered between the time they left seller and reached plaintiff (3) plaintiff was injured by goods (4) goods were unreasonably dangerous (most states) and (5) were proximate cause of injury.

T

Telephone Consumer Protection Act Federal law regulating telephone solicitations that use prerecorded voices, automatic dialing systems and ads transmitted by fax.

Tenants in common Joint owners of real property whose individual share of ownership will pass to the deceased owner's heirs. There is no right of survivorship for tenants in common.

Testate Refers to an individual dying with a valid will designating who will inherit the deceased's property.

Testator An individual who leaves a will designating who will inherit the deceased's property.

Title VII Provision of the U.S. Civil Rights Act of 1964 prohibiting employment discrimination based on sex, religion, race, color, or national origin.

Tort A private wrong committed against the injured party's person or property.

Trademark A particular name, picture, mark or logo that identifies a specific product or service.

Trade secret Information or process that gives one business an advantage over the competition.

Treaty Source of international law based on a formal agreement between two or more sovereign countries.

Trespass The wrongful crossing over or use of another's real or personal property.

Truth in Lending Act Federal law requiring lenders and sellers to disclose all relevant terms of a credit sale or loan to a consumer.

U

Unconscionable contract Contract where parties are in unequal bargaining position and the party with excess power takes unfair advantage of the weaker party. Courts frequently refuse to enforce an unconscionable contract.

Undisclosed principal In agency law, a principal is described as undisclosed when the third party is unaware of the agency relationship and does not know the principal's identity.

Undue influence Excessive influence one party to a contract exercises over another party who is vulnerable to the first party's influence.

Unenforceable contract A contract that has all the elements of a valid contract but for some other reason cannot be enforced. For example, a verbal contract to sell land may not be enforceable because the statute of frauds requires the contract be in writing.

Unilateral contract   A contract involving the exchange of a promise for an act.

V

Valid contract   An agreement that meets all the legal requirements for a contract and is enforceable by either party in a court of law.

Void contract   A contract that does not meet all of the legal requirements for a contract and that is not enforceable by either party. For example, a contract to commit a crime or a tort is void.

Voidable contract   A contract where one or both parties have the power to avoid performing the contract without suffering any legal consequence. For example, most contracts entered into by a minor are voidable on the minor's part (but not the adult's part).

W

Warranty of fitness for a particular purpose   Implied warranty imposed on the seller of goods when the seller selects the particular goods for the consumer after the consumer informs the seller of the particular purpose for the goods.

Warranty of merchantability   Implied warranty accompanying sales of goods by merchants that guarantees the goods are fit for their ordinary use and are acceptable within the trade.

Wrongful discharge   Refers to the firing of an employee without valid cause.

Wrongful interference with a contractual relationship   An intentional tort based on the defendant knowingly interfering with an existing contract the plaintiff had with a third party. The purpose of the interference is to benefit the defendant's pecuniary interest.

Wrongful interference with an economic expectation   Intentional tort based on defendant's predatory behavior in interfering with a relationship the plaintiff has with a potential customer or client.